RAND McNALLY

the road atlas

DELUXE MIDSIZE

CONTENTS

Travel Information

Maps and Indexes

Best of the Road®

RAND McNALLY
BEST OF THE ROAD

Each year our editors drive five new road trips to share with you those special things we call *Best of the Road*.

MORE pictures, MORE attractions, MORE at go.randmcnally.com/br

CENTER STAGE

Winnipeg, Manitoba, to Bismarck, North Dakota

The prairie is deceiving: what at first appears to be a wide expanse of flat nothing reveals itself, with a closer look, to be a teeming ecological system full of beautiful scenery, interesting stops, and tasty cuisine. All of that is enjoyed here via a look at North America's First Peoples and the settlers who came later, a jaunt through Canada's Manitoba province, and a hop across the border and into North Dakota. This journey takes in Manitoba's capital and largest city, Winnipeg, explores Riding Mountain National Park's vast wilderness, and looks at the bi-national International Peace Garden before ending with another capital, Bismarck.

Best known: Manitoba Museum and the Royal Winnipeg Ballet in Winnipeg; North Dakota State Capitol in Bismarck.

EDITOR'S PICKS

Manitoba Children's Museum (Winnipeg, MB)

Kids have too much fun to realize they're learning, while parents are happy to have the younger set along as an excuse to enjoy the vintage diesel locomotive, working TV studio, and various other exhibits and educational diversions at Winnipeg's Manitoba Children's Museum. *Kinsmen Building, 45 Forks Market Rd., (204) 924-4000, www.childrensmuseum.com*

Five Nations Gallery & Gifts (Mandan, ND)

Housed in a former railroad depot, the Five Nations retail arm of the Fort Abraham Lincoln Foundation provides a place for artists and musicians to sell a wide variety of CDs, paintings, beadwork, footwear, and more. *401 West Main St., (701) 663-4663, www.fortlincoln.com/five_nations_art.aspx*

More Great Stops

■ **Mondragon Bookstore and Coffee House**
91 Albert St.
Winnipeg, MB
(204) 946-5241
www.mondragon.ca

■ **Le Musée de Saint-Boniface Museum**
494 Tache Ave.
Saint-Boniface, MB
(204) 237-4500
www.msbm.mb.ca

■ **FortWhyte Alive**
1961 McCreary Rd.
Winnipeg, MB
(204) 989-8364
www.fortwhyte.org

MORE pictures, MORE attractions, MORE at go.randmcnally.com/br

North Dakota Heritage Center (Bismarck, ND)

An array of exhibits presents the North Dakota story at the Heritage Center, part of the state capitol complex, from the fossils of prehistoric beasts to the implements and artifacts of the humans who arrived and settled long after. *612 East Boulevard Ave., (701) 328-2666, www.nd.gov/hist/hcenter.htm*

Mariaggi's Theme Suite Hotel (Winnipeg, MB)

Travelers in the know use this kitschy-hip, surprisingly posh spot and its internationally themed rooms as home base for adventures in the surrounding counter-culture of the Exchange District. *231 McDermot Ave., (204) 947-9447, www.mariaggis.com*

EDITOR'S PICKS

Riding Mountain National Park (Wasagaming, MB)

Riding Mountain provides a natural nirvana for hikers, bikers, geocachers, snowshoers, bird watchers, and skiers, with almost 1,200 square miles of protected wilderness to explore and a wide variety of wildlife to see. *(204) 848-7275, www.pc.gc.ca/ridingmountain*

International Peace Garden (Dunseith, ND)

Begun as a 2,300-acre border-straddling statement about U.S.-Canadian friendship, the garden now includes a 9-11 Memorial, comprised of twisted girders from New York's World Trade Center. Visitors also take in a wildlife museum, café, gift shop, 1.5-mile hiking trail, and interpretive center. *10939 Highway 281, (701) 263-4390, www.peacegarden.com*

The Current Restaurant and Lounge
75 Forks Market Rd.
Winnipeg, MB
(204) 942-6555
www.innforks.com/dining/

Ft. Abraham Lincoln State Park
4480 Fort Lincoln Rd.
Mandan, ND
(701) 667-6380
www.fortlincoln.com

MORE pictures, **MORE** attractions, **MORE** at go.randmcnally.com/br

Blackstone Hotsprings (Truth or Consequences)

Blackstone Hotsprings lures travelers with more than just 104-degree natural mineral water streaming directly into private, oversized tubs. Guests can stay in TV-show-inspired theme rooms, such as the Roy Rogers Suite and The Jetsons.
410 Austin St., (575) 894-0894, www.blackstonehotsprings.com

EDITOR'S PICKS

Palma's Italian Grill (Deming)

Palma's Italian Grill is a popular dining spot both for the building's historical significance and for the friendly service. Made-from-scratch menu favorites include lasagna, manicotti, and southwestern chicken pasta (with green chiles mixed into the alfredo sauce).
110 S. Silver Ave., (575) 544-3100

THE LASTING LANDSCAPE

Truth or Consequences to Las Cruces, New Mexico

This enchanting land reminds all who traverse here that the Old West is alive. It's a place where frontier is not a historical term. A trip through the serene wilderness of southwestern New Mexico starts in the quirky town of Truth or Consequences, winds and twists westward through the mountains to Silver City, then loops south and east to Deming and Las Cruces. By the time this rustic journey concludes, visitors to the Land of Enchantment return to civilization with a renewed sense of country, culture, and self.

Best known: Elephant Butte Lake State Park; New Mexico State University in Las Cruces; Spaceport America* in Sierra County.

*At press time, Spaceport America was scheduled to open in early 2010, and hundreds of tickets had already been sold for Virgin Galactic commercial space tourism flights. Keep up with the progress at www.spaceportamerica.com.

More Great Stops

■ **Little Sprout Market and Juice Bar**
400 N. Broadway St.
Truth or Consequences, NM
(575) 894-4114

■ **Palace Hotel**
106 W. Broadway St.
Silver City, NM
(575) 388-1811
www.zianet.com/palacehotel

■ **Deming Luna Mimbres Museum and Custom House**
310 S. Silver Ave.
Deming, NM
(575) 546-2382
www.deminglunamimbresmuseum.com/

MORE pictures, MORE attractions, MORE at go.randmcnally.com/br

Nambé (Old Mesilla)

New Mexico treasure Nambé is beautiful and useful: it retains hot or cold temperatures and resembles silver but does not chip or tarnish. The Nambé store on the Old Mesilla square offers the complete line of products, including the eight-metal Nambé Alloy. *2109 Calle de Parian, (575) 527-4623, www.nambe.com*

EDITOR'S PICKS

Silver City Museum (Silver City)

The Silver City Museum serves as the "Treasure Vault of New Mexico," with more than 20,000 artifacts in its collection. A third-floor cupola overlooks the hill where silver was originally discovered and where the Legal Tender mine was located in 1870. *312 W. Broadway St., (575) 538-5921, www.silvercitymuseum.org*

Chile Pepper Institute (Las Cruces)

The Chile Pepper Institute enlightens visitors about the "hottest" crop around. The institute sells seeds for growing chile peppers and cookbooks for preparing them, and provides guided tours of a colorful chile garden filled with more than 200 types of chile pepper. *College St. and Knox St. MSC 3Q, New Mexico State University, (575) 646-3028, www.chilepepperinstitute.org*

■ **New Mexico Farm & Ranch Museum**
4100 Dripping Springs Rd.
Las Cruces, NM
(575) 522-4100
www.nmfarmandranchmuseum.org

■ **La Posta de Mesilla**
2410 Calle de San Albino
Mesilla, NM
(575) 524-3524
www.laposta-de-mesilla.com

6

Corning Museum of Glass (Corning)

Inside a landmark glass building, the Corning Museum of Glass demonstrates glassblowing and glass breaking. Visitors can make their own glass objects ($10-$27) or purchase an heirloom at the GlassMarket.
One Museum Way, (800) 732-6845, www.cmog.org

EDITOR'S PICKS

New York Wine & Culinary Center (Canandaigua)

At the New York Wine & Culinary Center, the LeCesse Garden shows off New York State crops, while the hands-on kitchen offers cooking classes. Meals at the Taste of New York Lounge feature New York ingredients and are paired with local beers and wine. *800 South Main St., (585) 394-7070, www.nywcc.com*

CULTIVATING NEW YORK

Canandaigua to Cooperstown, New York

There's no straight shot through upstate New York, not with those lakes in the way. But with all the good food to sample, it's worth taking the drive easy along the Finger Lakes, over the hills, through the farmland, and into river valleys. This road trip begins in Canandaigua, at the northern end of a western Finger Lake, and meanders south to Corning, then north to Ithaca, and gradually east toward Herkimer until it ends near the other great New York waterway, the Mohawk River Valley. New Yorkers and visitors are renewing attention to the land: the food grown here, the ecology that sustains farms and wildlife populations, and the waterways that fostered and transported culture across the state.

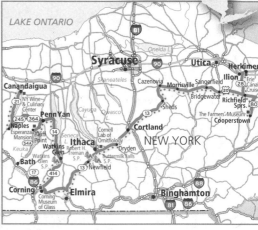

Best known: Watkins Glen International Raceway; Glenora Wine Cellars in Dundee; Baseball Hall of Fame in Cooperstown.

More Great Stops

Bully Hill Vineyards
8843 Greyton H. Taylor Memorial Drive
Hammondsport, NY
(607) 868-3210
www.bullyhill.com

Seward House
33 South St.
Auburn, NY
(315) 252-1283
www.sewardhouse.org

Oneida Community Mansion House
170 Kenwood Ave.
Oneida, NY
(315) 363-0745
www.oneidacommunity.org

The Farmers' Museum (Cooperstown)

At The Farmers' Museum, costumed interpreters carry out daily tasks in many of the 26 historic buildings. Twenty-four hand-carved animals carry children around the Empire State Carousel while parents read about famous New Yorkers on the carousel's frieze. *5775 NY 80, (888) 547-1450, www.farmersmuseum.org*

Cornell Lab of Ornithology (Ithaca)

At the Cornell Lab of Ornithology Visitors' Center, sample birdsong and make your own in the replica sound studio, try out powerful scopes, and stock up on birding equipment. Four-and-a-half miles of easy trails wind through 220-acre Sapsucker Woods. *159 Sapsucker Woods Rd., (800) 843-2473, www.birds.cornell.edu*

EDITOR'S PICKS

Erie Canal Cruise (Herkimer)

For 90 minutes aboard the *Lil' Diamond II* cruise boat, Captain Jerry entertains with tales of the Erie Barge Canal. When the Lock 18 doors close, the lock house seems to rise into the air as slimy walls creep up alongside the boat. *800 Mohawk St., (315) 715-0350, www.eriecanalcruises.com*

Esperanza Mansion (Bluff Point)

Esperanza Mansion overlooks Keuka Lake; its kitchen offers meals inside the Greek Revival house, outside on the patio, or aboard the *Esperanza Rose* tour boat. Puff pastry enfolds the warm turkey and brie sandwich, a local favorite ($14). *3456 NY 54A, (866) 927-4400, www.esperanzamansion.com*

Erie Canal Village

5789 Rome New London Rd. (NY 46/49)
Rome, NY
(315) 337-3999
www.eriecanalvillage.net

Fly Creek Cider Mill and Orchard

288 Goose St.
Fly Creek, NY
(800) 505-6455
www.flycreekcidermill.com

8

Upper Klamath National Wildlife Refuge canoe trail (Rocky Point, OR)

Rent a canoe (at The Ledge in Klamath Falls or from Rocky Point Resort) or bring your own craft for a paddle along a waterway trail where wildlife abounds. Look for osprey, white pelicans, even eagles fishing. *Rocky Point Resort, 28121 Rocky Point Rd., (530) 667-2231, www.fws.gov/klamathbasinrefuges/*

EDITOR'S PICKS

Nibbley's Cafe (Klamath Falls, OR)

Oatcakes, a substantial pancake that can be topped with blueberries, pecans, or bananas, are the house specialty for breakfast at this friendly local hangout. Lunch staples include fresh oat bread sandwiches and wraps. *2650 Washburn Way, Ste. 120, (541) 883-2314*

VOLCANIC LEGACY

Crater Lake, Oregon, to Mt. Shasta, California

Poor Lewis and Clark. They culminated their 1804 cross-country trek in a miserable nonstop rainy season at Ft. Clatsop, in the far northwestern corner of Oregon. If they'd only come down to south-central Oregon, starting just past present-day Eugene, they would have found abundant wildlife and rivers, spied the beautiful blue of Crater Lake, seen amazing formations in Oregon Caves just west of today's Medford. Further south, in California, they would have walked the eerie landscape that is now Lava Beds National Monument and hiked the majestic Shasta Cascade Mountains. Today's visitor can circle back up into Oregon for stops at wineries, cheese factories, and boutique chocolate producers along with gourmet restaurants in the Medford/Ashland area. Adventurous types go for the river rafting and jetboating (in Grants Pass), kayaking and canoeing wilderness trails, bicycling rail trails, a treehouse resort or even a railroad car motel. It's truly an explorer's paradise.

Best known: Crater Lake; Lava Beds National Park; Mt. Shasta; Ashland Shakespeare Festival in Ashland.

More Great Stops

■ **Hi-Lo Cafe**
88 S. Weed Blvd.
Weed, CA
(530) 938-2904
www.sisdevco.com/cafe.html

■ **Sundial Bridge at Turtle Bay**
1335 Arboretum Drive
Redding, CA
(530) 242-3143
www.turtlebay.org

■ **Oregon Caves National Monument Big Tree Loop Trail**
19000 Caves Hwy.
Cave Junction, OR
(541) 592-2100
www.nps.gov/orca

MORE pictures, MORE attractions, MORE at go.randmcnally.com/br

Railroad Park Resort and RV Campground (Dunsmuir, CA)

Spend the night in your own caboose or rail car, all outfitted as motel rooms. The Shasta Cascades serve as a gorgeous natural backdrop for the resort. The RV Campground features an old-time popular "swimming hole" and sandy beach. *100 Railroad Park Rd., (530) 235-4440, www.rrpark.com*

Harry & David Country Village (Medford, OR)

Tour the famed and extensive catalog operations, past rows of chocolate dippers and fruit and basket packers, then use the $5 tour fee toward purchasing fresh pears or other food goodies at the store afterward. *1314 Center Dr., (877) 322-8000, www.harryanddavid.com*

EDITOR'S PICKS

Happy Trails Cowboy Campground (Chiloquin, OR)

Sign up for a custom trail ride into Winema National Forest, enjoy a cowboy steak dinner by the campfire, and sleep in a platform tent or in your own RV at this horse-friendly campground that also welcomes your family pet. *46925 Hwy. 97 North, (541) 783-3559, www.happytrailscowboycampground.com*

Hellgate Jetboat Excursions (Grants Pass, OR)

Ride the wild Rogue River at breakneck speeds in a jetboat. The pace slows only to check out osprey nests, beaver dams, and other wildlife. Excursions range from two-hour blasts to five-hour power rides ($37 to $62 for adults). *966 SW 6th St., (800) 648-4874, www.hellgate.com*

Rogue Creamery Store
311 N. Front St.
Central Point, OR
(541) 665-1155
www.roguecreamery.com

Dragonfly Café and Gardens
241 Hargadine St.
Ashland, OR
(541) 488-4855
www.dragonflyashland.com

Kudzu Kabin Designs (Walhalla)

Native American and local fiber artist Nancy Basket finds practical use for each part of the Japanese-import kudzu plant. Visitors can create their own baskets, learn the paper-making process, and choose from dozens of prints, art cards, baskets, soaps, and jellies in her shop. *1105 E. Main St., (864) 718-8864, www.nancybasket.com*

Old Town Bistro (Rock Hill)

The Old Town Bistro honors the 1961 Friendship Nine civil rights protest with the original barstools at the counter. Patrons learn about the event through photos and a historical marker, then enjoy Southern-style classics such as broasted chicken with fried okra and fried squash. *135 E. Main St., (803) 327-9222, www.rholdtownbistro.com*

SOUTHERN CHARM

Rock Hill to Greenwood, South Carolina

Tucked neatly between the Appalachian Mountains and the Atlantic Ocean is humble Upcountry South Carolina. Revolutionary War and Civil War battlefields engage generations of history enthusiasts, while forests, rivers, and steep waterfalls create a natural playground. Beginning in Rock Hill, this drive along rolling country roads heads north to follow the Cherokee Foothills National Scenic Highway (SC 11), then continues south to Abbeville and Greenwood. The scenery and adventure opportunities abound amid the Deep South's truest charms: history and hospitality.

Best known: Carowinds amusement park in Charlotte; Chattooga River (film site for *Deliverance*); Cowpens National Battlefield in Gaffney; Clemson University in Clemson.

More Great Stops

Sanders Farm Stand
2275 Filbert Hwy.
Filbert, SC
(803) 684-9156
www.dorisanders.com

Carolina Foothills Artisan Center
124 W. Cherokee St.
Chesnee, SC
(864) 461-3050
www.cfac.us

Hagood Mill
307 Johnson St.
Pickens, SC
(864) 898-2936
www.co.pickens.sc.us/culturalcommission/

MORE pictures, MORE attractions, MORE at go.randmcnally.com/br

Historic Brattonsville (McConnells)

Costumed interpreters enlighten visitors about Historic Brattonsville's role in history, especially the Revolutionary War and slavery. An eight-and-a-half-mile network of hiking/mountain bike trails includes a battlefield trail and a nature trail.
1444 Brattonsville Rd., (803) 684-2327, www.chmuseums.org

Park Seed Co. (Hodges)

A tour of the Park Seed Co.'s headquarters reveals a horticulture wonderland, with more than 48,000 flowers, vegetables, shrubs, and trees. The on-site Garden Center sells seeds, unusual plants and bulbs, and unique and useful gardening accessories.
3507 Cokesbury Rd., (864) 223-8555, www.parkseed.com

Upcountry History Museum (Greenville)

Upcountry history comes to life via multimedia and sound and light presentations, covering everything from wars and textiles to Shoeless Joe Jackson. Children enjoy having their picture taken with the iconic pigs in the lobby, then taking a souvenir pig mascot home ($5).
540 Buncombe St., (864) 467-3100, www.upcountryhistory.org

EDITOR'S PICKS

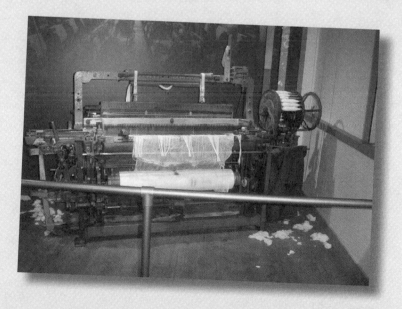

Table Rock State Park (Pickens)

In the deep, densely forested foothills of the Blue Ridge Mountains, visitors to Table Rock State Park enjoy swimming, canoeing and paddle boating, fishing, and hiking a variety of trails, including to the top of Table Rock Mountain.
158 E. Ellison Ln., (864) 878-9813, www.southcarolinaparks.com

---

■ **Split Creek Farm**
3806 Centerville Rd.
Anderson, SC
(864) 287-3921
www.splitcreek.com

■ **Hearthside Manor**
1304 N. Main St.
Abbeville, SC
(864) 366 6555
www.hearthsidemanorbedandbreakfast.com

ROAD WORK

Road construction and road conditions resources

Road closed. Single lane traffic ahead. Detour.

When you are on the road, knowledge is power. Let Rand McNally help you avoid situations that can result in delays, or worse.

There are ways to prepare for construction traffic and avoid the dangers of poor road conditions. Read on:

1. Use the state and province websites and hotlines listed on this page for road construction and road conditions information.

2. Visit go.randmcnally.com/roadconstruction for current U.S. and Canadian road construction information.

Get the Info from the 511 hotline

The U.S. Federal Highway Administration has begun implementing a national system of highway and road conditions/construction information for travelers. Under the new plan, travelers can dial 511 and get up-to-date information on roads and highways.

Implementation of 511 is the responsibility of state and local agencies.

For more details, visit:
www.fhwa.dot.gov/trafficinfo/511.htm.

Get updated road construction info and get rolling.
Register your 2010 Rand McNally Road Atlas and get FREE access to premium road construction information.
• Road construction maps
• Detailed, accurate information
• Project dates
• Trip-specific information
go.randmcnally.com/roadatlas

❇ Road conditions
⛰ Road construction
● Both

United States

Alabama
www.dot.state.al.us/docs ●

Alaska
511 ●
(866) 282-7577 ●
511.alaska.gov ●
In AK: (800) 478-7675 ❇

Arizona
511 ●
(888) 411-7623 ●
www.az511.com ●

Arkansas
(800) 245-1672 ❇
(501) 569-2000 ❇
(501) 569-2227 ●
www.arkansashighways.com ●

California
(916) 445-7623 ⛰
www.dot.ca.gov ●
San Francisco Bay area: 511 ●,
www.511.org ●
Sacramento Region: 511 ●,
www.sacregion511.org ●
San Diego: 511,
www.511sd.com ●
In CA: (800) 427-7623 ❇

Colorado
511 ●
(303) 639-1111 ●
www.cotrip.org ●
In CO: (877) 315-7623 ●

Connecticut
(860) 594-2000 ❇
www.ct.gov/dot ●
In CT: (800) 443-6817 ●

Delaware
www.deldot.net ●
In DE: (800) 652-5600 ●
Out of state: (302) 760-2080 ●

Florida
511 ●
www.fl511.com ●
www.dot.state.fl.us ●

Georgia
511 ●
(877) 694-2511 ●
(404) 635-8000 ●
www.511ga.org ●
www.georgia-navigator.com ●

Hawaii
(808) 536-6566 ⛰
www.hawaii.gov/dot/highways/roadwork/ ⛰

Idaho
511 ●
(888) 432-7623 ●
511.idaho.gov ●

Illinois
(800) 452-4368 ●
www.gettingaroundillinois.com ●

Indiana
(800) 261-7623 ❇
(317) 232-5533 ❇
www.in.gov/dot ●

Iowa
511 ●
(800) 288-1047 ●
www.511ia.org ●

Kansas
511 ●
(800) 585-7623 ●
511.ksdot.org ●

Kentucky
511 ●
(866) 737-3767 ●
www.511.ky.gov ●

Louisiana
(888) 762-3511 ●
www.511la.org ●

Maine
511 ●
(866) 282-7578 ●
(207) 624-3595 ●
www.511maine.gov ●

Maryland
(800) 543-2515 ●
(410) 582-5650 ●
www.chart.state.md.us ●

Massachusetts
511 ●
(617) 374-1234 ●
www.mhd.state.ma.us/ ●

Michigan
(800) 381-8477 ●
www.michigan.gov/mdot/ ●
Metro Detroit: (800) 641-6368 ⚑

Minnesota
511 ●
(800) 657-3774 ●
(651) 296-3000 ●
www.511mn.org ●

Mississippi
(601) 359-7017 ●
www.mstraffic.com ●

Missouri
(800) 222-6400 ⚑
(888) 275-6636 ●
(573) 751-2551 ●
St. Louis Gateway: 511 ●,
(877) 478-5511 ●,
www.gatewayguide.com/atis/
index.html ●
www.modot.mo.gov ●

Montana
511 ●
(800) 226-7623 ●
www.mdt.mt.gov/travinfo/511 ●

Nebraska
511 ●
(800) 906-9069 ●
(402) 471-4533 ●
www.nebraskatransportation.
org ●

Nevada
511 ●
(877) 687-6237 ●
www.safetravelusa.com/nv/ ●

New Hampshire
511 ●
(866) 282-7579 ●
www.nh.gov/dot/511 ●

New Jersey
511 ●
www.state.nj.us/transportation/
commuter/511/conditions.shtm ●
Turnpike: (800) 336-5875 ●,
www.state.nj.us/turnpike/ ●
Garden State Parkway:
(732) 727-5929 ●,
www.state.nj.us/turnpike/gsp-
conditions.htm ●

New Mexico
(800) 432-4269 ●
www.nmroads.com ●

New York
www.nysdot.gov ●
(518) 457-6195
Thruway: (800) 847-8929 ●,
www.thruway.state.ny.us ●

North Carolina
511 ●
(877) 511-4662 ●
www.ncdot.org/traffictravel ●

North Dakota
511 ●
(866) 696-3511 ●
www.dot.nd.gov/divisions/
maintenance/511_nd.html ●

Ohio
(614) 644-7031 ⚑
www.buckeyetraffic.org ●
Cincinnati/northern Kentucky
area: 511 ●, (513) 333-3333 ●,
www.artimis.org ●
Turnpike: (440) 234-2030 ⚑,
(888) 876-7453 ●,
www.ohioturnpike.org ●
In OH: (888) 264-7623 ●

Oklahoma
(888) 425-2385 ⚑
(405) 425-2385 ⚑
www.okladot.state.ok.us ●

Oregon
511 ●
(800) 977-6368 ●
(503) 588-2941 ●
www.tripcheck.com ●

Pennsylvania
(717) 783-5186 ●
www.dot7.state.pa.us/
TravelerInformation/ ●
In PA: (888) 783-6783 ●

Rhode Island
511 ●
Outside RI: (888) 401-4511 ●
www2.tmc.state.ri.us ●

South Carolina
www.dot.state.sc.us ●

South Dakota
511 ●
(866) 697-3511 ●
www.sddot.com/travinfo.asp ●

Tennessee
511 ●
(877) 244-0065 ●
www.tn511.com ●

Texas
(800) 452-9292 ●
www.dot.state.tx.us/travel/ ●

Utah
511 ●
(800) 492-2400 ●
(866) 511-8824 ●
www.utahcommuterlink.com ●

Vermont
511 ●
(800) 429-7623 ●
www.aot.state.vt.us/
travelinfo.htm ●
www.511vt.com ●

Virginia
511 ●
(800) 578-4111 ●
(800) 367-7623 ●
www.511virginia.org ●

Washington
511 ●
(800) 695-7623 ●
www.wsdot.wa.gov/traffic/ ●

Washington, D.C.
311 ●
(202) 727-1000 ●
www.ddot.dc.gov/ ●

West Virginia
(877) 982-7623 ✳
www.wvdot.com ●

Wisconsin
(800) 762-3947 ●
www.dot.state.wi.us/travel/
incident-alerts.htm ●

Wyoming
511 ✳
(888) 996-7623 ✳
www.dot.state.wy.us ●
www.wyoroad.info ●

Canada
Alberta
(403) 246-5853 ●
(877) 262-4997 ●
www.trans.gov.ab.ca ●
www.ama.ab.ca ●

British Columbia
(800) 550-4997 ●
www.drivebc.ca/ ●

Manitoba
(204) 945-3704 ●
www.gov.mb.ca/roadinfo/ ●
In MB: (877) 627-6237 ●

New Brunswick
www1.gnb.ca/cnb/
transportation/index-e.asp ●
In NB: (800) 561-4063 ✳

Newfoundland & Labrador
www.roads.gov.nl.ca ●

Nova Scotia
511 ●
(902) 424-3933 ✳
www.gov.ns.ca/tran ●
In NS: (800) 307-7669 ✳

Ontario
www.mto.gov.on.ca/english/
traveller/ ●
In ON: (800) 268-4686 ●
In Toronto: (416) 235-4686 ●

Prince Edward Island
(902) 368-4770 ●
(Nov–May 24 hours;
Jun-Oct daytime only)
www.gov.pe.ca/roadconditions ✳

Québec
(888) 355-0511 ●
www.inforoutiere.qc.ca ●
In Québec: (877) 393-2363 ●

Saskatchewan
(888) 335-7623 ●
www.highways.gov.sk.ca/
road-conditions ●

Mexico
www.sct.gob.mx ●
(in Spanish only)

HOTEL RESOURCES

Adam's Mark Hotels & Resorts
(800) 444-2326
www.adamsmark.com

America's Best Inns & Suites
(800) 237-8466
www.americasbestinns.com

AmericInn
(800) 396-5007
www.americinn.com

Baymont Inn & Suites
(877) 229-6668
www.baymontinn.com

Best Western
(800) 780-7234
www.bestwestern.com

Budget Host
(800) 283-4678
www.budgethost.com

Clarion Hotels
(877) 424-6423
www.clarionhotel.com

Coast Hotels & Resorts
(800) 716-6199
www.coasthotels.com

Comfort Inn
(877) 424-6423
www.comfortinn.com

Comfort Suites
(877) 424-6423
www.comfortsuites.com

Courtyard by Marriott
(888) 236-2427
www.courtyard.com

Crowne Plaza Hotel & Resorts
(877) 227-6963
www.crowneplaza.com

Days Inn
(800) 329-7466
www.daysinn.com

Delta Hotels & Resorts
(888) 890-3222
www.deltahotels.com

Doubletree Hotels, Guest Suites, Resorts & Clubs
(800) 222-8733
www.doubletree.com

Drury Hotels
(800) 378-7946
www.druryhotels.com

Econo Lodge
(877) 424-6423
www.econolodge.com

Embassy Suites Hotels
(800) 362-2779
www.embassysuites.com

Extended Stay Hotels
(800) 804-3724
www.extstay.com

Fairfield Inn by Marriott
(800) 228-2800
www.fairfieldinn.com

Fairmont Hotels & Resorts
(800) 257-7544
www.fairmont.com

Four Points by Sheraton
(800) 368-7764
www.fourpoints.com

Four Seasons Hotels & Resorts
(800) 819-5053
www.fourseasons.com

Hampton Inn
(800) 426-7866
www.hamptoninn.com

Hilton Hotels
(800) 445-8667
www.hilton.com

Holiday Inn Hotels & Resorts
(888) 465-4329
www.holidayinn.com

Homewood Suites
(800) 225-5466
www.homewood-suites.com

Howard Johnson
(800) 446-4656
www.hojo.com

Hyatt Hotels & Resorts
(888) 591-1234
www.hyatt.com

InterContinental Hotels & Resorts
(888) 424-6835
www.intercontinental.com

Jameson Inns
(800) 526-3766
www.jamesoninns.com

Knights Inn
(800) 843-5644
www.knightsinn.com

La Quinta Inns & Suites
(800) 753-3757
www.lq.com

Le Méridien Hotels & Resorts
(800) 543-4300
www.lemeridien.com

Loews Hotels
(866) 563-9792
www.loewshotels.com

MainStay Suites
(877) 424-6423
www.mainstaysuites.com

Marriott International
(888) 236-2427
www.marriott.com

Microtel Inns & Suites
(800) 771-7171
www.microtelinn.com

Motel 6
(800) 466-8356
www.motel6.com

Omni Hotels
(888) 444-6664 (U.S. only)
(402) 952-6664 (outside U.S.)
www.omnihotels.com

Park Inn
(888) 201-1801
www.parkinn.com

Preferred Hotels & Resorts
(800) 323-7500
www.preferredhotels.com

Quality Inn & Suites
(877) 424-6423
www.qualityinn.com

Radisson Hotels & Resorts
(888) 201-1718
www.radisson.com

Ramada Worldwide
(800) 272-6232
www.ramada.com

Red Lion Hotels
(800) 733-5466
www.redlion.com

Red Roof Inn
(800) 733-7663
www.redroof.com

Renaissance Hotels & Resorts by Marriott
(800) 468-3571
www.renaissancehotels.com

Residence Inn by Marriott
(800) 331-3131
www.residenceinn.com

The Ritz-Carlton
(800) 542-8680
www.ritzcarlton.com

Rodeway Inn
(877) 424-6423
www.rodeway.com

Sheraton Hotels & Resorts
(800) 325-3535
www.sheraton.com

Sleep Inn
(877) 424-6423
www.sleepinn.com

Super 8
(800) 800-8000
www.super8.com

Travelodge Hotels
(800) 578-7878
www.travelodge.com

Westin Hotels & Resorts
(800) 937-8461
www.westin.com

Wyndham Hotels & Resorts
(877) 999-3223
www.wyndham.com

To find a bed-and-breakfast at your destination, log on to www.bedandbreakfast.com.®

NOTE: All toll-free reservation numbers are for the U.S. and Canada unless otherwise noted. These numbers were accurate at press time, but are subject to change. Find more listings or book a hotel online at randmcnally.com.

RENTAL CAR RESOURCES

**Advantage
Rent-A-Car**
(800) 777-5500
www.arac.com

Alamo Rent A Car
(800) 462-5266
www.alamo.com

Avis Rent A Car
(800) 331-1212
www.avis.com

Budget Rent A Car
(800) 527-0700
(U.S. & Canada)
(800) 472-3325
(International)
www.budget.com

**Enterprise
Rent-A-Car**
(800) 261-7331
www.enterprise.com

Hertz Car Rental
(800) 654-3131
(U.S. & Canada)
(800) 654-3001
(International)
www.hertz.com

National Car Rental
(800) 227-7368
www.nationalcar.com

Payless Car Rental
(800) 729-5377
(U.S., Canada & Mexico)
www.paylesscarrental.com

Thrifty Car Rental
(800) 847-4389
www.thrifty.com

CELL PHONE EMERGENCY NUMBERS

Alabama
*47

Alaska
911

Arizona
911

Arkansas
911

California
911

Colorado
911, *277

Connecticut
911

Delaware
911

District of
Columbia
911

Florida
911; *347

Georgia
911; *477

Hawaii
911

Idaho
*477

Illinois
911

Indiana
911

Iowa
911; *55

Kansas
911; *47

Kentucky
(800) 222-5555
(in KY)

Louisiana
911; *577 (road
emergencies)

Maine
911

Maryland
911

Massachusetts
911

Michigan
911

Minnesota
911

Mississippi
911

Missouri
*55

Montana
911

Nebraska
*55

Nevada
*647

New Hampshire
*77

New Jersey
911, *77

New Mexico
911

New York
911

North Carolina
911; *47

North Dakota
*2121

Ohio
911

Oklahoma
911

Oregon
911

Pennsylvania
911

Rhode Island
911

South Carolina
911

South Dakota
911

Tennessee
911; *847

Texas
911

Utah
911; *11

Vermont
911

Virginia
911

Washington
911

West Virginia
911; *77

Wisconsin
911

Wyoming
911

Map Legend

Roads and related symbols

Free limited-access highway

Toll limited-access highway

New road (under construction as of press time)

Other multilane highway

Principal highway

Other through highway

Other road (conditions vary — local inquiry suggested)

Unpaved road (conditions vary — local inquiry suggested)

One way route; ferry

Interstate highway; Interstate highway business route

U.S. highway; U.S. highway business route

Trans-Canada highway; Autoroute

Mexican highway or Central American highway

State or provincial highway

Secondary state, secondary provincial, or county highway

County trunk highway

Toll booth or fee booth

Tunnel; mountain pass

Interchanges and exit numbers (For most states, the mileage between interchanges may be determined by subtracting one number from the other.)

Highway miles between arrows (Segments of one mile or less not shown.)

Comparative distance
1 mile = 1.609 kilometers   1 kilometer = 0.621 mile

Cities & towns (size of type on map indicates relative population)

National capital; state or provincial capital

County seat or independent city

City, town, or recognized place; neighborhood

Urbanized area

Separate cities within metropolitan area

Parks, recreation areas, & points of interest

U.S. or Canadian national park

U.S. or Canadian national monument, other National Park Service facility, state or provincial park, or recreation area

Park with camping facilities; park without camping facilities

National forest, national grassland, or city park; wildlife refuge

Point of interest, historic site or monument

Airport

Campsite; golf course or country club

Hospital or medical center

Indian reservation

Information center or Tourist Information Center (T.I.C.)

Military or governmental installation; military airport

Physical features

Dam

Mountain peak; highest point in state/province

Lake; dry lake

River; intermittent river

Desert; glacier

Swamp or mangrove swamp

Other symbols

Area shown in greater detail on inset map

Inset map page indicator

Intracoastal waterway

County or parish boundary and name

State or provincial boundary

National boundary

Continental divide

Time zone boundary

Population figures are from the latest available census or are Census Bureau or Rand McNally estimates.

For a complete list of abbreviations that appear on the maps, visit
go.randmcnally.com/ABBR.

©2010 Rand McNally

81 GREAT DESTINATIONS

Ready for a road trip? Our North American city guide will make mapping your route and filling your vacation itinerary super easy. We've put together profiles of **81** cities in the United States, Canada, and Mexico, including detailed maps to help you get around town and suggestions for nearby excursions. For attractions, shopping, and tourism information, start turning the pages. Whether you're searching for Sue, the *T. rex* at the Field Museum in Chicago; hoping to catch a glimpse of the stars shopping along Rodeo Drive in L.A.; or looking to check out the view from atop the CN Tower in Toronto, your vacation starts right here.

▶ DON'T MISS DRIVE

A visit to certain cities wouldn't be complete without a drive down its most famous or scenic street. Look for these routes throughout the guide for memorable moments while on the move.

▶ DIVERSION

Even on vacation, you may want to get out of town. Many other engaging destinations are often just a short drive away. Look for these diversions and directions on how to get there inside the guide, too.

ALBUQUERQUE, New Mexico

This desert city mixes Native American and Hispanic influences with a liberal dose of modern science. Exhibits and live performances at the Indian Pueblo Cultural Center introduce visitors to the ancient ways of the area's pueblo communities, while Petroglyph National Monument is the site of ancient rock etchings. In Old Town, the National Atomic Museum tells the story of New Mexico's role in the development of modern weaponry. The climb to Sandia Crest by either road or aerial tramway leads to spectacular views and exceptional skiing. *Tax: 12.88% hotel, 6.875% sales. For local weather, call (505) 821-1111.*

Old Town Plaza

► SELECTED ATTRACTIONS

Albuquerque Aquarium
2601 Central Ave. NW
in Albuquerque BioPark
(505) 764-6200

Albuquerque Museum of Art and History
2000 Mountain Rd. NW
(505) 243-7255

Cliff's Amusement Park
4800 Osuna Rd. NE
(505) 881-9373

¡Explora! Science Center and Children's Museum of Albuquerque
1701 Mountain Rd. NW
(505) 224-8300

Indian Pueblo Cultural Center
2401 12th St. NW
(505) 843-7270

National Hispanic Cultural Center
1701 4th St. SW
(505) 246-2261

National Museum of Nuclear Science & History
Eubank and Southern SE
(505) 245-2137

New Mexico Museum of Natural History and Science
1801 Mountain Rd. NW
(505) 841-2800

Petroglyph National Monument
6001 Unser Blvd. NW
(505) 899-0205

Rio Grande Botanic Garden
2601 Central Ave. NW
in Albuquerque BioPark
(505) 764-6200

Rio Grande Nature Center State Park
2901 Candelaria Rd. NW
(505) 344-7240

Rio Grande Zoo
903 10th St. SW in Albuquerque BioPark
(505) 764-6200

Sandia Peak Aerial Tramway
Skiing, restaurant, and tramway
10 Tramway Loop NE
(505) 856-7325

► SHOPPING

Coronado Center Mall
Department stores and specialty shops
6600 Menaul Blvd. NE
(505) 881-4600

Fashion Outlets Santa Fe
Brand-name and designer outlet stores
8380 Cerrillos Rd.
(505) 474-4000

Historic Nob Hill
Upscale boutiques, eclectic shops, art galleries, and restaurants
Central Ave. between Girard Blvd. and Washington St.
(505) 265-0433

Old Town
Arts and crafts shops, boutiques, and galleries
Bounded by Rio Grande Blvd., Central Ave., Mountain Rd., and 19th St.
(505) 319-4087

► VISITOR INFORMATION

Albuquerque Convention and Visitors Bureau
20 First Plaza NW, Ste. 601
Albuquerque, NM 87102
(505) 842-9918 or (800) 284-2282
www.itsatrip.org

Airport Information Center
Located in the lower level of the airport in the baggage claim area

Old Town Information Center
Plaza Don Luis on Romero St. NW, across from the San Felipe de Neri church

► DON'T MISS DRIVE

Central Avenue is old Route 66, with all of its neon, nostalgia, and distinctive architecture. Central runs through the heart of Albuquerque.

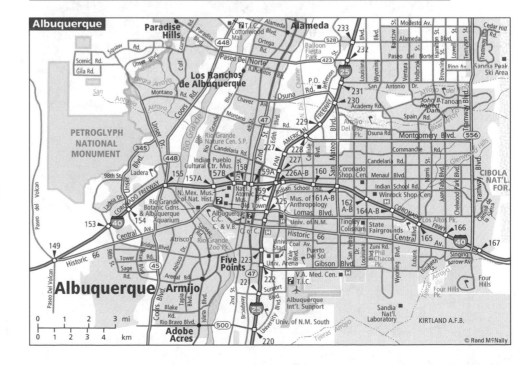

ATLANTA, Georgia

Centennial Olympic Park

Atlanta reached the pinnacle of homegrown success when the Olympic Games were held here in 1996. Visitors can stroll through the grounds at Centennial Olympic Park. Atlanta is also home to companies such as CNN and Coca-Cola, both of which feature tours and exhibits for the public. Sites dedicated to the life of Dr. Martin Luther King, Jr. offer a more somber reflection. For old-fashioned amusements, visitors and locals head to Six Flags Over Georgia. *Tax: 15% hotel, 8% sales. For local weather, call (770) 632-1837.*

▶ SELECTED ATTRACTIONS

Centennial Olympic Park
Park honoring the 1996 Olympic Summer Games
265 Park Avenue West NW
(404) 222-7275

CNN Center
Global headquarters and studio tours
One CNN Center
(404) 827-2300

Georgia Aquarium
World's largest
225 Baker St.
(404) 581-4000

High Museum of Art
1280 Peachtree St. NE
(404) 733-4444

Imagine It! The Children's Museum of Atlanta
275 Centennial Olympic Park Dr. NW
(404) 659-5437

Jimmy Carter Library and Museum
441 Freedom Pkwy.
(404) 865-7100

Martin Luther King, Jr. National Historic Site
450 Auburn Ave. NE
(404) 331-5190

World of Coca-Cola Atlanta
121 Baker St.
(404) 676-5151 or (800) 676-2653

▶ SHOPPING

Mall of Georgia
More than 225 stores and an amphitheater
3333 Buford Dr., Buford
(678) 482-8788

Phipps Plaza
World-class shops and fine dining
3500 Peachtree Rd. NE
(404) 262-0992

Peachtree Center
Specialty shops and dining
225 Peachtree St. NE
(404) 654-1296

▶ VISITOR INFORMATION

Atlanta Convention and Visitors Bureau
233 Peachtree St. NE, Ste. 1400
Atlanta, GA 30303
(404) 521-6600 or (800) 285-2682
www.atlanta.net

▶ DIVERSION

Stone Mountain Park is best known for its Confederate Memorial carving. The Park also has its own museums, gondola ride, and even water slides. 16 miles east of Atlanta, off US 78 at Stone Mountain. (770) 498-5690 or (800) 317-2006

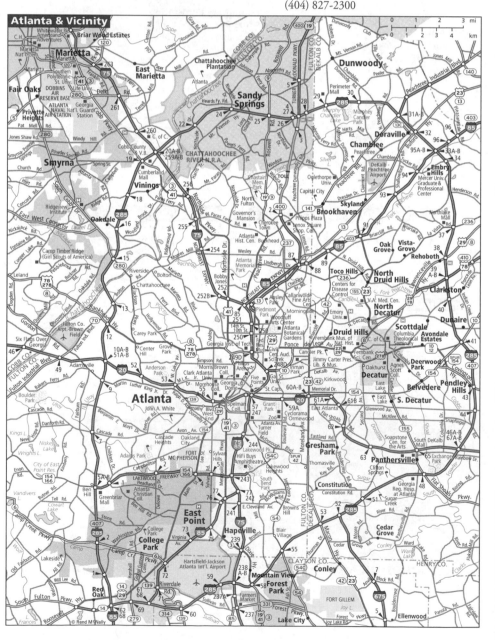

Atlanta & Vicinity

ATLANTIC CITY, New Jersey

A classic seaside resort with a history going back to the mid-1800s, Atlantic City became the first "Las Vegas East" with the introduction of casino gambling in 1978. Stories of the city's early days are preserved at the Atlantic City Historical Museum, where displays include memorabilia from the Miss America Pageant. One early attraction is still open for tours—Lucy, a giant elephant made of wood. More modern amusements and rides crowd the Steel Pier. *Tax: 14% hotel, 7% food and non-alcoholic beverage state sales tax for consumption on premises; 10% tax on alcoholic beverages consumed on premises. For local weather, call (609) 261-6600.*

Atlantic City Beach

▶ SELECTED ATTRACTIONS

Absecon Lighthouse
New Jersey's tallest lighthouse
31 S. Rhode Island Ave.
(609) 449-1360

Atlantic City Aquarium
800 N. New Hampshire Ave. at
Gardner's Basin
(609) 348-2880

Atlantic City Art Center on Garden Pier
Boardwalk at New Jersey Ave.
(609) 347-5837

Atlantic City Historical Museum
Garden Pier at New Jersey Ave.
(609) 347-5839

Atlantic City Miniature Golf
Boardwalk at Mississippi Ave.
(609) 347-1661

Central Pier Arcade & Speedway
NASCAR go-karts and paintball
1400 Boardwalk
(609) 345-5219

Civil Rights Garden at Carnegie Library
Seasonal garden and monument
Pacific Ave. at Martin Luther King Jr. Blvd.
(609) 347-0500

Lucy the Margate Elephant
Historic building shaped like an elephant
9200 Atlantic Ave., Margate
(609) 823-6473

Steel Pier
Family entertainment, rides for kids and adults
Virginia Ave. and the Boardwalk
(609) 345-4893 or (866) 386-6659

Storybook Land
Family fun park with storybook attractions and rides
6415 Black Horse Pike,
Egg Harbor Township
(609) 646-0103

▶ SHOPPING

"The Walk," Atlantic City Outlets
Outlet stores, restaurants, and nightclubs
1931 Atlantic Ave.
(609) 872-7002

Hamilton Mall
Specialty shops, restaurants, and food court
4403 Black Horse Pike, Mays Landing
(609) 646-8326

Shore Mall
Shops and restaurants
6725 Black Horse Pike,
Egg Harbor Township
(609) 484-9500

▶ VISITOR INFORMATION

Atlantic City Convention & Visitors Authority
2314 Pacific Ave.
Atlantic City, NJ 08401
(609) 348-7100 or (888) 228-4748
www.atlanticcitynj.com

Visitor Centers
The Atlantic City Expressway,
mile marker 3.5
The Boardwalk at Mississippi Avenue
(888) 228-4748

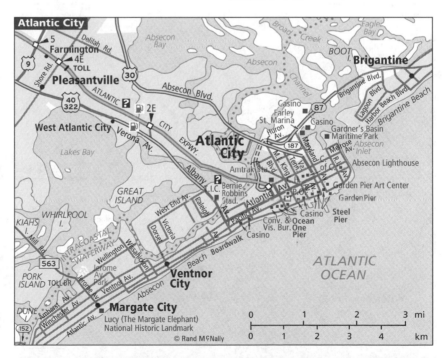

▶ DIVERSION

Step back in time and spend the day at the "Jersey Shore" as it was in the early days at Tuckerton Seaport in Tuckerton. See the lighthouse and other local landmarks. From Atlantic City, take the Garden State Parkway north to exit 50 to Tuckerton. (609) 296-8868

AUSTIN, Texas

Texas State Capitol

Austin enjoys a reputation as both a seat of state government and a powerful force in the world of popular music. Thousands trek here each year for the annual South by Southwest Music Festival. Visitors drawn to all things political will want to tour the State Capitol with its soaring marble dome as well as the Lyndon Baines Johnson Library and Museum. The Umlauf Sculpture Garden offers beauty in an all-natural setting. *Tax: 15% hotel, 8.25% sales. For local weather, call (830) 609-2029.*

DON'T MISS DRIVE

A ride down the city's famous Sixth Street places you in the middle of some 50 nightclubs and restaurants, with live music offerings of every genre and a host of colorful street characters. The Warehouse District between 4th and 6th Streets near Guadalupe also offers plenty of clubs and dining. (512) 478-0098

SELECTED ATTRACTIONS

Austin American-Statesman Bat Observation Center
305 S. Congress Ave.
(512) 327-9721

Barton Springs Pool
2101 Barton Springs Rd.
in Zilker Park
(512) 476-9044

Bob Bullock Texas State History Museum
1800 N. Congress Ave.
(512) 936-8746 or (866) 369-7108

Elisabet Ney Museum
Sculpture studio and portrait collection
304 E. 44th St.
(512) 458-2255

Harry Ransom Center
Art museum, rare books, and manuscripts
21st and Guadalupe Sts. at the University of Texas
(512) 471-8944

Lady Bird Johnson Wildflower Center
4801 LaCrosse Ave. off Loop 1
(512) 232-0100

Lyndon Baines Johnson Library and Museum
2313 Red River St.
(512) 721-0200

Texas State Capitol
1100 Congress Ave.
(512) 463-0063

Umlauf Sculpture Garden and Museum
605 Robert E. Lee Rd.
(512) 445-5582

SHOPPING

Arboretum at Great Hills
Specialty shops
10000 Research Blvd.
(512) 338-4437

Central Market
Old World marketplace grocery
4477 S. Lamar Blvd. and
4001 N. Lamar Blvd.
(512) 206-1000 or (800) 360-2552

South Congress Avenue (SoCo)
Antiques, folk art, and boutiques
S. Congress Ave., south of Town Lake to Johanna St.

West End
Art galleries and upscale antique shops
5th and 6th Sts. west of Lamar Blvd.

VISITOR INFORMATION

Austin Convention and Visitors Bureau
301 Congress Ave., Ste. 200
Austin, TX 78701
(512) 474-5171 or (800) 926-2282
www.austintexas.org

Visitor Center
209 E. 6th St.
(866) 462-8784

DIVERSION

Pack in a full day on 63-mile-long, 4.5-mile-wide Lake Travis for water sports, lakeside dining, and picnicking by the shore. From downtown Austin, travel north on Loop 1 (MoPac) to FM 2222. Go west on 2222 out to FM 620 south; Lake Travis is on the right.

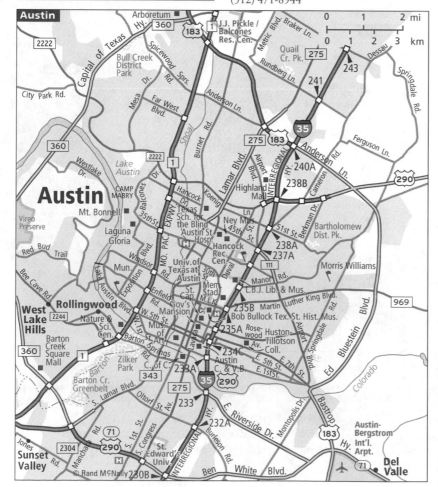

BALTIMORE, Maryland

With Chesapeake Bay at its front door, Baltimore takes full advantage of all that water has to offer. The National Aquarium draws millions to its coral reef. Nearby, the Maryland Science Center's motion simulator transports visitors on virtual space walks. On the harbor's far side lies Fort McHenry, site of the War of 1812 battle during which Francis Scott Key wrote the national anthem. And food lovers can revel in soft-shell crabs (eaten whole!). *Tax: 13.5% hotel, 6% sales. For local weather, call (410) 936-1212 or (703) 996-2200.*

Baltimore's Inner Harbor

▶ SELECTED ATTRACTIONS

Babe Ruth Birthplace Museum
216 Emory St.
(410) 727-1539

Baltimore Maritime Museum
Piers 3 & 5, Inner Harbor
(410) 396-3453

Baltimore Museum of Art
10 Art Museum Dr.
(443) 573-1700

Fort McHenry
2400 East Fort Ave.
(410) 962-4290

Harbor Cruises
561 Light St. at the Inner Harbor
(866) 312-2469

Maryland Science Center/IMAX
601 Light St.
(410) 685-5225

National Aquarium in Baltimore
501 E. Pratt St. on Pier 3
(410) 576-3800

**Sports Legends Museum
at Camden Yards**
301 W. Camden St.
(410) 727-1539

▶ SHOPPING

Fells Point
Antiques and collectibles
Fleet St. at Broadway
(410) 675-4776

Harborplace
Specialty shops and restaurants
200 E. Pratt St.
(410) 332-4191

Lexington Market
Fresh food market
400 W. Lexington St.
(410) 685-6169

▶ VISITOR INFORMATION

**Baltimore Area Convention and
Visitors Association**
100 Light St., 12th Fl.
Baltimore, MD 21202
(410) 659-7300 or (877) 225-8466
www.baltimore.org

Visitor Center
401 Light St.
(877) 225-8466

BILOXI/GULFPORT, Mississippi

A Biloxi Shrimping Trip expedition

Led by its resurgent casinos and the efforts of hundreds of thousands of volunteers, these towns have worked hard to bounce back from the devastating 2005 hurricane season. Within two years, 11 casinos had returned to full operation with many others on the drawing board. New family-oriented attractions are also being worked into the redevelopment mix. Originally known for its fishing fleet, Biloxi's charter boats offer a golden chance to catch snapper, amberjack, and even shark. *Tax: 12% hotel, 7% sales.*

In Gulfport, watery thrills can be enjoyed at the Gulf Islands Waterpark, while further inland, the StenniSphere allows visitors to see actual space shuttle engines and occasionally witness their testing. The Lynn Meadows Discovery Center keeps young minds engaged through role-playing activities and the ever-popular Super Colossal Climbing Structure. *Tax: 12% hotel, 7% sales.*

▶ SELECTED ATTRACTIONS

BILOXI

Biloxi Shrimping Trip
70-minute family shrimping excursion
693 Beach Blvd.
(228) 385-1182

Gulf Islands National Seashore
3500 Park Rd., Ocean Springs
(228) 875-9057

Hard Rock Hotel & Casino Biloxi
777 Beach Blvd.
(228) 374-7625

IP Casino Resort Spa
850 Bayview Ave.
(228) 436-3000

Ohr-O'Keefe Museum of Art
1596 Glenn Swetman St.
(228) 374-5547

Palace Casino Resort
158 Howard Ave.
(228) 432-8888

Walter Anderson Museum of Art
510 Washington Ave., Ocean Springs
(228) 872-3164

▶ SHOPPING

BILOXI

Edgewater Mall
Department stores and specialty shops
2600 Beach Blvd.
(228) 388-4636

Edgewater Village Shopping Center
Specialty shops
2650 Beach Blvd.

▶ SELECTED ATTRACTIONS

GULFPORT

Gulf Islands Waterpark
17200 16th St.
(228) 328-1266

Gulfport Dragway
Drag racing track
17085 Race Track Rd.
(228) 863-4408

Gulfport Little Theatre
Live performances
2600 13th St.
(228) 864-7983

Lynn Meadows Discovery Center
Children's museum
246 Dolan Ave.
(228) 897-6039

Seabee Heritage Center
U.S. Naval base, Atlantic home of Seabees
4902 Marvin Shields Blvd., Bldg. 1
(228) 871-3619

StenniSphere
Visitor Center at NASA Stennis Space Center
25 miles west of Gulfport off I-10, exit 2
(228) 688-2370 or (800) 237-1821

▶ SHOPPING

GULFPORT

Crossroads Mall
Department stores and specialty shops
I-10 at US 49

Prime Outlets at Gulfport
Designer outlet shops
10000 Factory Shops Blvd.
(228) 867-6100

▶ VISITOR INFORMATION

Mississippi Gulf Coast Convention and Visitors Bureau
11975 Seaway Rd.
Gulfport, MS 39503
(228) 896-6699 or (888) 467-4853
www.gulfcoast.org

Biloxi Visitor Center
932 Howard Ave.
(228) 435-6339

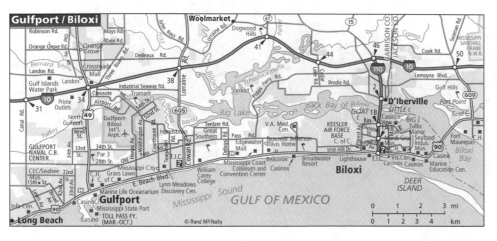

BOSTON, Massachusetts

A modern city of commerce, finance, and institutions of higher learning, Boston is inextricably linked to the Revolutionary War. A walk along Freedom Trail leads to birthplaces of the Revolution such as Paul Revere's House and the Old North Church. The city's museums include the Isabella Stewart Gardner, where works by Botticelli and Vermeer are displayed in a palatial setting, and the Institute of Contemporary Art in its new, dramatically cantilevered home by the docks. *Tax: 12.45% hotel, 5% sales. For local weather, call (508) 822-0634.*

Sailing in Boston

▶ SELECTED ATTRACTIONS

Boston Children's Museum
300 Congress St.
(617) 426-6500

The Freedom Trail
Self-guided historic walking tour
Tours begin at the Boston National
Historical Park Visitor Center
15 State St.
(617) 242-5642

Harvard Museum of Natural History
26 Oxford St., Cambridge
(617) 495-3045

Institute of Contemporary Art
100 Northern Ave.
(617) 478-3100

continued on the next page

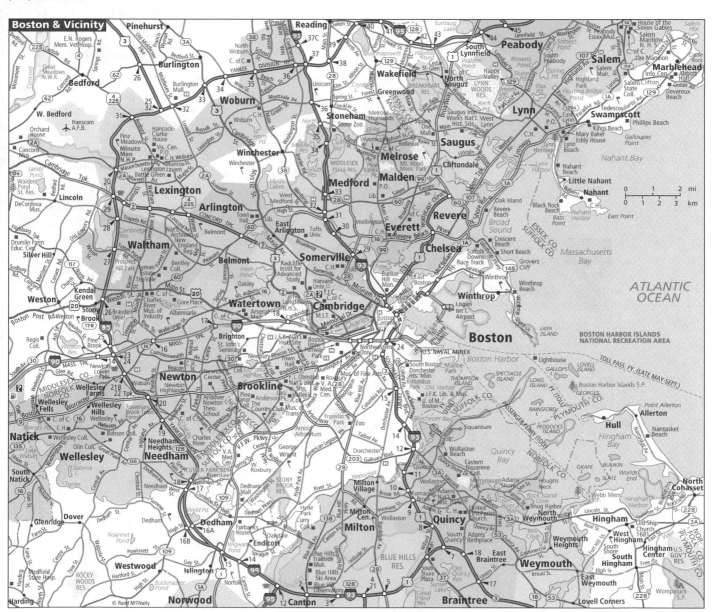

Boston attractions continued

Isabella Stewart Gardner Museum
Art museum in re-created Venetian palace
280 The Fenway
(617) 566-1401

John F. Kennedy Library and Museum
Off I-93 near Columbia Point
(617) 514-1600 or (866) 535-1960

Mary Baker Eddy Library for the Betterment of Humanity
Hall of ideas and Mapparium walk-through globe
200 Massachusetts Ave.
(617) 450-7000 or (888) 222-3711

Museum of Fine Arts
465 Huntington Ave.
(617) 267-9300

Museum of Science
O'Brien Hwy. between Storrow Dr. and Land Blvd.
(617) 723-2500

New England Aquarium
Central Wharf off Atlantic Ave.
(617) 973-5200

Old North Church
Boston's oldest church and its historic steeple
193 Salem St.
(617) 523-6676

Skywalk Observatory, Prudential Tower
800 Boylston St., 50th floor
(617) 859-0648

USS *Constitution* Ship and Museum
At the Charlestown Navy Yard
(617) 242-5671

DIVERSION

Just beyond Boston proper, connect to MA 1A and spend the day driving to Salem (perhaps with a stop at the House of the Seven Gables) and beyond on MA 127. The route hugs the rocky coast through Gloucester and beyond to Rockport and Andrews Point.

SHOPPING

CambridgeSide Galleria
Riverfront mall with department stores, specialty shops, and restaurants
100 CambridgeSide Place, Cambridge
(617) 621-8666

Copley Place
Department stores and designer boutiques
2 Copley Pl.
(617) 369-5000

Downtown Crossing
Department stores and specialty shops
Washington, Winter, and Summer Sts.
(617) 482-2139

Faneuil Hall Marketplace
Restaurants, galleries, and specialty shops
Congress and State Sts.
(617) 523-1300

The Shops at the Prudential Center
Department stores and retailers
800 Boylston St.
(617) 236-3100

VISITOR INFORMATION

Greater Boston Convention and Visitors Bureau
2 Copley Place, Ste. 105
Boston, MA 02116-6501
(617) 536-4100 or (888) 733-2678
www.bostonusa.com

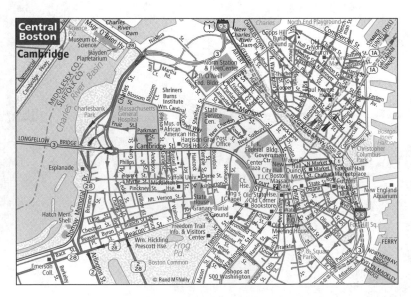

BRANSON, Missouri

More than 100 different theatrical entertainments have made this Ozark Mountain town one of the most popular vacation stops in middle America. But the comedians, singers, and diverse musical sounds filling the theaters along "The Strip" aren't the only shows in town. Silver Dollar City theme park offers high-speed thrill rides in a 19th-century setting, while the 95-acre Branson Landing features a $7 million water display amidst upscale lakefront shopping and dining. *Titanic:* The World's Largest Museum Attraction features a half-scale replica of the ship, interactive exhibits, and more than 400 artifacts. *Tax: 11.6% hotel, 8.6% sales, 8.975% food and beverage. For local weather, call (417) 336-5000.*

The Branson Strip

▶ SELECTED ATTRACTIONS

Baldknobbers Jamboree
Music theater and comedy
2835 W. MO 76
(417) 334-4528

Celebration City
Theme park with rides
1383 MO 376
(417) 336-7100 or (800) 831-4386

Dogwood Canyon Nature Park
2038 W. MO 86, Lampe
(417) 779-5983

Dolly Parton's Dixie Stampede
Dinner theater and horse show
1525 W. MO 76
(417) 336-3000 or (800) 520-5544

Grand Country Square
Dining, specialty shops, and family fun centers
1945 W. MO 76
(888) 514-1088

Ride the Ducks
City tours in land/water vehicles
2320 W. MO 76
(417) 336-7100 or (877) 887-8225

The Shepherd of the Hills Homestead
History and outdoor theater
5586 W. MO 76
(417) 334-4191

The Showboat Branson Belle
Show and lunch/dinner cruises
4800 MO 165
(800) 831-4386

Silver Dollar City
1880s theme park with rides
399 Indian Point Rd.
(417) 336-7100 or (800) 831-4386

Table Rock State Park
5272 MO 165
(417) 334-4704

The Track Family Fun Park
Go-karts, mini-golf, arcade, and more
3525 W. MO 76
(417) 334-1612

Welk Resort Branson
Musical variety shows
1984 MO 165
(417) 336-3575 or (800) 505-9355

White Water
12-acre water park
3505 W. MO 76
(417) 336-7100 or (800) 831-4386

▶ SHOPPING

Branson Mall
Shops, dining, and live music theater
2206 W. MO 76
(417) 334-5412

Dick's Old Time 5 & 10
Traditional dime store
103 W. Main St.
(417) 334-2410

Factory Merchants Branson
Outlet stores
1000 Pat Nash Dr.
(417) 335-6686

The Shoppes at Branson Meadows
Outlet stores
4562 Gretna Rd.
(417) 339-2580

Tanger Outlet Center
Outlet stores
300 Tanger Blvd.
(417) 337-9328

▶ VISITOR INFORMATION

Branson Lakes Area Chamber of Commerce and Convention and Visitors Bureau
269 MO 248
Branson, MO 65616
(417) 334-4136 or (800) 214-3661
www.explorebranson.com

▶ DIVERSION

Springfield, Missouri is only about 35 miles north of Branson and has a number of interesting attractions, including the first Bass Pro Shop. Also check out Wonders of Wildlife Museum and Aquarium, Wilson's Creek National Battlefield (site of a Civil War battle), and the Dickerson Park Zoo, which has breeding programs for several endangered species. Also, Fantastic Caverns offers ride-through cave tours. Springfield CVB: (417) 881-5300 or (800) 678-8767

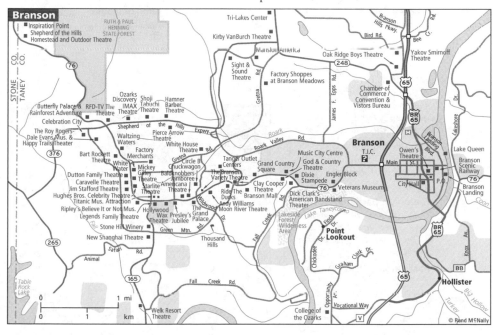

CALGARY, Alberta, Canada

Calgary occupies the western edge of the Canadian plains, the commercial center of a vast empire of cattle ranches, wheat farms, and oil and gas fields. Each year, hundreds of thousands attend the Calgary Stampede, one of the largest rodeo events in the world. For sweeping views of the mountains and plains, visitors ride to the observation deck and restaurant at the top of the Calgary Tower. The daring find even bigger thrills at Shaw Millennium Park, which offers the largest free outdoor skate park in the world, and at Canada Olympic Park, where visitors can take a turn on the luge. *Tax: 4% provincial tourism levy, 1% destination marketing fee, 5% GST.*

Eau Claire Festival Market

▶ SELECTED ATTRACTIONS

Aero Space Museum
4629 McCall Way NE
(403) 250-3752

Butterfield Acres Children's Farm
Family farm and petting zoos
254077 Rocky Ridge Rd.
(403) 547-3595

Calaway Park
Amusement park
245033 Range Rd. 33
(403) 240-3822

Calgary Chinese Cultural Centre
197 1st St. SW
(403) 262-5071

Calgary Stampede
Held every July, includes entertainers, cowboys, parades, chuck wagon races, and free pancake breakfasts
Calgary Stampede Park
1410 Olympic Way SE
(403) 261-0101 or
(800) 661-1260

Calgary Tower
Views of Calgary and the Canadian Rockies
101 9th Ave. SW
(403) 266-7171

Calgary Zoo, Botanical Garden, and Prehistoric Park
1300 Zoo Rd. NE at
Memorial Dr.
(403) 232-9300 or
(800) 588-9993

Canada Olympic Park
88 Canada Olympic Rd. SW
along Trans-Canada Hwy. 1
(403) 247-5452

Devonian Gardens
Indoor gardens with waterfalls, playground, artwork, and sculptures
317 7th Ave. SW, 4th level
(403) 268-2489

Fort Calgary Historic Park
750 9th Ave. SE
(403) 290-1875

Glenbow Museum
Exhibits on Western settlement and international art
130 9th Ave. SE
(403) 268-4100

Head-Smashed-In Buffalo Jump
Prehistoric archaeological site
On Hwy. 785, Fort Macleod
(403) 553-2731

Heritage Park Historical Village
Early 1900s village
1900 Heritage Dr. SW
(403) 268-8500

Inglewood Bird Sanctuary & Nature Center
2425 9th Ave. SE
(403) 268-2489

Shaw Millennium Park
Beach volleyball courts, skate park
1220 9th Ave. SW
(403) 268-2489

Telus World of Science – Calgary
701 11th St. SW
(403) 268-8300

▶ SHOPPING

Chinook Centre
Calgary's largest shopping center, with stores, theaters, and IMAX theater
6455 Macleod Trail SW
(403) 259-2022

Eau Claire Festival Market
Boutiques, produce, and restaurants
2nd Ave. and 2nd St. SW
(403) 264-6450

Kensington District
Upscale arts and crafts, retail stores, and restaurants
10th St. and Kensington Rd. NW
(403) 283-4810

Stephen Avenue Walk
Specialty boutiques and department stores
8th Ave. SW from 1st St. SE to 4th St. SW
(403) 215-1570

Uptown 17th Avenue
Antiques, art galleries, and boutiques
17th Ave. between 2nd St. SW and 14th St. SW
(403) 245-1703

Willow Park Village
Outdoor mall with shops and restaurants
10816 Macleod Trail SE
(403) 214-7565

▶ VISITOR INFORMATION

Tourism Calgary
238 11th Ave. SE, Ste. 200
Calgary, AB T2G 0X8 Canada
(403) 263-8510 or (800) 661-1678
www.tourismcalgary.com

Visitor Centers
Calgary International Airport, Arrivals Level
(403) 735-1234

Calgary Tower, 101 9th Ave. SW
(403) 750-2362

Southcentre Mall
100 Anderson Rd.
(403) 271-7670

▶ DIVERSION

Spend a day at the Royal Tyrrell Museum of Paleontology in Drumheller, 84 miles northeast of Calgary. Watch technicians restore dinosaur skeletons or sign up for a simulated dinosaur dig. Take AB 2 to AB 72 (it will turn into AB 9) and head east. (403) 823-7707

CHARLESTON, South Carolina

An immaculately preserved antebellum city of restored homes and winding streets, Charleston is often regarded as the epitome of gracious living. Historic attractions abound: Charles Towne Landing, where the city first took root in the 1600s; the well-tended grounds of Magnolia Plantation, Middleton Place, and Drayton Hall; and Fort Sumter, site of the momentous events that ignited the American Civil War. On a contemporary note, the new millennium brought with it the South Carolina Aquarium, with exhibits of creatures from the state's five regions. *Tax: 10.5%-12% hotel, 7.5% sales. For local weather, call (843) 744-0303.*

Middleton Place Gardens

▶ SELECTED ATTRACTIONS

Calhoun Mansion
Victorian manor house
14-16 Meeting St.
(843) 722-8205

Charles Towne Landing
State historic site and nature preserve
1500 Old Towne Rd.
(843) 852-4200

Charleston Museum
Regional history museum
360 Meeting St.
(843) 722-2996

Cypress Gardens
Swamp tours, aquarium, and butterfly house
3030 Cypress Gardens Rd., 24 miles north off US 52, Moncks Corner
(843) 553-0515

Drayton Hall
18th-century plantation
3380 Ashley River Rd.
(843) 769-2600

Fort Sumter National Monument Visitor Education Center
340 Concord St.
Ferries leave from locations at Liberty Square and Patriots Point complex
(843) 883-3123

Gibbes Museum of Art
135 Meeting St.
(843) 722-2706

Heyward-Washington House
18th-century house museum
87 Church St.
(843) 722-2996

Magnolia Plantation and Gardens
Oldest major public garden in America
3550 Ashley River Rd.
(843) 571-1266 or (800) 367-3517

Middleton Place
18th-century plantation
4300 Ashley River Rd.
(843) 556-6020 or (800) 782-3608

Old Exchange and Provost Dungeon
Customs house and Revolutionary War prison
122 E. Bay St.
(843) 727-2165 or (888) 763-0448

Patriots Point Naval and Maritime Museum
40 Patriots Point Rd., Mt. Pleasant
(843) 884-2727

South Carolina Aquarium
100 Aquarium Wharf
(843) 720-1990

▶ SHOPPING

Citadel Mall
Department stores and specialty shops
2070 Sam Rittenberg Blvd.
(843) 766-8511

Historic King Street
Upscale boutiques, antique shops, and galleries
King St. north of Broad St.

Old City Market
Artisan shops and boutiques
Market St. between Meeting and East Bay Sts.
(843) 973-7236

▶ VISITOR INFORMATION

Charleston Area Convention and Visitors Bureau
423 King St.
Charleston, SC 29403
(843) 853-8000 or (800) 868-8118
www.charlestoncvb.com

Visitor Centers
375 Meeting St., Charleston
22 Beachwalker Dr., Kiawah Island
Hwy 17N, Mt. Pleasant
4975-B Centre Point Dr., North Charleston

▶ DON'T MISS DRIVE

King Street is the major road that runs from I-26 through the downtown historic district, all the way to The Battery, where cargo ships come into port. You'll see plenty of shops, restaurants, historic homes, and buildings, as well as art galleries and museums.

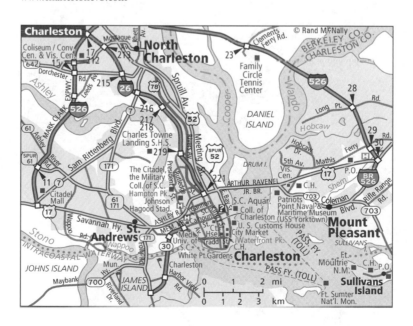

CHARLOTTE, North Carolina

The nation's second-largest financial center has been a fiscal hub since gold was discovered here in 1799. Amidst the city's glittering financial skyscrapers, the Mint Museum of Art displays a significant collection of pre-Columbian works and traditional European ceramics. Racing enthusiasts enjoy NASCAR and dirt track events as well as frequent car shows at Lowe's Motor Speedway. High-speed thrills of another kind draw huge crowds to Carowinds theme park. *Tax: 15.25% hotel, 7.25% sales. For local weather, call (864) 848-3859.*

Paramount's Carowinds water and theme park

DON'T MISS DRIVE

Prepare to be wowed by dream homes of nearly every architectural style on Charlotte's Queens Road West. Start your drive from uptown Charlotte, following 3rd Street east to Queens Road.

▶ SELECTED ATTRACTIONS

Afro-American Cultural Center
401 N. Myers St.
(704) 374-1565

Carowinds
Water and theme park
14523 Carowinds Blvd., 15 miles south off I-77
(704) 588-2600 or (800) 888-4386

Charlotte Museum of History and Hezekiah Alexander Homesite
Heritage museum and Colonial-era home
3500 Shamrock Dr.
(704) 568-1774

Charlotte Nature Museum
1658 Sterling Rd.
(704) 372-6261

Discovery Place
Hands-on science museum, planetarium, and Omnimax theater
301 N. Tryon St.
(704) 372-6261 or (800) 935-0553

Historic Latta Plantation
Living history farm
5225 Sample Rd., 13 miles north off I-77, Huntersville
(704) 875-2312

Levine Museum of the New South
200 E. 7th St.
(704) 333-1887

Lowe's Motor Speedway
5555 Concord Parkway S., 12 miles northeast off US 29, Concord
(704) 455-3200 or (800) 455-3267

Mint Museum of Art
2730 Randolph Rd.
(704) 337-2000

Mint Museum of Craft and Design
220 N. Tryon St.
(704) 337-2000

North Carolina Blumenthal Performing Arts Center
Opera, symphony, and theater
130 N. Tryon St.
(704) 372-1000

Ray's Splash Planet
Indoor water park
215 N. Sycamore St.
(704) 432-4729

Reed Gold Mine State Historic Site
9621 Reed Mine Rd., 30 miles east off Albemarle Rd., Midland
(704) 721-4653

▶ SHOPPING

Concord Mills
Outlet stores and specialty shops
8111 Concord Mills Blvd., 17 miles north off I-85, exit 49, Concord
(704) 979-3000

Founders Hall
Specialty shops
100 N. Tryon St.
(704) 716-8649

SouthPark Mall
Designer and department stores
4400 Sharon Rd.
(704) 364-4411

▶ VISITOR INFORMATION

Visit Charlotte
500 S. College St., Ste. 300
Charlotte, NC 28202
(704) 334-2282 or (800) 722-1994
www.visitcharlotte.com

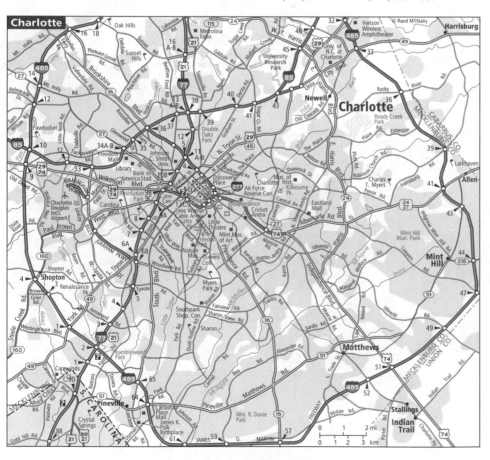

CHICAGO, Illinois

Known as the Windy City for both the challenges of its weather and the oratory of its officials, Chicago welcomes visitors with first-class architecture, renowned theater, and much-loved sports teams. Among the many museums here is the Field Museum, home of Sue, the biggest *Tyrannosaurus rex* skeleton in the world. Giant sculptures and a flashy amphitheater draw crowds to the new Millennium Park, while the joys of Navy Pier include a children's museum, the Chicago Shakespeare Theater, and a giant Ferris wheel. Countless restaurants around the city offer a taste of Chicago's famous stuffed pizza. Baseball fans head to the meccas of Wrigley Field and U.S. Cellular Field. *Tax: 15.4% hotel, 10.25% sales. For local weather, call (815) 834-0675.*

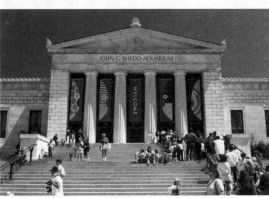
Shedd Aquarium

▶ SELECTED ATTRACTIONS

Adler Planetarium and Astronomy Museum
Free admission on Monday and Tuesday*
1300 S. Lake Shore Dr.
(312) 922-7827

Art Institute of Chicago
Free admission Thursday 5-8pm
111 S. Michigan Ave.
(312) 443-3600

Brookfield Zoo
Free admission on Tuesday and Thursday, October through February
1st Ave. and 31st St., Brookfield
(708) 688-8000

Chicago Architecture Foundation/ ArchiCenter
Guided tours of Chicago's architectural masterpieces and neighborhoods
224 S. Michigan Ave.
(312) 922-3432 ext. 240

Chicago Botanic Garden
1000 Lake Cook Rd., Glencoe
(847) 835-5440

Chicago Children's Museum
Free admission 5 to 8 p.m. on Thursday
700 E. Grand Ave. on Navy Pier
(312) 527-1000

Chicago Cultural Center
Architectural showplace for the arts
Free admission daily
78 E. Washington St.
(312) 744-6630

Chicago History Museum
1601 N. Clark St.
(312) 642-4600

Chicago Neighborhood Tours
Guided tours of the city's ethnic areas
Tours depart from the Chicago Cultural Center
78 E. Washington St.
(312) 742-1190

DuSable Museum of African American History
Free admission on Sunday
740 E. 56th Pl.
(773) 947-0600

Field Museum
Natural history exhibits
1400 S. Lake Shore Dr. at Roosevelt Rd.
(312) 922-9410

John Hancock Observatory
875 N. Michigan Ave.
(312) 751-3680

Lincoln Park Zoo
Free admission daily
2001 N. Clark St.
(312) 742-2000

Millennium Park
Amphitheater, restaurant, fountain, sculptures, and skating rink
Bounded by Michigan Ave., Columbus Dr., Randolph St., and Monroe St.
(312) 742-1168

Museum of Contemporary Art
Free admission on Tuesday
220 E. Chicago Ave.
(312) 280-2660

Museum of Science and Industry
Free admission 52 days each year
5700 S. Lake Shore Dr.
(773) 684-1414

National Museum of Mexican Art
Free admission daily
1852 W. 19th St.
(312) 738-1503

Navy Pier
Rides, museums, restaurants, IMAX theater, and family entertainment
600 E. Grand Ave.
(312) 595-7437

Peggy Notebaert Nature Museum
Free admission on Thursday
2340 N. Cannon Dr. at Fullerton Pkwy.
(773) 755-5100

Sears Tower Skydeck
233 S. Wacker Dr.
(312) 875-9696

Shedd Aquarium
Exhibits in main building free on Discount Days (call for details)
1200 S. Lake Shore Dr.
(312) 939-2438

Spertus Museum
History of Judaism and children's center
Free admission on Tuesday 10am-noon, Thursday 3-7pm
610 S. Michigan Ave.
(312) 322-1700

* *Various weeks in January, February, September, October, and November*

continued on page 31

Free every day

In Chicago, it is free day at least one day a week at most of the many museums and cultural centers that dot the city. Free day policies may change from time to time, so check before you go. Visit **www. choosechicago.com** for more information and locations:

- ABA Museum of Law
- ArchiCenter of Chicago Architecture Foundation
- CenterSpace at Gallery 37
- Chicago Cultural Center
- Chicago Public Library's Harold Washington Center
- City Gallery at the Historic Water Tower
- Garfield Park Conservatory
- Intuit: The Center for Intuitive and Outsider Art
- Jane Addams Hull House Museum
- Lincoln Park Zoo
- Museum of Contemporary Photography
- National Museum of Mexican Art
- Smart Museum of Art
- Smith Museum of Stained Glass Windows

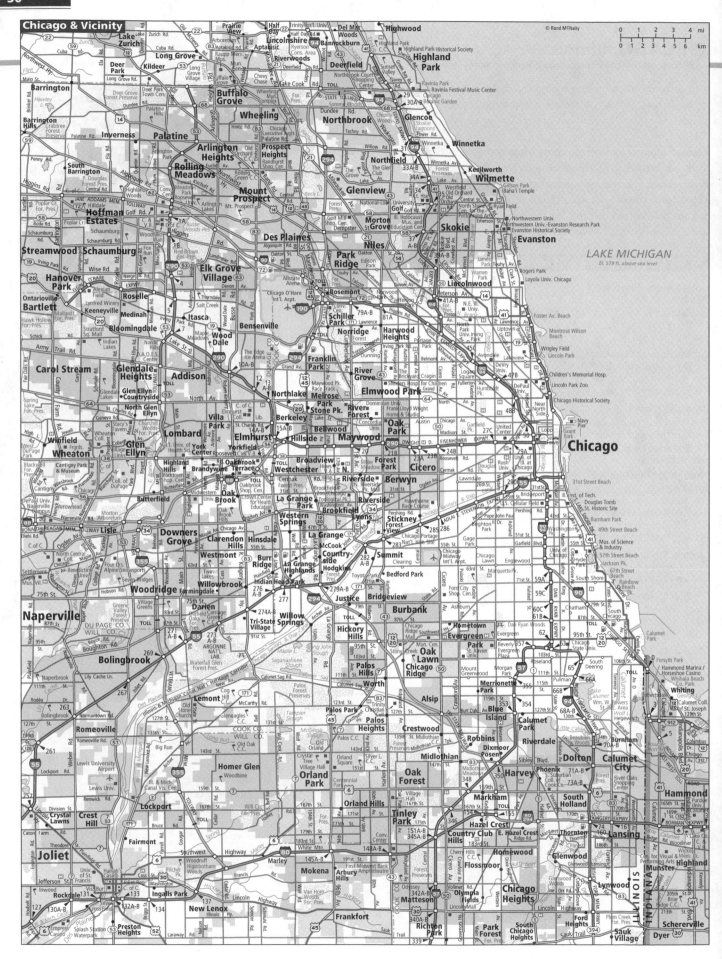

Chicago & Vicinity

© Rand McNally

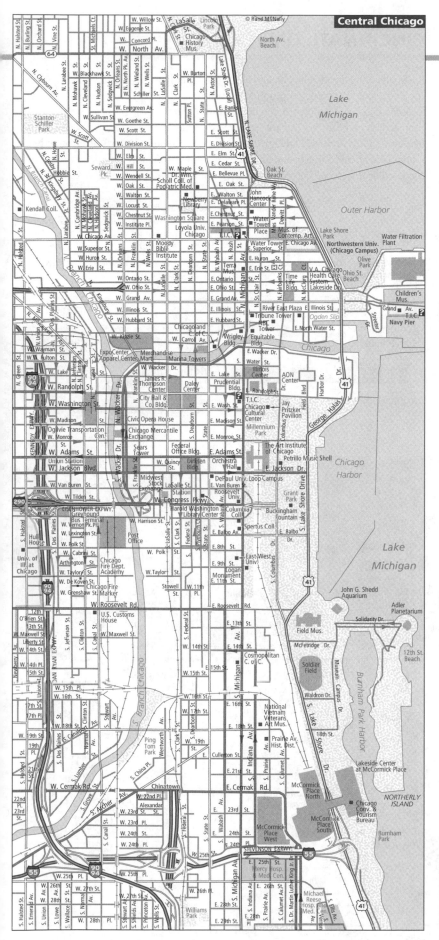

Central Chicago

© Rand McNally

Chicago attractions continued

Swedish American Museum Center

Free admission on the second Tuesday of each month
5211 N. Clark St.
(773) 728-8111

SHOPPING

Magnificent Mile

Upscale department stores and boutiques
N. Michigan Ave. from the Chicago River to Oak St.
(312) 642-3570

Shops at The Mart

Shops and restaurants in a huge wholesale design center
222 Merchandise Mart Plaza
(800) 677-6278

State Street

Department stores and boutiques
State St. between Randolph and Adams Sts.
(312) 782-9160

Water Tower Place

Department stores and specialty shops
835 N. Michigan Ave.
(312) 440-3166

VISITOR INFORMATION

Chicago Convention and Tourism Bureau

McCormick Complex-Lakeside Center
2301 S. Lake Shore Dr.
Chicago, IL 60616
(312) 567-8500
www.choosechicago.com

Chicago Office of Tourism

78 E. Washington St.
Chicago, IL 60602
(312) 744-2400 or (877) 244-2246

Chicago Cultural Center

77 E. Randolph St.

Chicago Water Works

163 E. Pearson

DON'T MISS DRIVE

It's been sung about and glorified on the big screen. Experience Chicago's famous Lake Shore Drive, which passes beaches, picturesque marinas, parks, and breathtaking views of the city's famed skyline.

CINCINNATI, Ohio

Taft Museum of Art

Railroads, interstate highways, and the Ohio River have all helped Cincinnati succeed as a hub of transportation and commerce. The restored Union Terminal houses three museums (history, natural history and science, and children's). Five thousand years of art history are represented at the expanded and renovated Taft Museum. The National Underground Railroad Freedom Center was inspired by Cincinnati's pivotal role in helping slaves find their way north in the years before the Civil War. *Tax: 17% hotel, 6.5% sales. For local weather, call (513) 241-1010.*

▶ SELECTED ATTRACTIONS

Cincinnati Art Museum
953 Eden Park Dr.
(513) 639-2984

Cincinnati Zoo and Botanical Garden
3400 Vine St.
(513) 281-4700 or (800) 944-4776

Great American Ball Park
Home of the Cincinnati Reds
100 Main St.
(513) 765-7000

Kings Island
Theme Park
24 miles north off I-71, Kings Island
(513) 754-5700

National Underground Railroad Freedom Center
50 E. Freedom Way
(513) 333-7500 or (877) 648-4838

Taft Museum of Art
316 Pike St.
(513) 241-0343

▶ SHOPPING

Cincinnati Mills Mall
600 Cincinnati Mills Dr.
(513) 671-7467

Kenwood Towne Centre
Upscale department stores and boutiques
7875 Montgomery Rd.
(513) 745-9100

Tower Place Mall at the Carew Tower
Fashion and gift boutiques
4th and Race Sts.
(513) 241-7700

▶ VISITOR INFORMATION

Cincinnati USA Convention & Visitors Bureau
525 Vine St., Ste. 1500
Cincinnati, OH 45202
(513) 621-2142 or (800) 543-2613
www.cincyusa.com

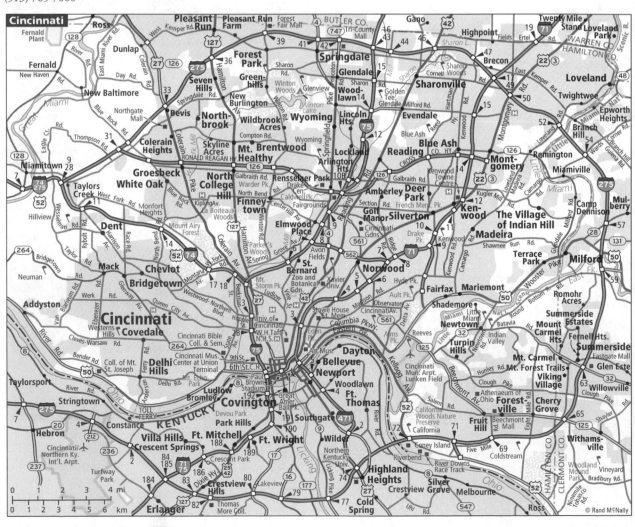

© Rand McNally

CLEVELAND, Ohio

A revitalized lakefront and riverway have helped reverse the fortunes of this Lake Erie port city. The Rock and Roll Hall of Fame and Museum draws fans from all over the world. Nearby, the Great Lakes Science Center provides its own brand of hair-raising excitement with more than 400 hands-on exhibits and demonstrations. Cultural institutions concentrated around University Circle include the Museum of Art and the Museum of Natural History. And some 600 separate species—3,000 animals in all—call the Metroparks Zoo home. *Tax: 15.25% hotel, 7.75% sales tax. For local weather, call (216) 265-2370.*

Rock and Roll Hall of Fame and Museum

▶ SELECTED ATTRACTIONS

Children's Museum of Cleveland
10730 Euclid Ave. in University Circle
(216) 791-7114

Cleveland Metroparks Zoo
3900 Wildlife Way
(216) 661-6500

Cleveland Museum of Art
11150 East Blvd. in University Circle
(216) 421-7350 or (888) 262-0033

Cleveland Museum of Natural History
1 Wade Oval Dr. in University Circle
(216) 231-4600 or (800) 317-9155

Cuyahoga Valley National Park
I-77 S to Rockside Rd. E., Valley View
(216) 524-1497

Great Lakes Science Center
Science exhibits and Omnimax theater
601 Erieside Ave.
(216) 694-2000

NASA Glenn Research Center
21000 Brookpark Rd. at Lewis Field
(216) 433-4000

Rock and Roll Hall of Fame and Museum
11100 Rock and Roll Blvd.,
E. 9th St. at Lake Erie
(216) 781-7625 or (888) 764-7625

The Warehouse District
Downtown along the Cuyahoga River
(216) 344-3937

Western Reserve Historical Society
Seven historic properties/museums
10825 East Blvd. in University Circle
(216) 721-5722

▶ SHOPPING

The Arcade
Restored shopping center that dates from 1890
401 Euclid Ave.
(216) 696-1408

Beachwood Place
Upscale department stores and specialty shops
26300 Cedar Rd., Beachwood
(216) 464-9460

The Galleria at Erieview
Specialty shops
1301 E. 9th St.
(216) 861-4343

▶ DIVERSION

Explore the largest Amish settlement in the world about an hour south of Cleveland in Wayne and Holmes counties. The area is dotted with craft shops, farms, and flea markets. Many Swiss-style buildings remind visitors of the Swiss ancestry of Ohio's Amish. (330) 674-3975 or (800) 362-6474

▶ VISITOR INFORMATION

Positively Cleveland and Visitors Center
100 Public Square, Ste. 100
Cleveland, OH 44113
(216) 875-6600 or (800) 321-1001
www.positivelycleveland.com

COLUMBUS, Ohio

Short North Arts District

More than a seat of government, Ohio's capital is a center of high-tech industrial development. It's also the home of enormous Ohio State University, which boasts an enrollment of more than 51,000. For an introduction to the joys of science, COSI Columbus (originally the Center of Science and Industry) includes more than 1,000 interactive exhibits. The city's historic German Village neighborhood offers distinctive homes, restaurants, and shops with an Old World flair, along with the Book Loft—a 32-room bookstore as long as a city block. *Tax: 16.75% hotel, 6.75% sales.*

DON'T MISS DRIVE

Travel 14 miles along High Street, which runs north to south past many of Columbus' main attractions. The drive takes visitors through several quaint suburbs and districts, past many popular sites, including the Ohio State University campus, Short North Arts District, Arena District, the Ohio state capitol building, German Village, and Brewery District.

SELECTED ATTRACTIONS

Arena District
Restaurants, bars, and nightclubs near Nationwide Arena
At Nationwide Blvd. and Front St.
(614) 857-2336

Columbus Museum of Art
480 E. Broad St.
(614) 221-6801

Columbus Zoo and Aquarium
9990 Riverside Dr., Powell
(614) 645-3550 or (800) 666-5397

COSI Columbus
333 W. Broad St.
(614) 228-2674 or (888) 819-2674

Franklin Park Conservatory
Botanical gardens
1777 E. Broad St.
(614) 645-8733 or (800) 214-7275

German Village
Historic German homes
588 S. 3rd St.
(614) 221-8888

Jack Nicklaus Museum
2355 Olentangy River Rd. at Ohio State University
(614) 247-5959

Ohio Historical Center and Ohio Village
1982 Velma Ave., 17th Ave. and I-71
(614) 297-2300

Ohio Statehouse
Broad and High Sts. in Capitol Square
(614) 752-9777 or (888) 644-6123

The *Santa Maria*
Replica of Christopher Columbus' flagship
25 Marconi Blvd in Battelle Riverfront Park
(614) 645-8760

Wexner Center for the Arts
1871 N. High St. at Ohio State University
(614) 292-3535

Zoombezi Bay
Water park at Columbus Zoo
10101 Riverside Dr., Powell
(614) 724-3600

SHOPPING

Easton Town Center
Department stores, specialty shops, restaurants, and entertainment
I-270 and Easton Way
(614) 416-7000

North Market
Fresh produce and specialty foods
59 Spruce St.
(614) 463-9664

Short North Arts District
Galleries, unique shops, and entertainment
N. High St. from Nationwide Blvd. to 11th Ave.
(614) 228-8050

VISITOR INFORMATION

Experience Columbus
277 W. Nationwide Blvd., Ste. 125
Columbus, OH 43215
(614) 221-6623 or (800) 354-2657
www.experiencecolumbus.com

Visitor Center
Easton Town Center, Easton Station Bldg.
(614) 416-8080

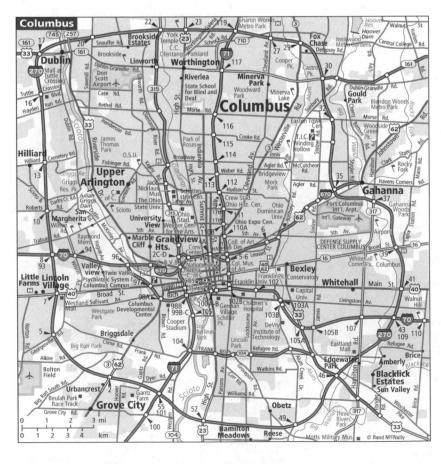

CORPUS CHRISTI, Texas

Miles of sandy beaches along Gulf Coast barrier islands make Corpus Christi a popular vacation retreat. Before heading to ocean shores, visitors can take in downtown waterfront attractions including the USS *Lexington*, a legendary World War II-era aircraft carrier that came to be known as the "Blue Ghost." Nearby, the Texas State Aquarium invites the curious to an underwater discovery of life below the Gulf's blue waters. Fans of the late Tejano singing star Selena will find personal memorabilia such as her concert dresses on display at the Selena Museum. *Tax: 15% hotel, 8.25% sales. For local weather, call (361) 814-9463 or (361) 289-0753.*

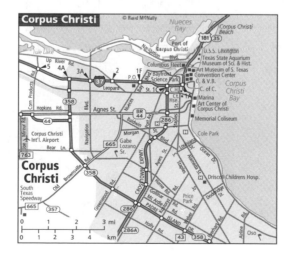

USS Lexington *Museum on the Bay*

▶ SELECTED ATTRACTIONS

Aransas National Wildlife Refuge
70 miles north off TX 35, Austwell
(361) 286-3559

Art Museum of South Texas
1902 N. Shoreline Blvd.
(361) 825-3500

Asian Cultures Museum
1809 N. Chaparral St.
(361) 882-2641

Corpus Christi Museum of Science and History
1900 N. Chaparral St.
(361) 826-4650

Hans and Pat Suter Wildlife Area
Off Ennis Joslin St. in South Guth Park
(361) 880-3460

Heritage Park
Restored historic homes
1581 N. Chaparral St.
(361) 826-3410

King Ranch
Working cattle and horse ranch
45 miles south off US 77, Kingsville
(361) 592-8055

Lake Corpus Christi State Park
35 miles northwest off TX 359, near Mathis
(361) 547-2635

Padre Island National Seashore Visitor Center
20402 Park Rd. 22, ten miles south of JFK Causeway
(361) 949-8068

Selena Museum
5410 Leopard St.
(361) 289-9013

South Texas Botanical Gardens & Nature Center
8545 S. Staples St.
(361) 852-2100

Texas State Aquarium
2710 N. Shoreline Blvd.
(361) 881-1200 or (800) 477-4853

USS *Lexington* Museum on the Bay
2914 N. Shoreline Blvd.
(361) 888-4873 or (800) 523-9539

▶ SHOPPING

Antique Row
Antiques and collectibles
Alameda and Robert Sts.

La Palmera Shopping Center
Department stores and specialty shops
5488 S. Padre Island Dr.
(361) 991-3755

Moore Plaza
Major national retailers
5425 S. Padre Island Dr.

Water Street Market
Boutiques, restaurants, and entertainment
Chaparral and Williams Sts.

▶ DON'T MISS DRIVE

Ocean Drive, lined with magazine-cover homes and mansions, runs along Corpus Christi Bay. The gardens and grounds are as impressive as the houses.

▶ VISITOR INFORMATION

Corpus Christi Area Convention and Visitors Bureau
101 N. Shoreline Blvd., Ste. 430
Corpus Christi, TX 78401
(361) 881-1888 or (800) 678-6232
www.corpuschristicvb.com

Visitor Centers
Downtown
1823 N. Chaparral St.
(800) 766-2322

On the Island
14252 S. Padre Island Dr.
(361) 949-8743

▶ DIVERSION

Padre Island National Seashore is only 15 minutes from Corpus Christi on TX 358. Birders have found the seashore to be a haven for their hobby as well as for migratory birds.

DALLAS/FORT WORTH, Texas

Dallas skyline at dusk

Sprawling Dallas rises from the Texas prairie to form the Southwest's largest center of finance and commerce. Two entertainment districts offer respite from the pressures of the boardroom: Deep Ellum is noted for funky shops and hip music clubs, while the West End features trendy restaurants and attractions. The home of the annual state fair, Fair Park also features a multitude of museums dedicated to women, African Americans, railroading, and other subjects. *Tax: 15% hotel, 8.25% sales. For local weather, call (214) 787-1111 or (817) 429-2631.*

Fort Worth might be known as a cowtown, but the city's wealth has brought with it a plethora of high culture. Its cultural district boasts one of the most renowned collections of museums in the nation, including the Modern Art Museum and the Kimbell Art Museum. For a taste of the West, visitors head to the National Cowgirl Museum and Hall of Fame or witness the twice-daily herding of cattle through Exchange Avenue in the Stockyards National Historic District. *Tax: 15% hotel, 8.25% sales. For local weather, call (817) 429-2631.*

DON'T MISS DRIVE

Main Street in Fort Worth runs from what was once "Hell's Half-Acre" through downtown's Sundance Square and the Historic Stockyards District, two of the largest entertainment districts in the city.

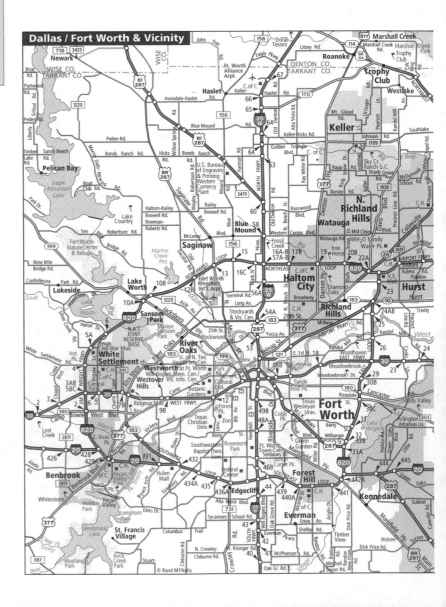

Dallas / Fort Worth & Vicinity

▶ SELECTED ATTRACTIONS

DALLAS

Dallas Arboretum
8525 Garland Rd.
(214) 515-6500

Dallas Museum of Art
1717 N. Harwood St.
(214) 922-1200

Dallas Theater Center
3636 Turtle Creek Blvd.
(214) 522-8499

Dallas World Aquarium
1801 N. Griffin St.
(214) 720-2224

Dallas Zoo
650 S. R.L. Thornton Frwy.
(214) 670-5656

Deep Ellum Historic District
Shops, restaurants, live music, and clubs
Elm St. and Good Latimer Expwy.
(214) 747-3337

Fair Park
State fairgrounds with nine museums
1300 Robert B. Cullum Blvd.
(214) 670-8400

Morton H. Meyerson Symphony Center
2301 Flora St.
(214) 670-3600

Museum of Nature and Science
*Hands-on exhibits, planetarium, and
IMAX theater*
3535 Grand Ave.
(214) 428-5555

Nasher Sculpture Center
Outdoor sculpture garden and center
2001 Flora St.
(214) 242-5100

Old City Park
Turn-of-the-century homes and structures
1515 S. Harwood
(214) 421-5141

Six Flags Over Texas
TX 360 and I-30, Arlington
(817) 530-6000

Sixth Floor Museum at Dealey Plaza
Exhibits about President John F. Kennedy
411 Elm St.
(214) 747-6660

West End Historical District
Shops, restaurants, and clubs
Ross at Market St.
(214) 741-7180

Women's Museum
3800 Parry Ave. in Fair Park
(214) 915-0860

▶ SHOPPING

DALLAS

Galleria Dallas
Upscale specialty stores
13350 N. Dallas Pkwy.
(972) 702-7100

continued on the next page

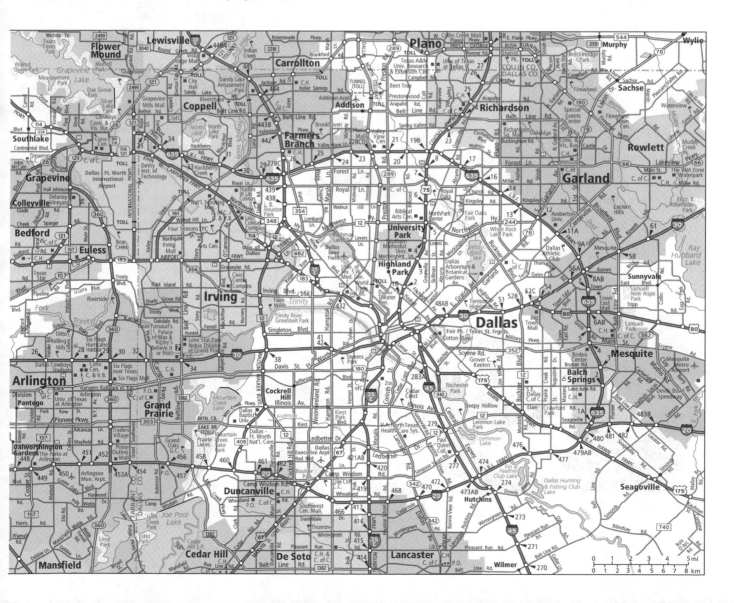

Dallas continued

Highland Park Village
Preston Rd. and Mockingbird Ln.
(214) 559-2740

NorthPark Center
Department stores and boutiques
8687 North Central Expwy.
(214) 361-6345

Victory Park
Upscale boutiques, dining, and entertainment
Museum Way and Victory Park Ln.
(214) 303-5572

▶ **SELECTED ATTRACTIONS**

FORT WORTH

American Airlines C.R. Smith Museum
Commercial aviation museum
4601 TX 360
(817) 967-1560

Amon Carter Museum
19th- and 20th-century American art
3501 Camp Bowie Blvd.
(817) 738-1933

Ball-Eddleman-McFarland House
Original Victorian home
1110 Penn St.
(817) 332-5875

Bass Performance Hall
4th and Calhoun Sts.
(817) 212-4325

Cattle Raisers Museum
1501 Montgomery St.
(817) 332-8551

Fort Worth Botanic Garden
3220 Botanic Garden Blvd.
(817) 871-7686

Fort Worth Museum of Science and History
1501 Montgomery St.
(817) 255-9300

Sundance Square in Fort Worth

Fort Worth Nature Center and Refuge
9601 Fossil Ridge Rd.
(817) 237-1111

Fort Worth Zoo
1989 Colonial Pkwy.
(817) 759-7555

Grapevine Vintage Railroad
21-mile historic railway excursion
140 E. Exchange Ave.
(817) 410-3123

Kimbell Art Museum
3333 Camp Bowie Blvd.
(817) 332-8451

Log Cabin Village
Living history in 1850s log cabins
2100 Log Cabin Village Ln. at University Dr.
(817) 926-5881

Modern Art Museum of Fort Worth
3200 Darnell St.
(817) 738-9215

National Cowboys of Color Museum and Hall of Fame
3400 Mount Vernon Ave.
(817) 534-8801

National Cowgirl Museum and Hall of Fame
1720 Gendy St.
(817) 336-4475

Sid Richardson Museum
309 Main St.
(817) 332-6554

Stockyards Historic District
130 E. Exchange Ave.
(817) 624-4741

Texas Motor Speedway
3601 TX 114, at I-35 W
(817) 215-8500

Thistle Hill
Historic cattle baron's mansion
1509 Pennsylvania Ave.
(817) 336-1212

Vintage Flying Museum
505 NW 38th St., adjacent to Meacham Airport
(817) 624-1935

Water Gardens
1502 Commerce St.
(817) 871-5755

▶ **SHOPPING**

FORT WORTH

Camp Bowie Boulevard
30 blocks of upscale specialty shops

North East Mall
Upscale department stores and shops
1101 Melbourne Rd., Hurst
(817) 284-3427

Ridgmar Mall
Department stores, shops, and restaurants
1888 Green Oaks Rd. at I-30
(817) 731-0856

▶ **DIVERSION**

Drive out to the Fossil Rim Wildlife Center, where endangered species run wild. A lodge offers overnight accommodations, and there are guided walking and mountain bike tours as well as day camps. Located in Glen Rose; take US 67 south and west to County Rd. 2008.
(254) 897-2960 or (888) 775-6742

Stockyards Station
Western shops, dining, and tours
130 E. Exchange Ave. off N. Main St.
(817) 625-9715

Sundance Square
Specialty shops and entertainment
Bounded by Belknap, Main, and 6th Sts.
(817) 255-5700

University Park Village
Upscale shops
1612 S. University Dr.
(817) 332-5700

▶ **VISITOR INFORMATION**

Dallas Convention and Visitors Bureau
325 North St. Paul St., Suite 700
Dallas, TX 75201
(214) 571-1000 or (800) 232-5527
www.visitdallas.com

Dallas Tourist Information Center
Old Red Courthouse
100 S. Houston St.
(800) 232-5527

Fort Worth Convention & Visitors Bureau
415 Throckmorton St.
Fort Worth, TX 76102
(817) 336-8791 or (800) 433-5747
www.fortworth.com

Fort Worth Visitor Centers
Sundance Square
415 Throckmorton St.
(817) 336-8791 or (800) 433-5747

Stockyards National Historic District
130 E. Exchange Ave.
(817) 624-4741

Cultural District
3401 W. Lancaster Ave.
(817) 882-8588

DENVER, Colorado

Colorado's capital city sits at the interface of high desert plains and the vertical rise of the Rocky Mountains. In City Park lies the Museum of Nature and Science, which features Egyptian mummies, wildlife dioramas, and dinosaur exhibits. The aquatic life of two very different river systems entertains visitors at Downtown Aquarium. Free tours of the U.S. Mint offer a look into the history of the country's currency. *Tax: 14.85% hotel, 7.72% sales. For local weather, call (303) 494-4221.*

Shops at the 16th Street Mall

▶ SELECTED ATTRACTIONS

Black American West Museum
History of African American migration to the West
3091 California St.
(303) 482-2242

Colorado History Museum
1300 Broadway
(303) 866-3682

Colorado State Capitol
200 E. Colfax Ave.
(303) 866-2604

Coors Brewery Tours
13th Ave. and Ford St., Golden
(303) 277-2337

Denver Museum of Nature & Science
2001 Colorado Blvd. in City Park
(303) 322-7009 or (800) 925-2250

Downtown Aquarium
700 Water St.
(303) 561-4450

Lower Downtown Historic District (LoDo)
Bounded by Larimer St., 20th St., Wynkoop St., and Speer Blvd.
(303) 628-5428

Tiny Town
Kid-size village and railroad
6249 S. Turkey Creek Rd., Morrison
(303) 697-6829

United States Mint
Free tours
320 W. Colfax Ave.
(303) 572-9500

▶ SHOPPING

16th Street Mall
Specialty shops in a pedestrian mall
Between Wynkoop and Broadway
(303) 534-6161

Cherry Creek North Shopping District
Galleries and boutiques
At 1st, 2nd, and 3rd Aves. between University Blvd. and Steele St.
(303) 394-2903

Cherry Creek Shopping Center
Department stores and specialty shops
3000 E. 1st Ave.
(303) 388-3900

Larimer Square Historic District
Specialty shops
Larimer St., between 14th and 15th Sts.
(303) 534-2367

▶ VISITOR INFORMATION

Denver Metro Convention and Visitors Bureau
1555 California St., Ste. 300
Denver, CO 80202
(303) 892-1112 or (800) 233-6837
www.denver.org

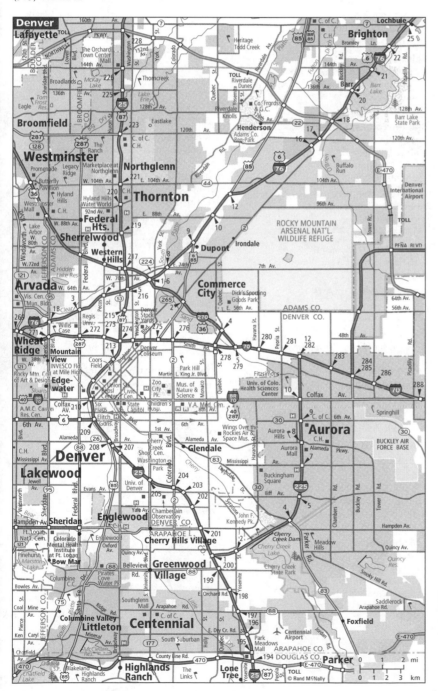

DETROIT, Michigan

Arctic Ring of Life exhibit at the Detroit Zoo

The promise embodied by the 30-year-old Renaissance Center, still gleaming at the Detroit River's edge, is beginning to take shape as Detroit slowly revitalizes itself. The wealth of the nation's automobile capital may be seen at historic homes such as Fair Lane, the estate of Henry Ford. Along with the Henry Ford Museum, Greenfield Village—a collection of historic buildings brought here from their original locations—celebrates both the spirit of innovation and the pastoral way of life. The high culture of the Renaissance and the Impressionist period is on view at the Institute of Arts, while Detroit's contribution to pop culture takes center stage at the Motown Historical Museum. *Tax: 15% hotel, 6% sales. For local weather, call (248) 620-2355.*

DON'T MISS DRIVE

The Nautical Mile is a peaceful drive down Jefferson Avenue from the stately lake mansions of Grosse Pointe, passing auto family Edsel and Eleanor Ford's mansion, through St. Clair Shores' picturesque boating community, and up to Metro Beach Metropark.

► SELECTED ATTRACTIONS

Automotive Hall of Fame
21400 Oakwood Blvd., Dearborn
(313) 240-4000

Belle Isle Park
Conservatory, nature zoo, and museum
Across the McArthur Bridge at the foot of E. Grand Blvd.
(313) 628-2081

Black Holocaust Museum
Located in the Shrine of the Black Madonna Cultural Center and Bookstore
13535 Livernois Ave.
(313) 491-0777

Charles H. Wright Museum of African-American History
315 E. Warren Ave.
(313) 494-5800

Cranbrook Art Museum
39221 Woodward Ave., Bloomfield Hills
(248) 645-3323

Detroit Institute of Arts
5200 Woodward Ave.
(313) 833-7900

Detroit Science Center
IMAX Dome Theatre, planetarium, and interactive exhibits
5020 John R St.
(313) 577-8400

Detroit Zoo
8450 W. Ten Mile Rd., Royal Oak
(248) 398-0900

Dossin Great Lakes Museum
100 Strand Dr., Belle Isle
(313) 852-4051

Edsel & Eleanor Ford House
Historic estate of auto baron family
1100 Lakeshore Rd., Grosse Pointe Shores
(313) 884-4222

GM Showroom
Vintage, specialty and production vehicles made by General Motors
Jefferson Ave. at Beaubien St. in Renaissance Center
(313) 667-7151

Henry Ford Estate
Former home of car manufacturing magnate
4901 Evergreen Rd. between Ford Rd. and Michigan Ave. at the University of Michigan, Dearborn
(313) 593-5590

The Henry Ford
Museum, Greenfield Village, IMAX theater, research center, and auto plant tour
20900 Oakwood Blvd., Dearborn
(313) 982-6001 or (800) 835-5237

Mexicantown
Authentic restaurants and shopping
At the foot of the Ambassador Bridge, bordered by Bagley, West Vernor Hwy., 16th, and Clark Sts.
(313) 967-9898

MGM Grand Detroit Casino
1777 3rd St.
(313) 393-7777 or (877) 888-2121

Motown Historical Museum
2648 W. Grand Blvd.
(313) 875-2264

Solanus Casey Center
Historic St. Bonaventure monastery, art gallery, and shrine to Detroit priest
1780 Mt. Elliott St.
(313) 579-2100

Tuskegee Airmen National Museum
6325 W. Jefferson
(313) 843-8849

► SHOPPING

Eastern Market
Indoor/outdoor century-old marketplace
2934 Russell St.
(313) 833-9300

Eastland Center
Department stores and specialty shops
18000 Vernier Rd., Harper Woods
(313) 371-1501

Fairlane Town Center
Department stores and specialty shops
18900 Michigan Ave. at Evergreen Rd., Dearborn
(313) 593-1370

GM Renaissance Center
Fine shops and boutiques
Jefferson Ave. at Beaubien St.
(313) 567-3126

Grosse Pointe Village
Specialty shops and services
Kercheval Ave. between Cadieux and Neff,
Grosse Pointe
(313) 886-7474

The Somerset Collection
*High-end department stores and
specialty shops*
2800 W. Big Beaver Rd., Troy
(248) 643-6360

VISITOR INFORMATION

**Detroit Metro Convention &
Visitors Bureau**
211 W. Fort St., Ste. 1000
Detroit, MI 48226
(313) 202-1800 or (800) 338-7648
www.visitdetroit.com

**Convention and Visitors Bureau
of Windsor**
333 Riverside Dr. W., Ste. 103
Windsor, ON, N9A 5K4 Canada
(519) 255-6530 or (800) 265-3633
www.visitwindsor.com

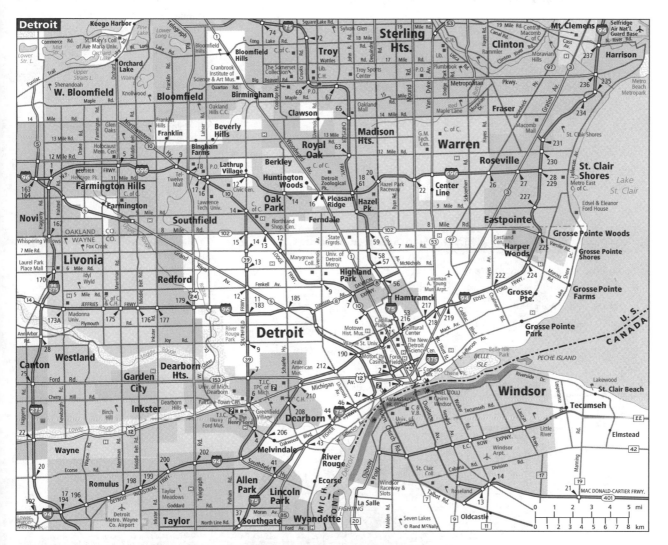

DIVERSION

Duty-free shopping is only minutes south of Detroit in Windsor, Ontario, Canada.
Windsor is just across the Detroit River via the Detroit-Windsor tunnel accessed
from Jefferson Avenue. Or take I-75 to the Porter St. exit and follow the signs to
the Ambassador Bridge.

EDMONTON, Alberta, Canada

Edmonton skyline

A major cross-Canada transportation hub, the capital of Alberta is noted for its extensive parklands and nearby huge oilfields. Many visitors make their first stop the West Edmonton Mall, the world's largest. This vast entertainment complex includes amusement parks, sports facilities, and a virtual reality playground. The city's other major attractions include the Telus World of Science-Edmonton, a space and science center with interactive exhibits, and Fort Edmonton Park, a living re-creation of the city in various phases of its short but remarkable history. *Tax: 10% hotel, 5% GST. For local weather, call (780) 468-4940.*

▶ SELECTED ATTRACTIONS

Alberta Railway Museum
24215 34 St.
(780) 472-6229

Art Gallery of Alberta
Enterprise Square
100-10230 Jasper Ave.
(780) 422-6223

Devonian Botanic Garden
40 km southwest on AB 60, north of Devon
(780) 987-3054

Elk Island National Park
45 km east on AB 16 (Yellowhead Hwy)
(780) 992-5790

Fort Edmonton Park
Historical park
Fox Dr. & Whitmund Dr.
(780) 496-8787

John Janzen Nature Centre
7000 143 St.
(780) 496-8787

John Walter Museum
Turn-of-the-century homes of early Edmonton entrepreneur
10661 91A Ave.
(780) 496-8787

Muttart Conservatory
Horticultural display garden
9626 96A St.
(780) 496-8755

Northlands Park
Horse races and home of the Edmonton Oilers
7300 116 Ave. NW
(780) 471-7210 or (888) 800-7275

Pysanka
World's largest Easter egg
100 km east of Edmonton on AB 16, Vegreville
(780) 632-3100

Royal Alberta Museum
12845 102 Ave.
(780) 453-9100

Telus World of Science–Edmonton
Space and science center
11211 142 St.
(780) 452-9100

Valley Zoo
13315 Buena Vista Rd.
(780) 496-8787

▶ SHOPPING

Edmonton City Centre
Department stores and specialty shops
102 St. and 102 Ave.
(780) 426-8444

Gallery Walk
Art galleries, gift shops, restaurants, and boutiques
124 St. from Jasper to 107 Ave.
(780) 452-9664

Old Strathcona
Fashion boutiques, specialty shops, and farmer's market
Whyte Ave. between 99 and 109 Sts.
(780) 437-4182

West Edmonton Mall
Shops, restaurants, indoor amusement park, mini golf, sea lions, and other family attractions
8882 170 St.
(780) 444-5200 or (800) 661-8890

▶ VISITOR INFORMATION

Edmonton Tourism
9990 Jasper Ave.
Edmonton, AB T5J 1P7 Canada
(780) 401-7696
www.edmonton.com/tourism

Gateway Park Visitor Ctr
2404 Gateway Blvd SW
(780) 496-8400 or (800) 463-4667

▶ DIVERSION

At the Ukrainian Cultural Heritage Village, open May to October, explore an open-air museum of 30 historic buildings, sample traditional Ukrainian food, or enjoy a horse-drawn wagon ride. 50 kilometers (about 31 miles) east of Edmonton on AB 16. (780) 662-3640

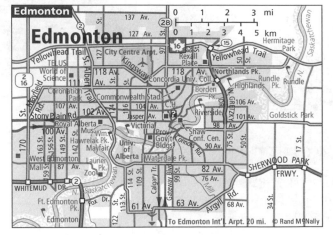

EL PASO, Texas

El Paso blends Native American, Spanish, Mexican, and Anglo cultures with a dose of the modern military. Worshippers attend services at three Spanish missions (still active after hundreds of years) along the Mission Trail. The Magoffin Homestead offers a peek into the lives of the first cowboy ranchers to settle here. The million-plus-acre expanse of Fort Bliss includes museums that cover its history and ongoing mission. And from downtown, trolley rides allow a quick jaunt over the river into Ciudad Juarez for authentic Mexican crafts and cuisine. *Tax: 15.5% hotel, 8.25% sales. For local weather, call (915) 533-7744 or (505) 589-4088.*

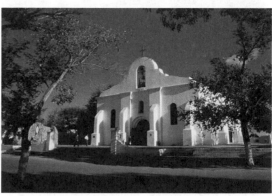

The Presidio along the Mission Trail

► SELECTED ATTRACTIONS

Border Jumper Trolleys
1 Civic Center Plaza at the El Paso
Convention Center
(915) 544-0062

Centennial Museum & Chihuahuan Desert Gardens
Natural and cultural history of the desert
Wiggins Rd. at University Ave.
(915) 747-5565

Chamizal National Memorial
Exhibits, art galleries, and performing arts theater in a park
800 S. San Marcial St.
(915) 532-7273

El Paso Museum of Archaeology
4301 Transmountain Rd.
(915) 755-4332

El Paso Museum of Art
Santa Fe and Main Sts.
(915) 532-1707

El Paso Museum of History
510 N. Santa Fe St.
(915) 351-3588

El Paso Zoo
4001 E. Paisano Dr.
(915) 521-1850

Fort Bliss Replica Museum
Adobe fort buildings and military artifacts
Pershing and Pleasonton Rds. at Ft. Bliss
(915) 568-4518

Insights El Paso Science Museum
505 N. Santa Fe St.
(915) 534-0000

Magoffin Homestead
Historic adobe-style hacienda with original furnishings
1120 Magoffin Ave.
(915) 533-5147

The Mission Trail
Historic missions on 9-mile route
Socorro Rd. at Zaragoza Rd.
(915) 851-9997

Tigua Indian Cultural Center
305 Yaya Ln.
(915) 859-7700

US Army Air Defense Artillery Museum
Building 1735 at Ft. Bliss
(915) 568-5412

Wet 'n Wild Waterworld
20 miles north off I-10, exit 0,
Anthony, Texas
(915) 886-2222

Wyler Aerial Tramway State Park
Aerial view of three states and Mexico
1700 McKinley Ave.
(915) 566-6622

► SHOPPING

Bassett Place
Department stores and specialty shops
6101 Gateway Blvd. W
(915) 772-7479

Cielo Vista Mall
Department stores and 140 retail stores
8401 Gateway Blvd. W
(915) 779-7070

Sunland Park Mall
Department stores and 100 specialty shops
750 Sunland Park Dr.
(915) 833-5596

Tony Lama Factory Stores
Outlet mall
7156 Gateway Blvd. E
(915) 772-4327

► VISITOR INFORMATION

El Paso Convention and Visitors Bureau
1 Civic Center Plaza
El Paso, TX 79901
(915) 534-0601 or (800) 351-6024
www.visitelpaso.com

DIVERSION

Drive out to the Cloudcroft-Ruidoso area in New Mexico for camping, skiing, fishing, even horse racing. It's less than 125 miles from El Paso. For Cloudcroft information: (505) 682-2733; for Ruidoso: (877) 784-3676

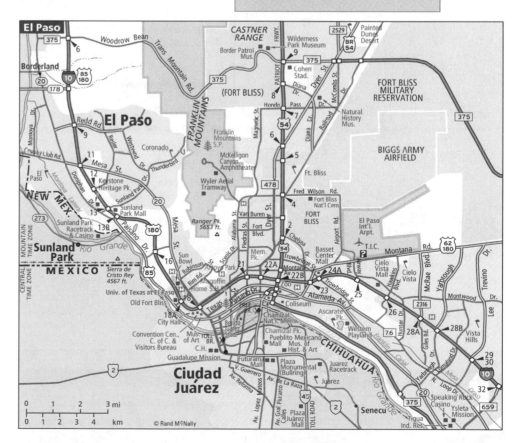

GATLINBURG, Tennessee

Ripley's Aquarium of the Smokies

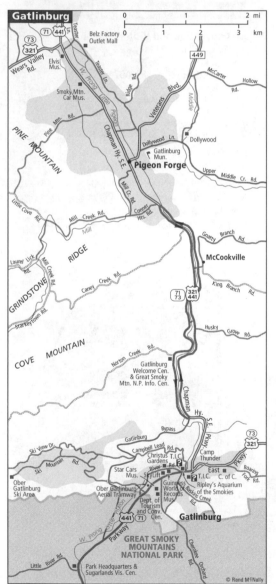

From Pigeon Forge to Gatlinburg, the road to Great Smoky Mountains National Park is awash with outlet stores, family attractions, restaurants, resorts, and motels. Gatlinburg, at the northern entrance to the park, is a hub of Southern craftsmanship. More than 100 different galleries and workshops occupy the loop through the Great Smoky Arts and Crafts Community. Dollywood's delights include live theatrical performers, a massive treehouse, and the Southern Gospel Music Hall of Fame & Museum. The Ober Gatlinburg Aerial Tramway starts on the sidewalk of downtown Gatlinburg and ferries riders to the top of Mt. Harrison, offering lofty mountain views along the way. *Tax: 12.5% hotel, 11% restaurants, 11.5% attractions, 9.5% retail sales. For local weather, call (800) 565-7330 ext. 5.*

▶ SELECTED ATTRACTIONS

Arrowmont School of Arts and Crafts
Art gallery
556 Parkway
(865) 436-5860

Camp Thunder Fun Center
Go-karts, mini golf, and motion simulator
542 Parkway
(865) 430-7223

Dollywood
Theme park with musical performances
1020 Dollywood Ln. off US 441,
Pigeon Forge
(865) 428-9488

Fort Fun Family Entertainment Center
Laser tag, 3D movies, and bumper cars
716 Parkway, Reagan Terrace Mall
(865) 436-2326

Gatlinburg Sky Lift
765 Parkway
(865) 436-4307

Great Smoky Arts and Crafts Community
8-mile loop of shops, studios, and galleries
Along Glades Rd. and Buckhorn Rd. east of
E. Parkway (US 321-N)

Guinness World Records Museum
631 Parkway
(865) 430-7800

Hollywood Star Cars Museum
Collection of cars used on TV and in movies
914 Parkway
(865) 430-2200

Ober Gatlinburg Aerial Tramway
Ski resort, tram rides, and amusement park
1001 Parkway
(865) 436-5423

Ripley's Aquarium of the Smokies
88 River Rd.
(865) 430-8808 or (888) 240-1358

Sweet Fanny Adams Theater
Live musical comedy
461 Parkway
(877) 388-5784

▶ SHOPPING

Calhoun's Village
Restaurants and several small shops
1004 Parkway
(865) 436-4100

Gatlinburg Aerial Tramway Mall
Crafts, gifts, and collectibles
1001 Parkway
(865) 436-5423

Mountain Mall
Small specialty shops
611 Parkway
(865) 436-5935

The Village
Boutiques, galleries, and arts and crafts outlets
634 Parkway
(865) 436-3995

▶ VISITOR INFORMATION

Gatlinburg Chamber of Commerce
811 E. Parkway
Gatlinburg, TN 37738
(865) 436-4178 or (800) 588-1817
www.gatlinburg.com

Gatlinburg Department of Tourism and Convention Center
303 Reagan Dr.
Gatlinburg, TN 37738
(865) 430-1052 or (800) 343-1475
www.gatlinburg-tennessee.com

Pigeon Forge Department of Tourism
2450 Parkway
Pigeon Forge, TN 37863
(865) 453-8574 or (800) 251-9100
www.mypigeonforge.com

Visitor Centers
Aquarium Welcome Center
Aquarium Plaza at Light #5
(865) 436-0535

Gatlinburg Welcome Center
1011 Banner Rd. at Hwy. 441 South
(865) 436-0519

Parkway Welcome Center
520 Parkway at Light #3
(865) 436-0504

DIVERSION

Treasured photographs of a vacation to Gatlinburg can be taken all along a 3.5-mile stretch called the Cherokee Orchard Road. Packed with scenery, it runs between Gatlinburg and Roaring Fork.

GUADALAJARA, Jalisco, Mexico

The historic birthplace of mariachi and tequila, Guadalajara is Mexico's second largest city, an enclave of traditional values coping with modern growth. Dominated by the city cathedral's twin towers, the old city center teems with colorful fountains and buildings dating back hundreds of years. In a city crammed with museums, one of the best—the Museo Regional de Guadalajara—exhibits archaeology, history, and fine arts including paintings by Jose Ibarra and Villalpando. Those in search of exceptional quality head to Tlaquepaque, where the craftspeople are famous for their ceramics as well as metal, glass, and leather goods. *Tax: 17% hotel (15% value-added, 2% lodging), 15% value-added sales tax is usually included in the retail price.*

The Cathedral and the Plaza de Armas

► SELECTED ATTRACTIONS

Calandria Tour
Carriage tour of the historic city center
Tours depart from the Regional Museum outside Liberty Market or at Jardín San Francisco by Corona St.

The Cathedral
Circa 1568-1618 church and a symbol of Guadalajara
Av. Alcalde between Av. Hidalgo and Calle Morelos
011-52-33-3942-4300*
011-52-33-3942-4306

Degollado Theater
Performing arts center
Degollado St., Av. Hidalgo, and Morelos St.
011-52-33-3030-9771*

Government Palace (Palacio de Gobierno)
State Capitol building with murals by Jose Clemente Orozco
Av. Corona at Morelos
011-52-33-3668-1800*

Guadalajara Regional Museum (Museo Regional de Guadalajara)
Calle Liceo, No. 60
011-52-33-3614-5257*

Guadalajara Zoo (Zoologico Guadalajara)
Zoo train and famous aviaries
Huentitan Canyon, Paseo del Zoologico No. 600
011-52-33-3674-1034*

Handicraft House (Casa de las Artesanias)
Blown glass, saddles, crafts, and papier-mâché
Constituyentes 21
011-52-33-3619-5402*

Lienzo Charro Jalisco
Charreadas, mariachi music, and competitions
Av. R. Michel No. 577
011-52-33-3619-0315*

► DIVERSION

Cobblestone streets, rustic white houses, and one of the most picturesque bays in the world are only three hours away in Puerto Vallarta. Take Mexico 15 with connections to Mexico 200. Don't miss the sculptures that line the boardwalk.

► SHOPPING

Mercado Libertad (San Juan de Dios)
Indoor market for handicrafts, clothes, souvenirs, and gifts
Calzada Independencia Sur and Av. Javier Mina

Tlaquepaque
Arts and crafts center
5 miles southwest of downtown Guadalajara

Shopping can also be found at:
Centro Magno
La Gran Plaza
Plaza del Sol
Plaza México
Plaza Pabellón
Plaza Patria
El Baratillo (flea market)
(Check with your hotel front desk for specific locations.)

► DON'T MISS DRIVE

Vallarta Avenue is one of the city's most beautiful streets. It brims with colorful shops and restaurants and is lined with historic monuments.

► VISITOR INFORMATION

Visitors and Convention Bureau at the Guadalajara Chamber of Commerce
Av. Guadalupe No. 5099
Zapopan, Jal. 45030
011-53-33-3628-4439

Jalisco State Tourism Ministry
102 Morelos (on Plaza Tapatia)
Guadalajara, Jal. 44100, Mexico
011-52-33-3668-1600

Mexico Tourism Board (U.S.)
(800) 446-3942
www.visitmexico.com

Number listed may or may not have an English-speaking person available.

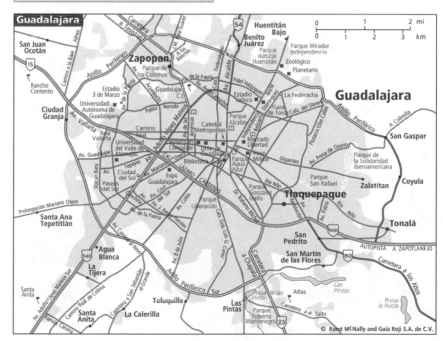

HONOLULU, Hawaii

Fire-knife dancer at the Polynesian Culture Center

The "Pearl of the Pacific" has lost none of its ability to enchant; a perfect climate, pristine beaches, and fabulous scenery induce visitors to return again and again. Hike to the 760-foot summit of Diamond Head Crater to take in the splendor of sunrise as well as 360-degree views of the island. The Bishop Museum is dedicated to telling the story of the natural and cultural history of Hawaii and the Pacific. The USS *Arizona* Memorial is a moving tribute to those who lost their lives at Pearl Harbor during the entrance of America into World War II. *Tax: 11.962% hotel, 4.712% sales, 0.5% Oahu county surcharge. For local weather, call (808) 973-4380 or (808) 973-5286.*

▶ SELECTED ATTRACTIONS

Bishop Museum
Natural and cultural history exhibits, garden shows, and planetarium
1525 Bernice St.
(808) 847-3511

Foster Botanical Garden
50 N. Vineyard Blvd.
(808) 522-7060

▶ DON'T MISS DRIVE

Nu'uanu Pali Lookout overlooks forested, near-vertical 600-foot cliffs on the windward side of O'ahu and provides one of the best views on the island. From Waikīkī, take H-1 west, then take Pali Highway, HI 61, via Nu'uanu Pali Drive. Half a mile beyond Queen Emma's Summer Palace, follow signs to the lookout.

Hawaii State Art Museum (HiSAM)
Contemporary Hawaiian artists
250 S. Hotel St., (808) 586-0900

Hawaiian Waters Adventure Park
400 Farrington Hwy., Kapolei
(808) 674-9283

Honolulu Academy of Arts
Western and Asian art collections
900 S. Beretania St.
(808) 532-8700

Honolulu Zoo
151 Kapahulu Ave.
(808) 971-7171

'Iolani Palace
364 S. King St.
(808) 522-0832

National Memorial Cemetery of the Pacific
Veterans' cemetery in Punchbowl Crater
2177 Puowaina Dr.
(808) 532-3720

Polynesian Cultural Center
55-370 Kamehameha Hwy., Lā'ie
(808) 293-3333 or (800) 367-7060

USS *Arizona* Memorial at Pearl Harbor
1 Arizona Memorial Pl. off H-1 Fwy.
(808) 422-0561

Waimea Valley Audubon Center
Botanical gardens and self-guided tours
59-864 Kamehameha Hwy., Hale'iwa
(808) 638-9199

▶ SHOPPING

Ala Moana Center
Open-air shopping center
1450 Ala Moana Blvd.
(808) 955-9517

Aloha Tower Marketplace
Specialty stores, restaurants, live concerts, and theater
1 Aloha Tower Dr.
(808) 528-5700

Bailey's Antiques and Aloha Shirts
Hawaiiana and more than 15,000 vintage shirts
517 Kapahulu Ave.
(808) 734-7628

International Marketplace
Open-air market
2330 Kalakaua Ave.
(808) 971-2080

Royal Hawaiian Shopping Center
Specialty shops and restaurants
2201 Kalakaua Ave.
(808) 922-2299

2100 Kalakaua Avenue
High-end merchants
2100 Kalakaua Ave. at Kalaimoku St.
(808) 541-5136

Ward Centers
Specialty shops, restaurants, and entertainment
Ala Moana Blvd. and Ward Ave.
(808) 591-8411

▶ VISITOR INFORMATION

Hawai'i Visitors and Convention Bureau
2270 Kalakaua Ave., Ste. 801
Honolulu, HI 96815
(808) 923-1811 or (800) 464-2924
www.gohawaii.com

▶ DIVERSION

Visit the "surfing capital of the world" on the North Shore of the island. The area is also home to Historic Hale'iwa Town. From Waikīkī, go west on H-1 and take exit 8-A, which will turn to H-2; then take exit 8, which becomes Kamehameha Hwy. Continue through Hale'iwa Town and on to the North Shore.

Honolulu

© Rand McNally

HOUSTON, Texas

Fifty miles from the Gulf and many more from the moon, Houston is both a major seaport and a familiar name in the exploration of space. The Menil Collection houses Byzantine and contemporary masterworks in a stunning building. For lighthearted entertainment, families head to Children's Museum of Houston or to the Houston Zoo, which hunkers down in the forests and trees of Hermann Park. For a trip a bit farther from home, visitors try a simulated journey to the stars at Space Center Houston. *Tax: 17% hotel, 8.25% sales. For local weather, call (281) 337-5074.*

Battleship USS Texas

▶ SELECTED ATTRACTIONS

Battleship *Texas*
3523 Battleground Rd.
San Jacinto Battleground State Historic Site, LaPorte
(281) 479-2431

Bayou Bend Collection and Gardens
American decorative arts collection in historic mansion
1 Westcott St.
(713) 639-7750

Children's Museum of Houston
1500 Binz St.
(713) 522-1138

Contemporary Arts Museum
5216 Montrose Blvd.
(713) 284-8250

George Ranch Historical Park
1830s stock farm with mansion and ranch house
10215 FM 762, six miles south of US 59 and Grand Parkway, Richmond
(281) 343-0218

The Health Museum
1515 Hermann Dr.
(713) 521-1515

The Heritage Society
Museum of Texas history and nine historic structures
1100 Bagby St. in Sam Houston Park
(713) 655-1912

continued on the next page

Houston City Hall

Houston attractions continued

Holocaust Museum Houston
5401 Caroline St.
(713) 942-8000

Houston Arboretum and Nature Center
4501 Woodway Dr.
(713) 681-8433

Houston Museum of Natural Science
1 Hermann Circle Dr.
(713) 639-4629

Houston Zoo
6200 Golf Course Dr. in Hermann Park
(713) 533-6500

The Menil Collection
Art museum
1515 Sul Ross St.
(713) 525-9400

Museum of Fine Arts
1001 Bissonnet St.
(713) 639-7300

Orange Show Center for Visionary Art
Eclectic arts center and monument
2402 Munger St.
(713) 926-6368

Sam Houston Boat Tour
Free public tour of the Houston Ship Channel
7300 Clinton Dr., Gate 8
(713) 670-2416

San Jacinto Monument and Museum of History
1 Monument Circle in the San Jacinto
Battleground State Historic Site, La Porte
(281) 479-2421

Space Center Houston
Museum, live shows, and tram tours of NASA's Johnson Space Center
3 miles east of I-45 on NASA Parkway,
25 miles southeast of downtown Houston
(281) 244-2100

SplashTown Water Park
21300 I-45 N., Spring, TX
(281) 355-3300

▶ SHOPPING

The Galleria
Upscale boutiques, shops, department stores, and restaurants
5085 Westheimer Rd.
(713) 622-0663

Highland Village
Department stores and specialty shops
4055 Westheimer Rd.
(713) 850-3100

Houston Tunnel System
Six-mile system of underground shops and restaurants, 55 entrances

Rice Village
Boutiques, retail stores, and restaurants
Kirby Dr. and University Blvd.

Uptown Park
Designer boutiques
Post Oak Blvd. at Loop I-610
(713) 850-1400

▶ VISITOR INFORMATION

Greater Houston Convention and Visitors Bureau
901 Bagby St., Ste. 100
Houston, TX 77002
(713) 437-5200 or (800) 446-8786
www.visithoustontexas.com

Houston Visitors Center
901 Bagby St. (Bagby and Walker Sts.)
(713) 437-5556

Bay Area Houston Visitors Center
20710 I-45, Webster
(281) 338-0333 or (800) 844-5253

Upper Kirby Visitors Center
3273B Southwest Freeway
(281) 833-3333

DIVERSION

Washington-on-the-Brazos State Historic Site north of Brenham, TX is where the treaty that declared Texas' independence from Mexico was signed. 80 miles west on US 290 to TX 105. Watch for signs.
(936) 878-2214

Blast off for Houston

Space Center Houston is NASA's official visitors center. It houses actual spacecraft such as the Mercury, Gemini, and Apollo capsules and provides an exclusive tram ride through the Johnson Space Center. Visitors can make a stop at the largest IMAX theater in Texas or try to "walk in space" via state-of-the-art simulators. The Astronaut Gallery features spacesuits dating back to the first American trip into space. Hands-on exhibits encourage visitors to test their skills at landing a spacecraft or retrieving a satellite through interactive computer simulators. It's a blast, and most visitors stay all day. Located at 1601 NASA Parkway, off I-45 South, in the Clear Lake area outside of Houston. Admission is $18.95 for adults, with discounts for children and senior citizens. For information, call (281) 244-2100 or visit **www.spacecenter.org**.

INDIANAPOLIS, Indiana

The roar of racing cars will forever be associated with this metropolis of the cornfields, but Indiana's capital offers subtler charms as well. The Children's Museum boasts 100,000 items to stimulate youngsters' interests in art, science, and the world around them. The Eiteljorg Museum displays an exceptional collection of Native American and Western-themed art. It's part of White River State Park, which is where visitors also find the zoo, the NCAA Hall of Fame, and a chance to paddle through downtown on the Central Canal. *Tax: 16% hotel, 7% sales. For local weather, call (317) 222-2222 or (317) 856-0664.*

Canal Walk in Indianapolis

► SELECTED ATTRACTIONS

Central Canal
Runs through downtown's White River State Park
Paddleboat rental at Ohio and West Sts.
(317) 767-5072

The Children's Museum of Indianapolis
3000 N. Meridian St.
(317) 334-3322

Congressional Medal of Honor Memorial
North bank of the Central Canal, next to Military Park
650 Washington St. in White River State Pk.
(317) 233-2434 or (800) 665-9056

Conner Prairie
Living history museum
13400 Allisonville Rd., Fishers
(317) 776-6000 or (800) 966-1836

Crispus Attucks Museum
History museum honoring African Americans
1140 Dr. Martin Luther King Jr. St.
(317) 226-2430

Eiteljorg Museum of American Indians and Western Art
500 W. Washington St.
(317) 636-9378

Freetown Village
Living history museum about African American life in 19th-century Indiana
625 Indiana Ave.
(317) 631-1870

Indiana Basketball Hall of Fame
408 Trojan Ln., New Castle
(765) 529-1891

Indiana State Museum and IMAX Theater
650 W. Washington St.
(317) 232-1637

Indianapolis Motor Speedway and Hall of Fame Museum
4790 W. 16th St.
(317) 492-6784

Indianapolis Museum of Art
Includes historic estate and gardens
4000 Michigan Rd.
(317) 920-2660

Indianapolis Zoo and White River Gardens
1200 W. Washington St.
(317) 630-2001

NCAA Hall of Champions
700 W. Washington St.
(317) 916-4255 or (800) 735-6222

President Benjamin Harrison Home
1230 N. Delaware St.
(317) 631-1888

Riley Museum Home
Historic home of poet James Whitcomb Riley
528 Lockerbie St.
(317) 631-5885

State Soldiers' and Sailors' Monument
Meridian and Market Sts. on Monument Circle
(317) 232-7615

Victory Field
Home of Minor League Baseball's Indianapolis Indians
501 W. Maryland St.
(317) 269-3545

White River State Park
Urban state park with museums, canal, greenways, and bike/hiking paths
801 W. Washington St.
(317) 233-2434 or (800) 665-9056

► SHOPPING

Castleton Square Mall
Department and specialty stores
6020 E. 82nd St.
(317) 849-9993

Circle Centre Mall
Shopping, dining, and entertainment complex
49 W. Maryland St.
(317) 681-8000

Fashion Mall at Keystone
Upscale department stores and specialty shops
8702 Keystone Crossing
(317) 574-4000

Fountain Square Merchants
Antique shops and specialty stores
Intersection of Virginia Ave., Shelby St., and Prospect St.
(317) 686-6010

Indianapolis City Market
Fresh foods and imported grocery items
222 E. Market St.
(317) 634-9266

Lafayette Square Mall
38th St. and Lafayette Rd.
(317) 291-6391

DON'T MISS DRIVE

Cruise Meridian Street between 38th and 86th Streets for a view of mansions built by the founders of Indianapolis. The Governor's Mansion is also on Meridian Street.

► VISITOR INFORMATION

Indianapolis Convention and Visitors Association
30 S. Meridian St., Ste. 410
Indianapolis, IN 46204
(317) 639-4282 or (800) 556-4639
www.indy.org

Indiana Convention Center Information Desk
200 S. Capitol Ave.
(317) 684-7574

Indianapolis Artsgarden Visitor Center
100 W. Washington St.
(317) 624-2563

IndyGo Transit Center at Indianapolis City Market
222 E. Market St.
(317) 635-3344

White River State Park Visitor Center
801 W. Washington St.
(317) 233-2434

See next page for Indianapolis vicinity map

DIVERSION

The Wholesale District Tour and Monument Circle Tour provide a 90-minute walk through restored and historic areas. The Monument Circle Tour includes Christ Church Cathedral (1857), the oldest church in the city. The Wholesale District Tour includes Union Station, the first centralized train station in the country. Tours also focus on noteworthy architecture. Call (317) 639-4534 or (800) 450-4534 for both tours.

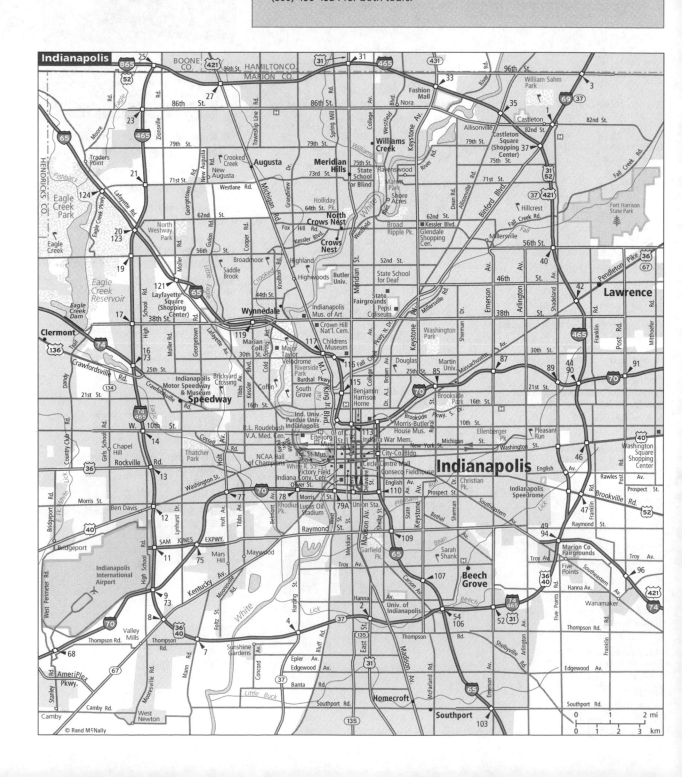

© Rand McNally

JACKSONVILLE, Florida

The most populous city in Florida, Jacksonville is a growing commercial and financial mecca. The city is home to the Cummer Museum of Art & Gardens, renowned for its collection of Meissen porcelain and the massive Cummer Oak that overspreads the grounds. The Jacksonville Zoo and Garden's rare and exotic fauna from around the world make it a favorite stop; take a walking safari through the African habitat or explore the Range of the Jaguar exhibit. Day or night, the Jacksonville Landing downtown on the riverbank offers a place to unwind with restaurants, shops, and live entertainment. *Tax: 13% hotel, 7% sales. For local weather, call (904) 741-4311.*

Lone Sailor *statue on The Riverwalk*

▶ SELECTED ATTRACTIONS

Adventure Landing
Laser tag, arcade, go-karts, and mini golf
4825 Blanding Blvd.
(904) 771-2803

Baseball Grounds of Jacksonville
Home of Minor League Baseball's Jacksonville Suns
301 A. Philip Randolph Blvd.
(904) 358-2846

Budweiser Brewery Tours
111 Busch Dr.
(904) 696-8373

Cummer Museum of Art & Gardens
829 Riverside Ave.
(904) 356-6857

The Downtown Riverwalks
Along the St. Johns River through downtown Jacksonville

Fort Caroline National Memorial
12713 Fort Caroline Rd.
(904) 641-7155

Jacksonville Veteran's Memorial Arena
300 A. Philip Randolph Blvd.
(904) 630-3900

Jacksonville Zoo and Gardens
370 Zoo Pkwy.
(904) 757-4463

Kathryn Abby Hanna Park
450-acre beachfront city park
500 Wonderwood Dr.
(904) 249-4700

Kingsley Plantation
Historic cotton and sugarcane plantation on Ft. George Island
11676 Palmetto Ave.
(904) 251-3537

Museum of Contemporary Art— Jacksonville
333 N. Laura St.
(904) 366-6911

Museum of Science and History (MOSH)
1025 Museum Circle
(904) 396-6674

Times-Union Center for the Performing Arts
300 W. Water St.
(904) 633-6110

▶ SHOPPING

Avonlea Antique Mall
200 antique dealers
8101 Phillips Hwy.
(904) 636-8785

The Avenues
Department stores and specialty shops
10300 Southside Blvd.
(904) 363-3060

Jacksonville Landing
A riverfront marketplace
2 Independent Dr.
(904) 353-1188

Orange Park Mall
Department stores and specialty shops
1910 Wells Rd., Orange Park
(904) 269-2422

Regency Square Mall
Department stores and specialty shops
9501 Arlington Expwy.
(904) 725-3830

San Marco District
Shopping and restaurants
San Marco and Atlantic Blvds.

▶ VISITOR INFORMATION

Jacksonville and the Beaches Convention and Visitors Bureau
550 Water St., Ste. 1000
Jacksonville, FL 32202
(904) 798-9111 or (800) 733-2668
www.visitjacksonville.com

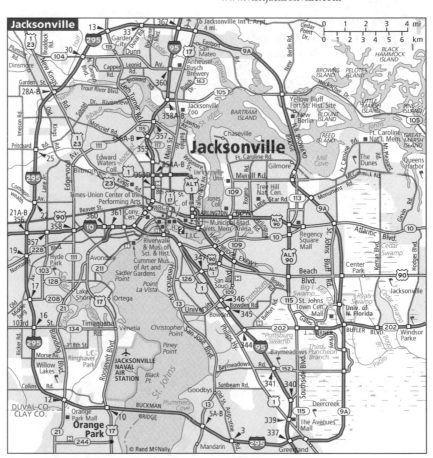

KANSAS CITY, Missouri

The Nelson-Atkins Museum of Art

The burghers of Kansas City, looking for a way to make their city stand out, came up with a winner: fountains, both large and small. They're now part of almost every developer's plans here—only Rome has more. With its rich musical past, the city makes a fitting home for the American Jazz Museum. It's part of the Museum Complex at 18th and Vine, which includes the Negro Leagues Baseball Museum, a memorial to the African American teams that played from the late 1800s until the 1960s. For great barbecue, everyone knows to head to Arthur Bryant's. *Tax 15.225% (15.725% downtown) hotel, 7.725% sales. For local weather, call (816) 540-6021.*

DIVERSION

Drive over to Independence to visit the Harry S. Truman National Historic Site, which preserves his home, the Truman Presidential Museum and Library, and the city's 15 other historic sites and museums. The National Frontier Trails Museum offers a history of wagon train journeys to the west. From Kansas City, take I-70 east to I-435 north to Winner Rd., US 24 east.
(816) 325-7111 or (800) 748-7323

► SELECTED ATTRACTIONS

American Jazz Museum
1616 E. 18th St.
(816) 474-8463

Arabia Steamboat Museum
400 Grand Blvd.
(816) 471-1856

Children's Fountain
The fountain of and for youth
32nd St. and N. Oak Trafficway
(816) 842-2299

J.C. Nichols Memorial Fountain
47th and Main St. at the entrance to the Plaza District
(816) 842-2299

The Kansas City Zoo
6800 Zoo Dr. in Swope Park
(816) 513-5700

Kemper Museum of Contemporary Art
4420 Warwick Blvd.
(816) 753-5784

Negro Leagues Baseball Museum
1616 E. 18th St.
(816) 221-1920

Nelson-Atkins Museum of Art
4525 Oak St.
(816) 751-1278

Starlight Theater
Large outdoor theater
4600 Starlight Rd. in Swope Park
(816) 363-7827 or (800) 776-1730

Thomas Hart Benton Home and Studio State Historic Site
3616 Belleview Ave.
(816) 931-5722

Truman Presidential Museum and Library
500 W. US Hwy. 24, Independence
(816) 268-8200 or (800) 833-1225

Union Station
Restored train station, home to science museum, shops, theaters, and restaurants
30 W. Pershing Rd.
(816) 460-2020

Vietnam Veterans Fountain
W. 42nd St. and Broadway
(816) 842-2299

Worlds of Fun/Oceans of Fun
Theme and water parks
I-435, exit 54 (Parvin Rd.)
(816) 454-4545

► SHOPPING

City Market
Shopping district with farmers' market
5th and Walnut Sts.
(816) 842-1271

Country Club Plaza
Upscale specialty shops and department stores
4745 Central St.
(816) 753-0100

Crown Center
Shopping, dining, entertainment, and hotels
2450 Grand Blvd.
(816) 274-8444

Independence Center
Department stores, specialty shops, and eateries
I-70 and MO 291, Independence
(816) 795-8600

Oak Park Mall
Department stores and specialty shops
11461 W. 95th St., Overland Park, KS
(913) 888-4400

► VISITOR INFORMATION

Kansas City Convention and Visitors Association
1100 Main St., Ste. 2200
Kansas City, MO 64105
(816) 221-5242 or (800) 767-7700
www.visitkc.com

Visitor Information Centers
County Club Plaza
4709 Central St.

City Center Square
1100 Main St., Ste. 2200

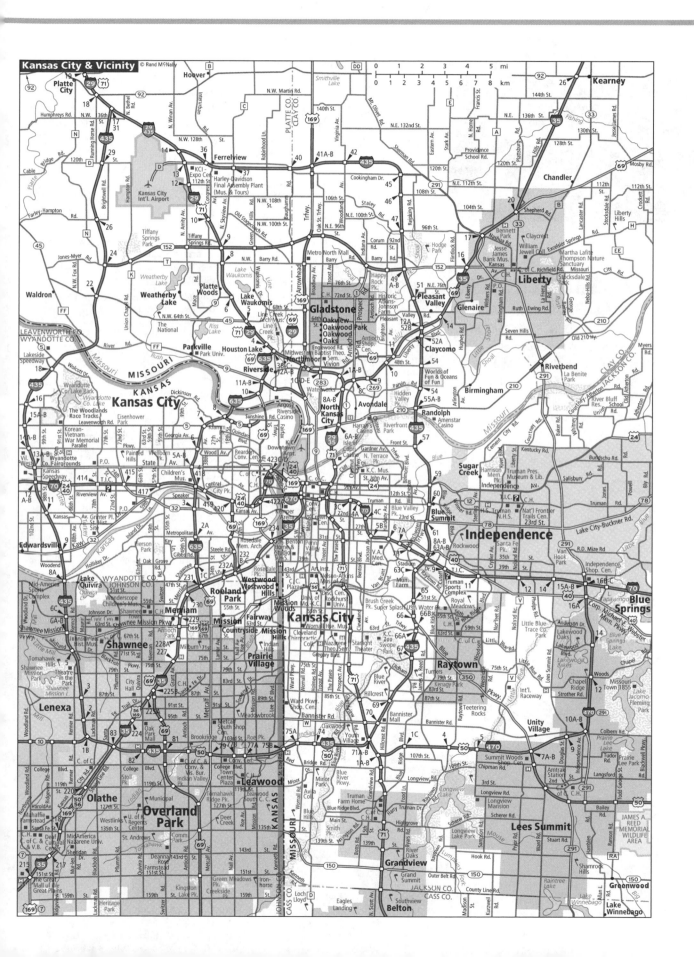

Kansas City & Vicinity
© Rand McNally

KEY WEST, Florida

Duval Street

In fun and funky Key West, the sunset is a big deal. Street performers of all kinds gather at Mallory Square for an informal, raucous celebration at the end of each day. The city's many cottages and fine mansions are forever in some stage of restoration. Work on Audubon House in the 1950s started the trend toward preservation; James Audubon's original watercolor paintings are among its treasures. Ernest Hemingway's home now houses a museum and some sixty felines. The Shipwreck Historeum looks back to the wrecking industry. *Tax: 11.5% hotel, 7.5% sales. For local weather, call (305) 295-1324.*

DON'T MISS DRIVE

You haven't seen Key West until you've seen Duval Street, with its architectural and botanical treasures. Take Duval to Mallory Square for the best view of Key West's famed sunsets.

SELECTED ATTRACTIONS

Audubon House & Tropical Gardens
205 Whitehead St.
(305) 294-2116 or (877) 294-2470

Dry Tortugas National Park
19th-century island fort
68 miles west in the Gulf of Mexico
(305) 242-7700

Ernest Hemingway Home and Museum
907 Whitehead St.
(305) 294-1136

Harry S Truman Little White House
Truman's winter White House
111 Front St. in Truman Annex
(305) 294-9911

Key West Aquarium
1 Whitehead St.
(305) 296-2051

Key West Butterfly and Nature Conservatory
1316 Duval St.
(305) 296-2988 or (800) 839-4647

Key West Lighthouse and Keeper's Quarters Museum
938 Whitehead St.
(305) 294-0012

Key West Museum of Art and History at the Custom House
281 Front St.
(305) 295-6616

Key West Shipwreck Historeum
1 Whitehead St.
(305) 292-8990

Mel Fisher Maritime Museum
200 Greene St.
(305) 294-2633

The Oldest House & Garden
Oldest house in Key West, historic exhibits
322 Duval St.
(305) 294-9501

Southernmost House in the U.S.
1400 Duval St.
(305) 296-3141

Sunset Celebration
Daily festivities with crafts and food
Mallory Square at the foot of Duval St. on the Gulf of Mexico
(305) 292-7700

SHOPPING

Clinton Square Market
Artisans, crafts, and specialty shops
291 Front St.
(305) 296-6825

Duval Street
Galleries, antiques, and specialty shops
Duval St. between South and Front Sts. in Old Town

VISITOR INFORMATION

Florida Keys Tourist Development Council
1201 White St.
Key West, FL 33040
(305) 296-1552 or (800) 352-5397
www.fla-keys.com

Key West Business Guild
513 Truman Ave.
Key West, FL 33040
(305) 294-4603 or (800) 535-7797
www.gaykeywestfl.com

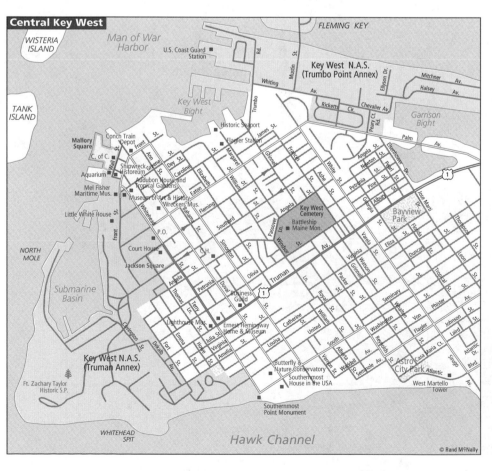

Central Key West

© Rand McNally

LAS VEGAS, Nevada

From one end to the other, the Strip in this legendary desert oasis throbs. Hotels and casinos compete for attention with dancing water displays, imitation cities, and exploding volcanoes. Downtown's Fremont Street, where the older gaming establishments are found, is topped with a multimedia canopy of high-tech effects. Thrill-seekers take the plunge from the top of the 1,149-foot Stratosphere Tower. At Star Trek: The Experience in the Las Vegas Hilton, visitors can meet a Klingon, check out the History of the Future exhibit, and have their picture taken in the captain's chair. *Tax: 11% hotel for downtown; 9% hotel for the Strip; 7.75% sales. For local weather, call (702) 263-9744 or 811.*

The Las Vegas Strip at night

▶ SELECTED ATTRACTIONS

The Adventuredome at Circus Circus
Amusement park
2880 Las Vegas Blvd. S
(702) 734-0410

Atomic Testing Museum
755 E. Flamingo Rd.
(702) 794-5161

The Auto Collections
3535 Las Vegas Blvd. S.
(702) 794-3174

Fountains of Bellagio
More than 1,000 fountains dance in sync to music
3600 Las Vegas Blvd. S.
(702) 693-7111

Fremont Street Experience
Canopy light show set to music
425 Fremont St.
(702) 678-5600

Liberace Museum
1775 E. Tropicana Ave.
(702) 798-5595

Red Rock Canyon National Conservation Area
17 miles west on Charleston Blvd.
(NV 159)
(702) 515-5350

Star Trek: The Experience
Las Vegas Hilton
3000 Paradise Rd.
(888) 462-6535

Stratosphere Casino Hotel and Tower
2000 Las Vegas Blvd S.
(702) 380-7777 or (800) 998-6937

▶ SHOPPING

Fashion Outlets
32100 Las Vegas Blvd. S., I-15 south to exit 1, Primm
(702) 874-1400 or (888) 424-6898

Fashion Show Mall
High-end retailers and weekend fashion shows, on the runway and projected onto the "cloud" screen
3200 Las Vegas Blvd. S.
(702) 369-8382

The Forum Shops at Caesars Palace
Designer boutiques
3500 Las Vegas Blvd. S.
(702) 893-4800

Grand Canal Shoppes at the Venetian
Upscale specialty shops and restaurants
3377 Las Vegas Blvd. S.
(702) 414-4500

Las Vegas Outlet Center
Outlet stores
7400 Las Vegas Blvd. S.
(702) 896-5599

Miracle Mile Shops at Planet Hollywood
Retails shops, restaurants, and entertainment
3663 Las Vegas Blvd. S.
(888) 800-8284

▶ VISITOR INFORMATION

Las Vegas Convention and Visitors Authority
3150 Paradise Rd.
Las Vegas, NV 89109
(702) 892-0711 or (877) 847-4858
www.visitlasvegas.com

DIVERSION

Take a 31-mile drive east on Boulder Hwy. to see gorgeous Lake Mead, the largest man-made lake in the country. Go another four miles to Boulder City and tour the impressive Hoover Dam, which is 726 ft. high and 660 feet wide at the base.
(702) 293-8906 (Lake Mead),
(702) 494-2517 (Hoover Dam)

LEXINGTON, Kentucky

Bronze horse statues at Thoroughbred Park

The unofficial capital of the Bluegrass region, Lexington is horse country. The area's most familiar symbol: miles and miles of white plank fencing enclosing equestrian pastures on hundreds of ranches. More than 30 breeds are represented at the Kentucky Horse Park, where exhibits include the International Museum of the Horse and the American Saddlebred Museum. The countryside is also rich with elegant homes such as Ashland, where 19th-century politician and presidential hopeful Henry Clay resided, and the childhood home of Mary Todd Lincoln. *Tax: 13.4% hotel, 6% sales. For local weather, call (859) 253-4444 or (859) 281-8131.*

▶ SELECTED ATTRACTIONS

Applebee's Park
Minor League Baseball
1200 N. Broadway
(859) 422-7867

Ashland
19th-century home of Henry Clay
120 Sycamore Rd.
(859) 266-8581

▶ DON'T MISS DRIVE

Old Frankfort Pike, or KY 1681, has been designated as one of Kentucky's Scenic Byways. The rolling hills found on either side of the road yield to vistas of house farms, limestone rockwalls, and flowering trees in spring.

Aviation Museum of Kentucky
4316 Hangar Dr., off US 60 at the Blue Grass Airport
(859) 231-1219

Headley-Whitney Museum
Art museum
4435 Old Frankfort Pike
(859) 255-6653

Keeneland Race Course
Horse racing
4201 Versailles Rd.
(859) 254-3412 or (800) 456-3412

Kentucky Horse Park and International Museum of the Horse
4089 Iron Works Pkwy.
(859) 233-4303 or (800) 678-8813

Lexington Cemetery
833 W. Main St.
(859) 255-5522

Mary Todd Lincoln House
Childhood home of former First Lady
578 W. Main St.
(859) 233-9999

Shaker Village of Pleasant Hill
3501 Lexington Rd., Harrodsburg
(859) 734-5411 or (800) 734-5611

The Thoroughbred Center
Horse training facility
3380 Paris Pike
(859) 293-1853

Thoroughbred Park
2.5-acre park with life-size bronze horses streaking toward the finish line
Main St. and Midland Ave.

Waveland State Historic Site
Plantation home and 10-acre park
225 Waveland Museum Ln.
off Nicholasville Rd.
(859) 272-3611

The Woodford Reserve Distillery
Bourbon distillery
7855 McCracken Pike, Versailles
(859) 879-1812

▶ SHOPPING

Clay Avenue Shops
Antiques and shops on historic street
Clay Ave. off E. Main St.

Fayette Mall
Department stores and specialty shops
3401 Nicholasville Rd.
(859) 272-3493 or (800) 972-9874

Heritage Antiques
Antiques and collectibles
380 E. Main St.
(859) 253-1035

Turfland Mall
Department and retail stores
2033 Harrodsburg Rd.
(859) 276-4411

Victorian Square
Specialty shops in renovated Victorian block
401 W. Main St.
(859) 252-7575

▶ VISITOR INFORMATION

Lexington Convention and Visitors Bureau
301 E. Vine St.
Lexington, KY 40507
(859) 233-7299 or (800) 845-3959
www.visitlex.com

▶ DIVERSION

Spend an afternoon touring the bluegrass countryside and passing horse farms. Self-drive tour directions are available. (800) 845-3959

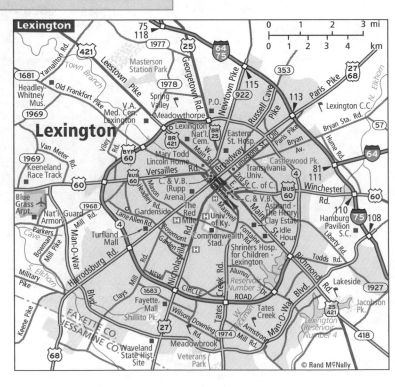

© Rand McNally

LITTLE ROCK, Arkansas

Fueled by development of the William J. Clinton Presidential Center and Park, Arkansas's capital city is undergoing a downtown renaissance. The presidential library and museum houses millions of documents, photographs, and artifacts from the Clinton administration. The Center has spurred growth in the River Market district, now the city's hot spot for restaurants, shops, and entertainment. Elsewhere, history buffs can tour the Old State House Museum and the present state capitol. *Tax: 11.5% hotel, 7.5% sales, 9.5% prepared food. For local weather, call (501) 371-7777 or (501) 834-0308.*

River Market

▶ SELECTED ATTRACTIONS

Aerospace Education Center and IMAX Theater
3301 E. Roosevelt Rd.
(501) 376-4232

Arkansas Arts Center
Art galleries, children's theatre, and museum school
501 E. 9th St.
(501) 372-4000

Arkansas State Capitol
1 Capitol Mall
(501) 682-5080

Central High School National Historic Site
History of the 1957 desegregation crisis
2120 Daisy L. Gatson Bates Dr.
(501) 374-1957

Empress of Little Rock
Elaborate Gothic Queen Anne-style bed-and-breakfast with historic tours
2120 Louisiana St.
(501) 374-7966

Historic Arkansas Museum
200 E. 3rd St.
(501) 324-9351

Little Rock Zoo
1 Jonesboro Dr.
(501) 666-2406

MacArthur Museum of Arkansas Military History
503 E. 9th St. in MacArthur Park
(501) 376-4602

Museum of Discovery
Science, history, and anthropology
500 President Clinton Ave.
(501) 396-7050 or (800) 880-6475

Old State House Museum
Arkansas's first state capitol building
300 W. Markham St.
(501) 324-9685

Quapaw Quarter
Historic district
Bounded by Arkansas River, the old Rock Island Railroad tracks, Fourche Creek, and Central High School
(501) 371-0075

William J. Clinton Presidential Center
Library and school of public affairs
1200 President Clinton Ave.
(501) 374-4242

▶ SHOPPING

Bowman Curve/West Markham
Shops and restaurants
W. Markham St. and Bowman Rd.

Kavanaugh Boulevard–The Heights
Boutiques and gift shops in historic area
Between 3000 block of Markham St. and University Ave.

Lakewood Village
Specialty shops, restaurants, and theaters
2800 Lakewood Village Dr., McCain Blvd. and Justin Matthews Dr., North Little Rock
(501) 758-3080

McCain Mall
McCain Blvd. and US 67, North Little Rock
(501) 758-6340

River Market
Farmers' market and enclosed market hall
400 President Clinton Ave.
(501) 375-2552

▶ VISITOR INFORMATION

Little Rock Convention and Visitors Bureau
Robinson Center, 426 W. Markham St.
Little Rock, AR 72201
(501) 376-4781 or (800) 844-4781
www.littlerock.com

Little Rock Visitor Information Center
Curran Hall, 615 E. Capitol Ave.
(501) 371-0076 or (877) 220-2568

DIVERSION

Experience the realities of global life in a variety of economically disadvantaged "villages" at Heifer Ranch and Global Village near Perryville. It's a learning center for sustainable solutions to global problems. AR 10 west to Perryville.
(800) 422-0474 or (501) 889-5124

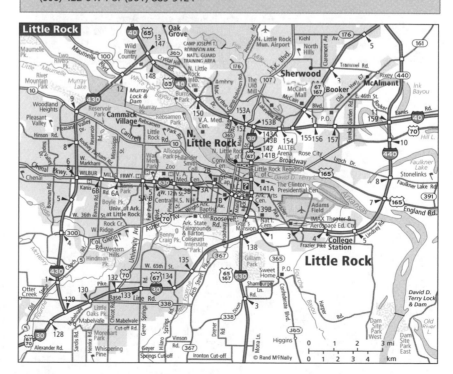

LOS ANGELES, California

Movie premiere in Hollywood

The city that sprawls from the ocean through valleys to mountain foothills is really a vast amalgamation of much smaller towns, including West Hollywood, Burbank, and Beverly Hills —home to the stars. Universal Studios and Warner Bros. offer tours of the sets and lots where feature films and television shows are made. High culture is on view at the imposing Getty Center. Kids old and young find all that hearts desire at the granddaddies of American theme parks—Disneyland and Knott's Berry Farm. *Tax: 10%-14% hotel, 8.25% sales for L.A. County; 10%-15% hotel, 7.75% sales for Orange County. For local weather, call (805) 988-6610.*

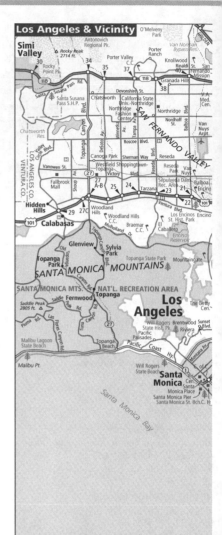

▶ DON'T MISS DRIVE

Ride the crest of the Santa Monica Mountains along the curves of Mulholland Drive for spectacular views, day or night. On one side is the San Fernando Valley; on the other side lies Hollywood. On a clear day, you can see as far as the Pacific Ocean.

▶ SELECTED ATTRACTIONS

Aquarium of the Pacific
At the south end of I-710 at Shoreline Dr., Long Beach
(562) 590-3100

California Science Center
Science exhibits and IMAX theater in Exposition Park
700 State Dr.
(323) 724-3623

Disneyland Resort
Original Disneyland, California Adventure, and Downtown Disney
1313 S. Harbor Blvd., Anaheim
(714) 781-4565

El Pueblo de Los Angeles
Historic monument at Olvera St.
125 Paseo de la Plaza
(213) 485-6855

Getty Center
Art museum and architectural wonder
1200 Getty Center Dr. near I-405 and Sunset Blvd.
(310) 440-7300

Grauman's Chinese Theatre
Celebrity handprints and footprints
6925 Hollywood Blvd.
(323) 464-8111

Hollywood Walk of Fame
Sidewalk of entertainment legends' names
Hollywood Blvd. from Gower to La Brea, and Vine St. from Yucca to Sunset
(323) 469-8311

Hollywood Wax Museum
6767 Hollywood Blvd.
(323) 462-8860

Knott's Berry Farm
Theme park
8039 Beach Blvd., Buena Park
(714) 220-5200

continued on page 60

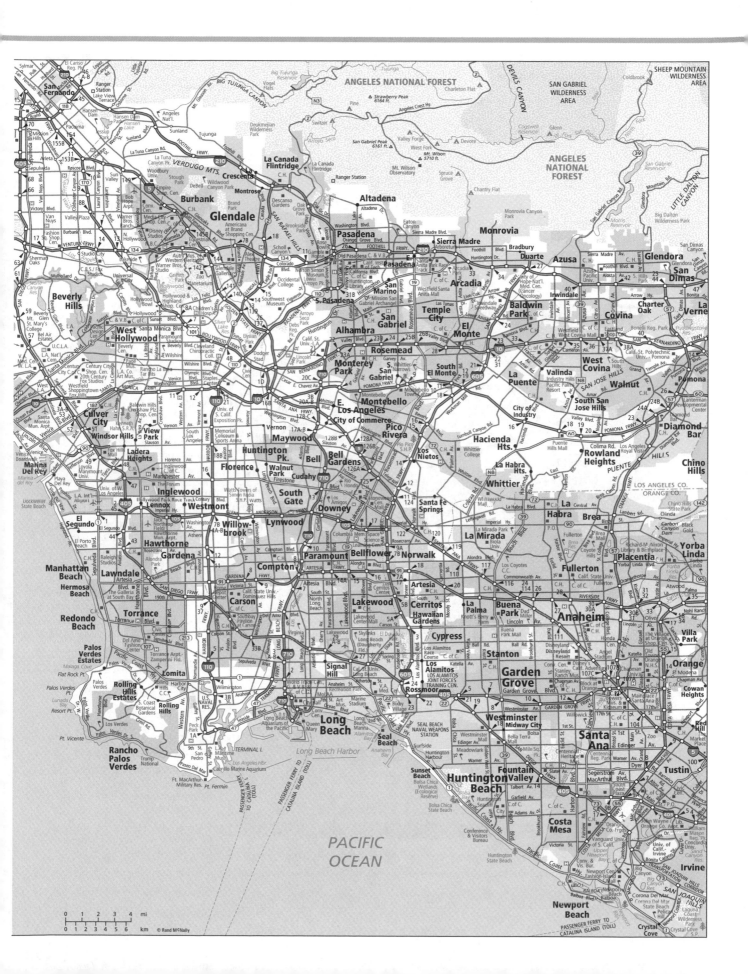

Los Angeles attractions continued

Los Angeles Maritime Museum
Berth 84, foot of 6th St.
San Pedro
(310) 548-7618

Los Angeles Zoo and Botanical Gardens
5333 Zoo Dr. in Griffith Park
(323) 644-4200

Museum of Tolerance
Exhibits on racism, prejudice, and the Holocaust
9786 W. Pico Blvd.
(310) 553-8403

Natural History Museum of Los Angeles County
900 Exposition Blvd. in Exposition Park
(213) 763-3466

Santa Monica Pier
Colorado Ave. at the Pacific Ocean,
Santa Monica
(310) 458-8900

Universal Studios Hollywood
Movie lot and theme park
Off US 101, Universal City
(800) 864-8377

Walt Disney Concert Hall
Home of the Los Angeles Philharmonic
111 S. Grand Ave.
(213) 972-7211

Warner Bros. Studio Tour
3400 W. Riverside Dr., Burbank
(818) 977-8687

SHOPPING

Beverly Center
Shops, department stores, and restaurants
8500 Beverly Blvd. between La Cienega and San Vicente Blvds.
(310) 854-0071

Farmers Market
Restaurants, cafés, and produce
6333 W. 3rd St. at Fairfax Ave.
(323) 933-9211

The Grove
Stores, restaurants, theaters, and fountains
189 The Grove Dr.
(323) 900-8080 or (888) 315-8883

Hollywood & Highland Center
Upscale shops, restaurants, entertainment, and the Kodak Theatre (home of the Oscars)
6801 Hollywood Blvd.
(323) 817-0200

Paseo Colorado
Urban village of shops, restaurants, and theaters along the Rose Parade route
280 E. Colorado Blvd., Pasadena
(626) 795-8891

Rodeo Drive
Upscale boutiques
Wilshire Dr. to Santa Monica Blvd.,
Beverly Hills

Universal CityWalk
Pedestrian promenade, shopping, entertainment, and dining
100 Universal City Plaza, Universal City
(818) 622-4455

Westfield Century City
Department stores, specialty shops, and restaurants
10250 Santa Monica Blvd.
(310) 277-3898

Westside Pavillion Shopping Center
Specialty shops, restaurants, and department stores
10800 W. Pico Blvd.
(310) 474-6255

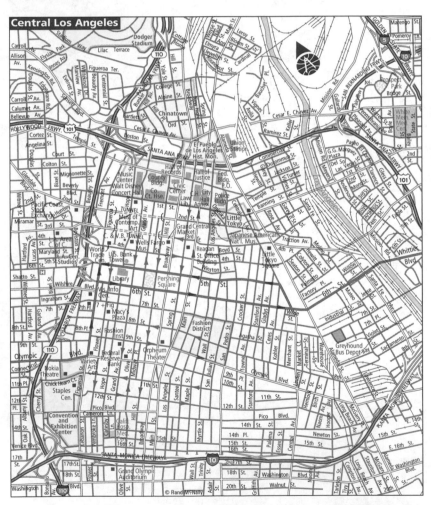

VISITOR INFORMATION

LA INC. The Convention and Visitors Bureau
333 S. Hope St., 18th Floor
Los Angeles, CA 90071
(213) 624-7300 or (800) 228-2452
www.discoverlosangeles.com

Visitor Information Centers
Downtown Los Angeles
685 S. Figueroa St.
(213) 689-8822

Hollywood & Highland Center
6801 Hollywood Blvd., Hollywood
(323) 467-6412

DIVERSION

Visit Venice, a beach resort modeled after its namesake in Italy at the beginning of the last century. Take the I-10 freeway west to I-405 south to Venice Blvd., then turn south.

LOUISVILLE, Kentucky

Recognized worldwide for the annual Kentucky Derby at Churchill Downs, this Ohio River port is also a respected center for theater and the arts. The Actors Theatre is celebrated for its annual Humana Festival of new plays, while exhibits at the Speed Art Museum survey art history from Egyptian antiquities to the present. The Kentucky Derby Museum is the only one dedicated to a single sporting event. The Muhammad Ali Center relates the story of boxing's greatest modern legend while promoting humanitarian ideals. *Tax: 15.01% hotel, 6% sales. For local weather, call (502) 968-6025.*

Downtown Louisville

▶ SELECTED ATTRACTIONS

Actors Theatre of Louisville
Regional theater
316 W. Main St.
(502) 584-1205

American Printing House for the Blind
Plant tours and museum
1839 Frankfort Ave.
(502) 895-2405 or (800) 223-1839

Churchill Downs
Home of the Kentucky Derby
700 Central Ave.
(502) 636-4400 or (800) 283-3729

Farmington Historic Plantation
Early 19th-century home
3033 Bardstown Rd.
(502) 452-9920

Frazier International History Museum
Artifacts and arms demonstrations
829 W. Main St.
(502) 753-5663

Gheens Science Hall and Rauch Planetarium
North end of Belknap Campus, University of Louisville
(502) 852-6664

Glassworks
Galleries, glassblowing classes, and tours
815 W. Market St.
(502) 584-4510

The Kentucky Center
Theater and music
501 W. Main St.
(502) 562-0100

Kentucky Center for African American Heritage
315 Guthrie Green
(502) 583-4100

Kentucky Derby Museum
704 Central Ave.
(502) 637-1111

Historic Locust Grove
1790 Georgian mansion on the Lewis and Clark National Historic Trail
561 Blankenbaker Ln.
(502) 897-9845

Louisville Science Center and IMAX
727 W. Main St.
(502) 561-6100

Louisville Slugger Museum
800 W. Main St.
(877) 775-8443 or (502) 588-7228

Louisville Zoo
1100 Trevilian Way
(502) 459-2181

Muhammad Ali Center
Immersive multimedia self-discovery exhibits
144 N. 6th St.
(502) 584-9254

Six Flags Kentucky Kingdom
937 Phillips Ln.
(502) 366-2231 or (800) 727-3267

The Speed Art Museum
2035 S. 3rd St.
(502) 634-2700

Whitehall
Antebellum home with Florentine garden
3110 Lexington Rd.
(502) 897-2944

▶ SHOPPING

Bardstown Road
Antique shops, boutiques, and restaurants
Bardstown Rd. east from downtown to Douglas Blvd. (Baxter Ave. in downtown)

Mall St. Matthews
Department and specialty stores
5000 Shelbyville Rd.
(502) 893-0311

The Summit Louisville
Shops and restaurants in Mediterranean setting
4300 Summit Plaza Dr.
(502) 425-3441

▶ VISITOR INFORMATION

Greater Louisville Convention and Visitors Bureau
401 W. Main St., Ste. 2300
Louisville, KY 40202
(502) 584-2121 or (888) 568-4784
www.gotolouisville.com

Visitor Information Center
4th and Jefferson Sts.
(502) 379-6109

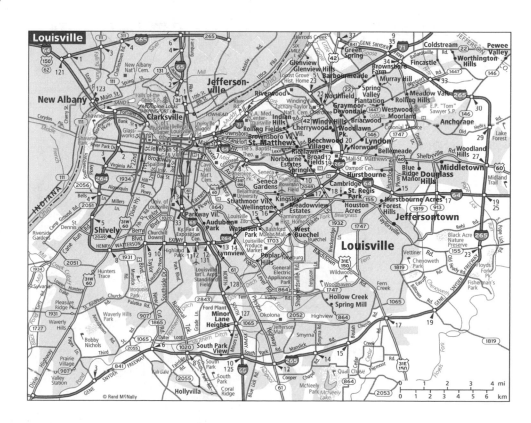

MEMPHIS, Tennessee

Graceland

Memphis means just two things in the popular mind: barbeque and roots music. The Memphis Rock 'n' Soul Museum traces the city's seminal influence on blues, country, gospel, rock and roll, and other musical genres. Historic recording studios, like the Stax Museum of American Soul Music, offer tours, as does Graceland, home of the oft-imitated, never-equaled king of rock and roll. More than 30 clubs and shops along Beale Street jump with the beat. Come springtime, the Memphis in May über-festival opens with the Beale Street Music Festival and closes with the World Championship Barbeque Cooking Contest. *Tax: 15.95% hotel, 9.25% sales. For local weather, call (901) 544-0399.*

▶ SELECTED ATTRACTIONS

Beale Street Entertainment District
Nightclubs, restaurants, and shopping
Beale St. and Third St.
(901) 526-0110

Chucalissa Museum
Archaeological exhibits and ancient village site
1987 Indian Village Dr.
(901) 785-3160

The Children's Museum of Memphis
2525 Central Ave.
(901) 458-2678

Dixon Gallery and Gardens
Impressionist and post-Impressionist art and gardens
4339 Park Ave.
(901) 761-5250

Graceland
Home of Elvis Presley
3734 Elvis Presley Blvd.
(901) 332-3322 or (800) 238-2000

Memphis Botanic Garden
750 Cherry Rd. in Audubon Park
(901) 576-4100

Memphis Brooks Museum of Art
1934 Poplar Ave. in Overton Park
(901) 544-6200

Memphis Pink Palace Museum
Regional history museum, Sharpe Planetarium, and IMAX theater
3050 Central Ave.
(901) 320-6320

Memphis Riverboats, Inc.
Riverboat cruise
Tickets and boat at 45 Riverside Dr.
(901) 527-2628 or (800) 221-6197

Memphis Rock 'n' Soul Museum
191 Beale St.
(901) 205-2533

Memphis Zoo
2000 Prentiss Pl.
(901) 333-6500

Mud Island River Park
125 N. Front St.
(901) 576-7241 or (800) 507-6507

National Civil Rights Museum
450 Mulberry St.
(901) 521-9699

The Peabody Ducks
Famous ducks that parade through the hotel lobby twice daily
Peabody Memphis Hotel, 149 Union Ave.
(901) 529-4000 or (800) 732-2639

Stax Museum of American Soul Music
926 E. McLemore Ave.
(901) 946-2535

▶ SHOPPING

Palladio International Antique Market
Unique antiques and collectibles
2169 Central Ave.
(901) 276-3808

Peabody Place
Retail shops, movie theaters, and restaurants
Peabody Pl. at 3rd St.
(901) 261-7529

South Main Arts District
Galleries and specialty shops
Bounded by Beale St., the Mississippi River, 4th St., and Crump Blvd.
(901) 578-7262

▶ VISITOR INFORMATION

Memphis Convention and Visitors Bureau
47 Union Ave., Memphis, TN 38103
(901) 543-5300 or (800) 873-6282
www.memphistravel.com

Memphis/Shelby County Visitor Center
12036 Arlington Trail (exit 25 on I-40)
(901) 543-5333

Memphis Visitor Center
3205 Elvis Presley Blvd.

Tennessee State Welcome Center
119 N. Riverside Dr.

DON'T MISS DRIVE

The heart and soul of Memphis is Beale Street, where music fills the air. You'll find everything from blues, pop, and rock to fusion jazz and reggae. Note that Beale Street is closed to cars Thursday-Sunday between 2nd St. and 4th St.

MEXICO CITY, Distrito Federal, Mexico

As one of the world's largest cities, Mexico City is fast, loud, and in a continuous state of flux. Unlimited opportunities for exploration begin in the old city center, where the Palacio National is adorned with murals by Diego Rivera, and the Templo Mayor archaeological site reveals life in the time of the ancient Aztecs. Major museums dot the 1,600-acre green space known as Bosque de Chapultepec, including the exceptional Museo Nacional de Antropologia. The Zona Rosa area maintains its popularity for finer shops, galleries, restaurants and nightspots. And everyone goes to the Xochimilco neighborhood, home of many canals and gardens, to float amidst the flowers. *Tax: 17% hotel, 15% value-added sales tax is usually included in the retail price.*

Palace of Fine Arts

▶ SELECTED ATTRACTIONS

**Chapultepec Park
(Bosque de Chapultepec)**
World's largest city park
Av. Constituyentes 1a Sección,
San Miguel Chapultepec

**Frida Kahlo Museum
(Museo de Frida Kahlo)**
Londres 247 at Allende,
El Carmen Coyoacán
011-52-55-5554-5999*

**National Museum of Anthropology
(Museo Nacional de Antropología)**
Paseo de la Reforma at Gandhi
011-52-55-5553-6386*

National Palace (Palacio Nacional)
Murals by Diego Rivera
Plaza de la Constitución, Zocalo
011-52-55-9158-1252 or
011-52-55-9158-1256*

**Palace of Fine Arts
(Palacio de Bellas Artes)**
Home of the Folkloric Ballet of Mexico
Central Lázaro Cárdenas at Av. Juárez
011-52-55-5512-2593*

**Rufino Tamayo Museum
(Museo Rufino Tamayo)**
Tamayo's contemporary paintings
Av. Reforma and Gandhi, Chapultepec Park
011-52-55-5286-6519*

Templo Mayor
Ancient Aztec city's main ceremonial pyramid
Seminario 8 at the Zócalo
011-52-55-5542-4943*

Turibus
Double-decker tour bus that stops at selected attractions
Tickets available on board; check with your hotel front desk for pick-up locations

Xochimilco
Floating gardens and boat rides
Los Embarcaderos (The Piers)
011-52-55-5676-0810*

▶ SHOPPING

Bazaar Sabado
Weekly artisan market
Plaza San Jacinto, San Angel

Polanco
Upscale shopping and dining
Av. Presidente Masaryk at
Arquimedes, Polanco

Zócalo
UNESCO World Heritage site; shops and cafés
Centro Histórico

Zona Rosa
Boutiques and lively entertainment area
Calle Amberes at Paseo de la Reforma

▶ VISITOR INFORMATION

Mexico City Tourist Office
Nuevo León 56, 4th floor
Colonia Condesa 06100
Mexico City, D.F., Mexico
011-52-55-5212-0260
www.mexicocity.gob.mx

Mexico Tourism Board (U.S.)
(800) 446-3942
www.visitmexico.com

DON'T MISS DRIVE

Built by Emperor Maximilian of Hapsburg, the elegance of Paseo de la Reforma is often compared to Les Champs-Elysées in Paris. A series of parks with world-class sculptures complement the boulevard that passes through the center of the city.

*Number listed may or may not have an English-speaking person available.

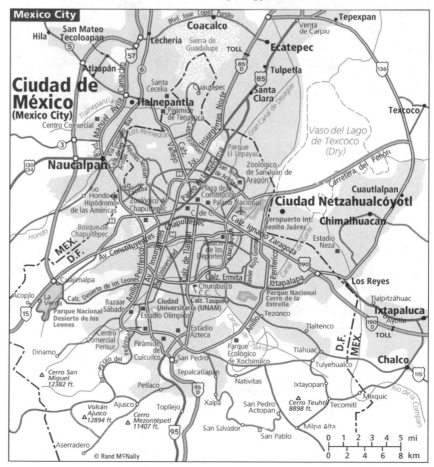
© Rand McNally

MIAMI, Florida

Miami skyline and marina

This busy seaport supports a huge fleet of cruise ships, but there's plenty to explore on land as well—like the Little Havana neighborhood's spicy foods, hot Latin music, and hand-embroidered guayabera shirts. Jungle Island hosts a one-ton crocodile dubbed "Crocosaurus" plus thousands of monkeys, reptiles, and birds. At its nearby home on Watson Island, the Miami Children's Museum has two floors of bilingual exhibits to stimulate young imaginations. *Tax: 13% hotel, 7% sales. For local weather, call (305) 229-4550.*

▶ SELECTED ATTRACTIONS

Art Deco District
1200 Ocean Dr. (Gift Shop)
(305) 672-2014

Bass Museum of Art
2121 Park Ave.
(305) 673-7530

Everglades National Park
40001 FL 9336, Homestead
(305) 242-7700

Fairchild Tropical Botanic Garden
10901 Old Cutler Rd., Coral Gables
(305) 667-1651

Jungle Island
Gardens, exotic animals, shows, and exhibits
1111 Parrot Jungle Trail, off MacArthur
Causeway (I-395)
(305) 400-7000

Little Havana District
SW 8th St. between SW 12th Ave.
and SW 27th Ave.

Miami Art Museum
101 W. Flagler St.
(305) 375-3000

Miami Children's Museum
980 MacArthur Causeway
(305) 373-5437

Miami Seaquarium
Exhibits, dolphin shows, and reef aquarium
4400 Rickenbacker Causeway
(305) 361-5705

Vizcaya Museum and Gardens
Italian Renaissance-style villa
3251 S. Miami Ave.
(305) 250-9133

▶ SHOPPING

Bal Harbour Shops
Upscale shops in an open-air setting
9700 Collins Ave., Bal Harbour
(305) 866-0311

Bayside Marketplace
Shopping, open-air market, waterfront dining
401 Biscayne Blvd.
(305) 577-3344

Coco Walk
Retail shops and entertainment
3015 Grand Ave., Coconut Grove
(305) 444-0777

Downtown Miami Shopping District
*Department stores, specialty shops,
and restaurants*
Biscayne Blvd. to 2nd Ave. W., SE 1st St. to
NE 3rd St.
(305) 379-7070

▶ VISITOR INFORMATION

**Greater Miami Convention and
Visitors Bureau**
701 Brickell Ave., Ste. 2700
Miami, FL 33131
(305) 539-3000 or (800) 933-8448
www.gmcvb.com

MILWAUKEE, Wisconsin

Only one giant brewery and a handful of its micro-cousins remain, but Milwaukee will always be known for beer. The Miller Brewing Company (now MillerCoors) offers daily tours of its huge facility, while a tour of the Pabst Mansion evokes the glory years of the city's most famous industry. Along the lakefront, the Henry Maier Festival Grounds host a series of annual ethnic festivals. An extraordinary wing-like moving sculpture above the Quaddracci Pavilion has brought worldwide cultural attention to the Milwaukee Art Museum. *Tax: 14.6% hotel, 5.6% sales. For local weather, call (414) 744-8000.*

Milwaukee Art Museum

▶ SELECTED ATTRACTIONS

The Basilica of St. Josaphat
Historic church
601 W. Lincoln Ave.
(414) 645-5623

Betty Brinn Children's Museum
929 E. Wisconsin Ave.
(414) 390-5437

Boerner Botanical Gardens
9400 Boerner Dr. in Whitnall Park,
Hales Corners
(414) 525-5600

The Captain Frederick Pabst Mansion
Flemish Renaissance Revival-style home
2000 W. Wisconsin Ave.
(414) 931-0808

Henry Maier Festival Grounds
200 N. Harbor Dr.
(414) 273-2680

MillerCoors Visitor Center
Free brewery tours
4251 W. State St.
(414) 931-2337

Milwaukee Art Museum
700 N. Art Museum Dr.
(414) 224-3200

Milwaukee County Historical Society
910 N. Old World 3rd St.
(414) 273-8288

Milwaukee Public Museum
800 W. Wells St.
(414) 278-2702

Mitchell Park Horticultural Conservatory
(*The Domes*)
524 S. Layton Blvd.
(414) 649-9800

RiverWalk
Eclectic shops, restaurants, nightlife, and art
Runs 13 blocks along the Milwaukee River
(414) 287-2623

▶ SHOPPING

Brady Street
Unique specialty shops, bars, and restaurants
From Van Buren St. to Farwell Ave.
(414) 272-3978

Historic Third Ward
Entertainment district in 1890s neighborhood
Bounded by Milwaukee River, St. Paul Ave.,
and Jackson St.
(414) 273-1173

Old World Third Street
Shops and restaurants with Wisconsin favorites
From Wisconsin to Juneau Ave.

▶ VISITOR INFORMATION

Greater Milwaukee Convention and Visitors Bureau
648 N. Plankinton Ave., Ste. 425
Milwaukee, WI 53203
(414) 273-7222 or (800) 554-1448
www.visitmilwaukee.org

MINNEAPOLIS/SAINT PAUL, Minnesota

The Twin Cities complement and complete each other with their individual personalities. In Minneapolis—all skyscrapers and modernity—the visually compelling Weisman Art Museum is noted for works by 20th-century American painters. The expanded Walker Art Center is ranked among the finest institutions of its kind. The highly respected Guthrie Theatre occupies impressive new digs on the banks of the Mississippi River. On Hennepin Avenue, the latest Broadway productions attract theatergoers. *Tax: 13.15% hotel, 10.15% restaurant, 12.65% downtown liquor tax, 6.5% state sales tax (excluding clothing), 0.5% city sales and use tax. For local weather, call (763) 512-1111 or (952) 361-6680.*

Saint Paul, more traditional in its outlook, is the seat of Minnesota state government. Tours of the capitol building include a visit to the golden horses overlooking the main steps. The Science Museum of Minnesota has tons of hands-on activities and an extensive collection of artifacts and curiosities. Shoppers nationwide are drawn to the Twin Cities by the lure of the massive Mall of America in nearby Bloomington. *Tax: 13% hotel (10% for establishments with less than 50 rooms), 7% sales. For local weather, call (763) 512-1111.*

Minneapolis Sculpture Garden at Walker Art Center

▶ SELECTED ATTRACTIONS

MINNEAPOLIS

American Swedish Institute
2600 Park Ave.
(612) 871-4907

The Bakken
Library and electrical science museum
3537 Zenith Ave. S.
(612) 926-3878

Bell Museum of Natural History
Corner of University and 17th Aves. SE at the University of Minnesota
(612) 624-7083

Frederick R. Weisman Art Museum
333 E. River Rd. at the University of Minnesota
(612) 625-9494

Mill City Museum
Hands-on exhibits about milling industry
704 S. 2nd St.
(612) 341-7555

Milwaukee Road Depot
Indoor water park and ice rink
225 3rd Ave. S
(612) 339-2253

Minneapolis Institute of Arts
2400 3rd Ave. S.
(888) 642-2787

Minneapolis Sculpture Garden
726 Vineland Pl.
(612) 375-7600

▶ DON'T MISS DRIVE

No one should leave Saint Paul without taking a drive along Summit Avenue, the longest remaining stretch of residential Victorian architecture in the United States, which includes the Governor's Mansion.

Theater District on Hennepin Ave.
Historic vaudeville theaters, currently home to Broadway productions and concerts
Orpheum Theatre: 910 Hennepin Ave.
Pantages Theater: 710 Hennepin Ave.
State Theater: 805 Hennepin Ave.
(651) 989-5151(Ticketmaster) or
(612) 673-0404 (box office)

Walker Art Center
1750 Hennepin Ave.
(612) 375-7600

▶ SHOPPING

MINNEAPOLIS

Gaviidae Common and City Center
Boutiques, restaurants, and trendy shops
651 Nicollet Mall
(612) 372-1222

Southdale Shopping Center
Retail stores, movie theaters, and restaurants
6601 France Ave., Edina
(952) 925-7874

▶ SELECTED ATTRACTIONS

SAINT PAUL

Alexander Ramsey House
Restored Victorian home of first territorial governor
265 S. Exchange St.
(651) 296-8760

Como Zoo and Marjorie McNeely Conservatory
1225 Estabrook Dr.
(651) 487-8200

Landmark Center
Arts center in restored federal courthouse
75 W. 5th St.
(651) 292-3225

Minnesota History Center
Exhibits, collection, and library of Minnesota's history
345 W. Kellogg Blvd.
(651) 259-3000 or (800) 657-3773

Minnesota Museum of American Art
50 W. Kellogg Blvd. at Market St.
(651) 266-1030

Minnesota State Capitol
75 Rev. Dr. Martin Luther King Jr. Blvd.
(651) 296-2881

Ordway Center for the Performing Arts
345 Washington St.
(651) 224-4222

Padelford Packet Boat Co.
Sternwheel riverboat cruises
Dr. Justus Ohage Blvd. on Harriet Island
(651) 227-1100

Saint Paul Public Library
Restored Italian Renaissance building
90 W. 4th St.
(651) 266-7000

Science Museum of Minnesota
120 W. Kellogg Blvd.
(651) 221-9444

▶ SHOPPING

SAINT PAUL

District del Sol
Specialty supermarkets, shops, and art
Cesar Chavez St. from Wabasha to Ada Sts.
(651) 222-6347

Grand Avenue
26 blocks of restaurants and specialty boutiques
Parallels Summit Avenue from the Mississippi River to downtown area
(651) 699-0029

Mall of America
Nation's largest mall and entertainment complex with stores, restaurants, theme park
I-494 and MN 77, Bloomington
(952) 883-8800 or (800) 879-3555

▶ DIVERSION

Take flight for a day to the Hiawatha Valley area in Red Wing. Scenic bluffs await. Located 50 miles southeast of Saint Paul on US 61.
(651) 385-5934 or (800) 498-3444

7th Avenue Antiques Mall
Antiques and collectibles
2563 7th Ave. E., North Saint Paul
(651) 773-7001

▶ VISITOR INFORMATION

Greater Minneapolis Convention & Visitors Association
250 Marquette Ave. S., Ste. 1300
Minneapolis, MN 55401
(612) 767-8000 or (888) 676-6757
www.minneapolis.org

Saint Paul Convention and Visitors Authority
175 W. Kellogg Blvd., Ste. 502
Saint Paul, MN 55102
(651) 265-4900 or (800) 627-6101
www.visitsaintpaul.com

Minneapolis Visitor Information Center
1301 2nd Ave. S. (in the Minneapolis Convention Center)
(612) 335-6337

Marjorie McNeely Conservatory, Saint Paul

MOBILE, Alabama

Bragg-Mitchell Mansion

Brimming with historic homes and neighborhoods, Mobile has managed to preserve much of its storied past, even as it has developed into a major industrial seaport. Flowers bloom year-round at the Bellingrath Gardens and Home in nearby Theodore, where 65 acres of plantings and aquatic features surround a mansion filled with decorative arts. Grand antebellum Bragg-Mitchell Mansion is celebrated for its period furnishings and décor. The contributions of black Mobilians to local and national history are recalled at the National African-American Archives Museum. Visitors can tour two World War II-era ships at the USS *Alabama* Battleship Memorial Park. *Tax: 14% hotel, 9% sales. For local weather, call (251) 478-6666 or (215) 633-6443.*

DIVERSION

Explore the wonders of the nation's second-largest delta system at the Five Rivers Delta Resource Center off the Mobile Bay Causeway in Spanish Fort, Ala. Visit the museum and exhibits or take a ride in an airboat, canoe, or kayak. (251) 625-0814

▶ SELECTED ATTRACTIONS

Bellingrath Gardens and Home
Historic home and gardens
12401 Bellingrath Gardens Rd., Theodore
(251) 973-2217

Bragg-Mitchell Mansion
Antebellum mansion and museum
1906 Springhill Ave.
(251) 471-6364

Fort Condé Museum
Reconstructed fort and 18th-century living history museum
150 S. Royal St.
(251) 208-7569

Gulf Coast Explorium Science Center
Interactive exhibits and IMAX theater
65 Government St.
(251) 208-6873

Mobile Botanical Gardens
5151 Museum Dr. in Langan Park
(251) 342-0555

Mobile Museum of Art
4850 Museum Dr., Langan Park
(251) 208-5200

National African-American Archives Museum
564 Dr. Martin Luther King Jr. Ave.
(251) 433-8511

Oakleigh Historic Complex
Antebellum mansion and two houses
300 Oakleigh Pl.
(251) 432-6161

Richards-DAR House Museum
19th-century Italianate home
256 N. Joachim St.
(251) 208-7320

USS *Alabama* Battleship Memorial Park and Pavilion
Vintage battleship, submarine, and aircraft
2703 Battleship Pkwy.
(251) 433-2703

▶ SHOPPING

Antiques at the Loop
Antiques and collectibles
2103 Airport Blvd.
(251) 476-0309

Bel Air Mall
Department stores and specialty shops
Airport Blvd. at I-65
(251) 478-1893

Cotton City Antique Mall
Antiques and collectibles
2012 Airport Blvd.
(251) 479-9747

▶ VISITOR INFORMATION

Mobile Bay Convention and Visitors Bureau
1 S. Water St., Mobile, AL 36602
(251) 208-2000 or (800) 566-2453
www.mobile.org

Fort Condé Welcome Center
150 S. Royal St.
(251) 208-7989

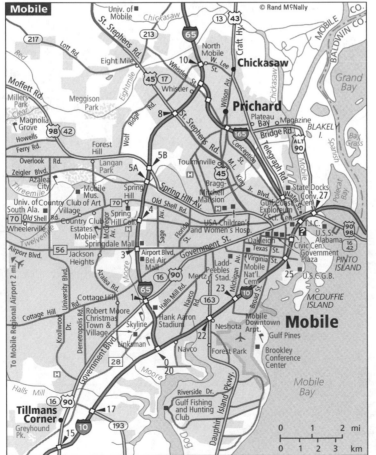

MONTRÉAL, Québec, Canada

This continent's most Continental city, Montréal boasts a deep connection with its French forebears. A state-of-the-art multimedia presentation enhances the already awe-inspiring interior of Notre Dame Basilica. In Old Montréal (Vieux Montréal), specialized street lighting adds charm to the narrow lanes of the city's historic center. *Tax: 15.5% hotel, 5% GST, 7.5% PST. For local weather, call (514) 283-4006 or (514) 283-3010.*

Montréal skyline from Jean-Drapeau Park

▶ SELECTED ATTRACTIONS

Biodome
4777 av. Pierre-de-Coubertin
(514) 868-3000

Jean-Drapeau Park
Biosphere, casino games, and amusement park
Île Ste-Hélène and Île Notre-Dame
(514) 872-6120

Montréal Olympic Park
4141 av. Pierre-de-Coubertin
(514) 252-4737 or (877) 997-0919

Mount Royal Park and St. Joseph's Oratory
Designed by Frederick Law Olmsted
Mount Royal neighborhood
(514) 843-8240

Notre-Dame Basilica
110, rue Notre-Dame Ouest in Old Montreal
(514) 842-2925

Old Montréal (Vieux Montréal)
Bounded approximately by rue McGill, rue Saint-Antoine, rue Berri, and the St. Lawrence River

Old Port of Montréal (Vieux-Port)
333 rue de la Commune Ouest between the St-Laurent River and Old Montreal
(514) 496-7678 or (800) 971-7678

Place Jacques-Cartier
Jugglers, artists, and restaurants
On Place Jacques-Cartier between rue Notre-Dame and rue Saint Paul
(877) 266-5687

▶ SHOPPING

Atwater Market
Farmers' market and specialty boutiques
138, av. Atwater
(514) 937-7754

Les Cours Mont-Royal
Upscale shops and boutiques
1455, rue Peel
(514) 842-7777

Promenades Cathédrale
Specialty shops
625 rue Ste-Catherine Ouest next to McGill Metro Station
(514) 845-8230

Sainte-Catherine and Crescent Street
Boutiques and upscale shopping
Between rue Guy and Berri

The Underground City
Interconnected downtown malls
Rue Ste-Catherine at McGill

▶ VISITOR INFORMATION

Ministère du Tourisme du Quebec
P.O. Box 979
Montréal, QC H3C 2W3 Canada
(514) 873-2015 or (877) 266-5687
www.tourisme-montreal.org

Infotourist Center
1255 rue Peel, Bureau 100

Tourist Welcome Office in Old Montreal
174 rue Notre-Dame Est

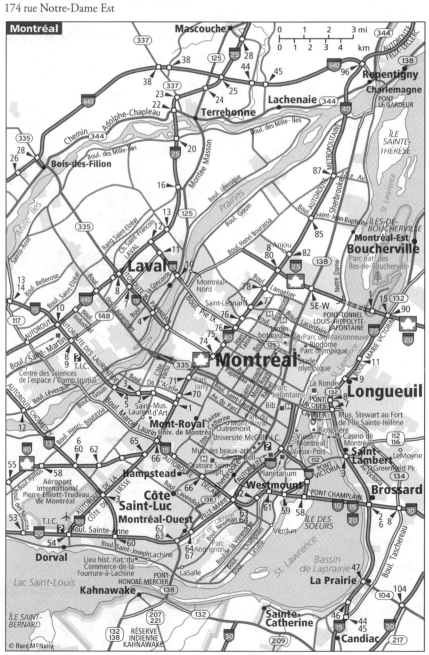

MYRTLE BEACH, South Carolina

Pier at Barefoot Landing

Myrtle Beach is one of the nation's most popular getaway locations. The area's plethora of attractions includes amusement parks such as Family Kingdom, which offers thrill rides and a water park, and the nightclubs, restaurants, and theaters at Broadway at the Beach. Nature lovers can retreat to the solitude of Brookgreen Gardens, a one-time rice plantation that boasts thousands of native and exotic species and some 550 works of sculpture. *Tax: 11% hotel, 7% retail sales, 9.5% restaurants. For local weather, call (843) 293-6600.*

SELECTED ATTRACTIONS

Alligator Adventure
US 17 at Barefoot Landing, N. Myrtle Beach
(843) 361-0789

Barefoot Landing
Dining, shopping, and entertainment
4898 US 17 S., N. Myrtle Beach
(800) 272-2320 or (843) 272-8349

Broadway at the Beach
Amusements, restaurants, and shops
US 17 Bypass between 21st and 29th Aves. N.
(843) 444-3200

Brookgreen Gardens
Sculpture gardens
1931 Brookgreen Dr., Murrells Inlet
(843) 235-6000

The Carolina Opry
Live musical performances
8901-A Business 17 N.
(843) 913-4000 or (800) 843-6779

Children's Museum of South Carolina
2501 N. Kings Hwy.
(843) 946-9469

Family Kingdom
Amusement and water parks
300 S. Ocean Blvd.
(843) 626-3447

Hobcaw Barony
Estate and wildlife refuge
35 miles south off US 17, Georgetown
(843) 546-4623

Myrtle Beach State Park
4401 S. Kings Hwy.
(843) 238-5325

Myrtle Waves Water Park
10th Ave. N. at US 17 Bypass
(843) 913-9260

The Palace Theater
Live music and dance performances
1420 Celebrity Cir. at Broadway at the Beach
(843) 448-9224

Waccatee Zoological Farm
8500 Enterprise Rd.
(843) 650-8500

SHOPPING

Coastal Grand Mall
Department stores, specialty shops, and restaurants
US 17 Bypass and Harrelson Blvd.
(843) 839-9100

Myrtle Beach Mall
Department stores, specialty shops, and restaurants
10177 N. Kings Hwy.
(843) 272-4040

Tanger Outlet Center
Factory outlet mall
US 501 at Waccamaw Pines Dr.
(843) 236-5100

VISITOR INFORMATION

Myrtle Beach Area Chamber of Commerce and Convention and Visitors Bureau
1200 N. Oak St.
Myrtle Beach, SC 29577
(843) 626-7444 or (800) 356-3016
www.myrtlebeachinfo.com

Myrtle Beach Welcome Center
1200 N. Oak St.
(843) 626-7444

Myrtle Beach Official Welcome Center
1800 US 501 W, Aynor
(843) 358-6100

South Strand Welcome Center
3401 US 17 Business S., Murrells Inlet
(843) 651-1010

Airport Welcome Center
1100 Jetport Rd.
(843) 626-7444

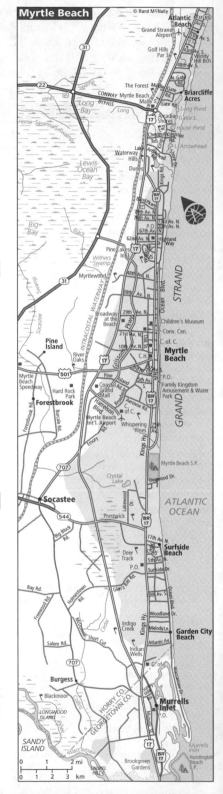

Myrtle Beach

DON'T MISS DRIVE

A trip to Myrtle Beach should begin with a windows-rolled-down cruise along Ocean Boulevard. This street borders the waterfront, or as the locals say, the "Grand Strand."

NASHVILLE, Tennessee

Universally familiar as the capital of country music, Nashville is also noted for its keen appreciation for education and the arts. For music fans, the city offers a multitude of clubs in the downtown entertainment district, the live broadcast of the Grand Ole Opry from its 4,400-seat auditorium at Opryland, and the regalia, instruments, and mementos displayed at the Country Music Hall of Fame. Art and history buffs can visit Cheekwood, where contemporary and traditional art is on exhibit, and the Hermitage, the restored and accurately furnished home of President Andrew Jackson. *Tax: 14.25% hotel, 9.25% sales. For local weather, call (615) 259-2222 or (615) 754-4633.*

Country Music Hall of Fame and Museum at night

▶ SELECTED ATTRACTIONS

Adventure Science Center
800 Fort Negley Blvd.
(615) 862-5160

Belle Meade Plantation
19th-century house museum
5025 Harding Rd.
(615) 356-0501

Cheekwood Botanical Garden and Museum of Art
1200 Forrest Park Dr.
(615) 356-8000

Country Music Hall of Fame and Museum
222 5th Ave. S.
(615) 416-2001 or (800) 852-6437

Frist Center for the Visual Arts
919 Broadway
(615) 244-3340

General Jackson Showboat
2812 Opryland Dr.
(615) 889-1000

Grand Ole Opry and Museum
Live country music performances
2802 Opryland Dr.
(615) 871-6779 or (800) 733-6779

The Hermitage
Historic home of Andrew Jackson
4580 Rachel's Ln.
(615) 889-2941

Nashville Zoo at Grassmere
3777 Nolensville Rd.
(615) 833-1534

The Parthenon
Art museum and full-scale reproduction of the Greek temple
West End and 25th Aves. in Centennial Park
(615) 862-8431

Tennessee State Capitol
Between 6th and 7th Aves. on Charlotte Ave.
(615) 741-2692

Tennessee State Museum
505 Deaderick St.
(615) 741-2692 or (800) 407-4324

▶ SHOPPING

Green Hills Antique Mall
4108 Hillsboro Rd.
(615) 383-3893

Lower Broadway
Records and music collectibles
100-600 Broadway

The Mall at Green Hills
Upscale boutiques, department stores, and restaurants
2126 Abbott Martin Rd.
(615) 298-5478

Opry Mills
Factory outlets and specialty shops
433 Opry Mills Dr.
(615) 514-1000

▶ VISITOR INFORMATION

Nashville Convention and Visitors Bureau
150 4th Ave. N., Ste. G-250
Nashville, TN 37219
(615) 259-4730 or (800) 657-6910
www.visitmusiccity.com

Nashville Visitor Information Center
501 Broadway
(615) 259-4747

DON'T MISS DRIVE

One section of Nashville is called Midtown, but locals refer to it only by its street names, like Broadway. For a taste of the honky-tonks made famous by local musicians, a drive down Broadway is a must.

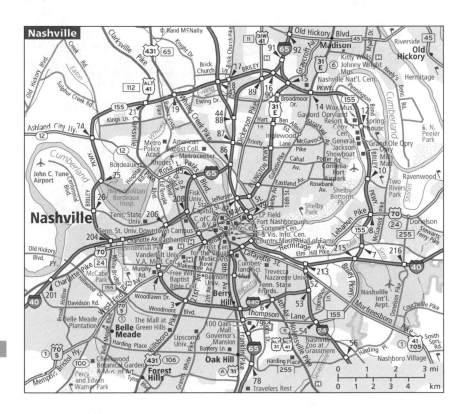

NEW ORLEANS, Louisiana

Mardi Gras festivities in the French Quarter

As the much-loved city of New Orleans continues on its path of restoration, the good times still roll for the thousands of music and party lovers who flock here for Mardi Gras and the Jazz and Heritage Festival. The colorful French Quarter, with its mix of cultural influences, boasts structures like the Cabildo and Presbytere where visitors can explore the city's historic roots, as well as the wealth of restaurants that lent the city its reputation for exceptionally delectable cooking. Shoppers at French Market and riverside malls take time for a coffee and beignet at Cafe Du Monde. *Tax: 13% hotel, with sliding scale of room-per-night charge: $1 (hotels with less than 300 rooms), $2 (hotels with less than 1000 rooms), or $3 (at hotels with 1000+ rooms). 9% sales. For local weather, call (504) 529-6259 or (504) 828-4000.*

▶ SELECTED ATTRACTIONS

Audubon Aquarium of the Americas
1 Canal St.
(800) 774-7394

Audubon Zoo
6500 Magazine St.
(800) 774-7394

Blaine Kern's Mardi Gras World
Tours of parade float studios
233 Newton St.
(504) 361-7821

Degas House
Historic home of artist Edgar Degas
2306 Esplanade Ave.
(504) 821-5009 or (800) 755-6730

French Quarter
Historic French and Spanish district
Canal St. to Esplanade Ave.
(Maps for self-guided walking tours available at the Visitors Bureau, 529 St. Ann St.)
(504) 568-5661

Harrah's New Orleans Casino
8 Canal St.
(504) 533-6000 or (800) 427-7247

Herman-Grima/Gallier Historic Houses
French Quarter landmark homes
820 St. Louis St.
(504) 525-5661

Lafayette Cemetery No. 1
Historic Garden District cemetery
1427 6th St.

Louisiana Children's Museum
420 Julia St.
(504) 523-1357

Louisiana State Museum
(504) 568-6968 or (800) 568-6968
• The Cabildo
  Site of the Louisiana Purchase transfer
  701 Chartres St. in Jackson Square
• The Presbytere
  751 Chartres St.
• Old U.S. Mint
  400 Esplanade Ave.

National WWII Museum
945 Magazine St.
(504) 527-6012

New Orleans Museum of Art
1 Collins C. Diboll Cir. in City Park
(504) 658-4100

New Orleans Pharmacy Museum
514 Chartres St.
(504) 565-8027

Ogden Museum of Southern Art
945 Camp St.
(504) 539-9600

Old Ursuline Convent
Oldest building in the Mississippi Valley
1100 Chartres St.
(504) 529-3040

St. Louis Cathedral
Jackson Square
(504) 525-9585

▶ DON'T MISS DRIVE

St. Charles Avenue is really a boulevard with a 115-year-old streetcar system winding down the middle. Other sights include huge oaks, period architecture, and the idyllic campuses of Tulane and Loyola Universities.

Central New Orleans
© Rand McNally

SHOPPING

The Esplanade Mall
140 specialty shops and restaurants
1401 W. Esplanade Ave., Kenner
(504) 465-2161

French Market
Arts and crafts, farmers' market, and souvenir stalls
1008 N. Peters St. between Barracks St. and Jackson Square
(504) 522-2621

French Quarter
Souvenir shops and specialty boutiques
84-block area bounded by Esplanade Ave., Rampart St., Canal St., and the Mississippi River

Jackson Brewery
Mall with shops and restaurants
600 Decatur St.
(504) 566-7245

Magazine Street
Six miles of antique shops, art galleries, restaurants, and specialty shops
From Canal St. to Audubon Park
(504) 342-4435

Riverwalk Marketplace
Specialty stores, boutiques, and restaurants
Between Poydras and Julia Sts. on the Mississippi River
(504) 522-1555

Royal Street
Antique stores and upscale galleries
Royal St. in the French Quarter

The Shops at Canal Place
Designer boutiques and department store
333 Canal St.
(504) 522-9200

VISITOR INFORMATION

New Orleans Metropolitan Convention and Visitors Bureau
2020 St. Charles Ave.
New Orleans, LA 70130
(504) 566-5011 or (800) 672-6124
www.neworleanscvb.com

NOMCVB Information Center
529 St. Ann St.
New Orleans, LA 70116
(504) 568-5661

NOMCVB Visitor Center
2020 St. Charles Ave.
New Orleans, LA 70130
(504) 566-5011

New Orleans © Rand McNally

Mardi Gras—Let the good times roll!

One of the signatures of Mardi Gras in New Orleans is a series of spectacular parades beginning 12 days before Mardi Gras. During that time, some 60 parades are held in the tour-parish area of Orleans, Jefferson, St. Bernard, and St. Tammany.

Mardi Gras parades follow a standard carnival format with a King and Queen in the lead. The royalty are followed by a procession of floats, krewes (organized parade groups), dancing groups, marching bands, clowns, sometimes motorcycle units . . . you name it. It is not uncommon for parade participants to total in the thousands.

Want to see an official New Orleans Mardi Gras parade? Parade routings are printed in advance, so it is easy to find out which street will be used as a route. Curbside seats are free of charge. Grandstand seats for the first week are free from City Hall at (504) 658-4927, and seats for the second week are available for advance purchase from Ticketmaster at (504) 522-5555. Upcoming Mardi Gras dates include February 16, 2010, and March 8, 2011.

DIVERSION

Drive out to Crawford Landing in Slidell for Dr. Wagner's Honey Island Swamp Tour. The two-hour boat tour explores the beauty of a cypress swamp. Only 30 minutes north of New Orleans, off I-10. (985) 641-1769

NEW YORK, New York

Central Park

New York's five distinctive boroughs come together to form one magnificent city. Many visitors stick to Manhattan to gawk in Times Square, shop on Fifth Avenue, gallery-hop in Soho, drop by the museums bordering Central Park, or take in Broadway's latest hit show. But when time allows, cross the Brooklyn Bridge to the Brooklyn Academy of Music. Take the subway to the Bronx Zoo or the Museum of the Moving Image in Queens. And don't forget chugging past the Statue of Liberty on the Staten Island Ferry; at $0 a ticket, it's by far the city's best sightseeing value. *Tax: 13.375% hotel tax plus a $3.50 per-room-per-night surcharge, 8.375% sales. For local weather, call (631) 924-0517.*

▶ SELECTED ATTRACTIONS

American Museum of Natural History
W. 79th and Central Park W.
(212) 769-5100

Broadway
Theater district
Roughly E. 42nd to W. 50th Sts.,
5th to 8th Aves.

Bronx Zoo/Wildlife Conservation Society
2300 Southern Blvd., Bronx
(718) 367-1010

Brooklyn Academy of Music
30 Lafayette Avenue, Brooklyn
(718) 636-4100

Carnegie Hall
Concert and recital hall
881 7th Ave.
(212) 247-7800

Cathedral of St. John the Divine
World's largest cathedral
1047 Amsterdam Ave.
(212) 932-7347

Central Park Zoo
830 5th Ave.
(212) 439-6500

Coney Island
Amusement park rides, famous boardwalk
1208 Surf Ave., Brooklyn
(718) 372-5159

Ed Sullivan Theater
"Late Show with David Letterman" tapings
1697 Broadway
(212) 247-6497

Ellis Island Immigration Museum
Ferry departs from Battery Park
(877) 523-9849

▶ DIVERSION

Visit the historic and breathtaking Hudson Valley. This is one of the oldest settled regions in the United States. Take in the mighty Hudson River, pass historic mansions on the Palisades, even tour a vineyard. Fifty miles north of New York City on I-87.

Empire State Building Observatory
350 5th Ave.
(212) 736-3100

Greenwich Village
Trendy shops, boutiques, and galleries
W. 14th St. to Houston St., and West St. to Ave. C

Guggenheim Museum
Art museum designed by Frank Lloyd Wright
1071 5th Ave. at 89th St.
(212) 423-3500

Harlem
Historic African American neighborhood
125th St. to 155th St.

Intrepid Sea, Air and Space Museum
Historic aircraft carrier
W. 46th St. at 12th Ave.
(212) 245-0072

Little Italy and NoLIta (North of Little Italy)
Boutiques, ethnic shops, and great eats
Houston St. to Canal St., and Cleveland to Bowery

Metropolitan Museum of Art
1000 Fifth Ave. at 82nd St.
(212) 535-7710

Museum of the Moving Image
35th Ave. at 36th St., Astoria
(718) 784-4520 or (718) 784-0077

NBC Tours
30 Rockefeller Plaza at 49th St.
(212) 664-3700

South Street Seaport Museum
12-square block district of galleries, historic ships, printing shop; harbor sails
12 Fulton St. (Tickets at Pier 16)
(212) 748-8600

Staten Island Ferry
Whitehall Terminal, Whitehall St. and South St., Lower Manhattan
St. George Ferry Terminal, Richmond Terrace, Staten Island

Times Square
Broadway from 42nd to 47th Sts.

▶ SHOPPING

Crystal District
High-end designer jewelry stores
Madison Ave. between 58th and 63rd Sts.

Fifth Avenue
High-end designer stores, jewelers, and department stores
5th Ave. between 50th and 59th Sts.

Grand Central Terminal
Renovated Beaux-Arts landmark with boutiques, restaurants, and gift stalls
42nd St. and Park Ave.
(212) 340-2347

Lower East Side
Discount specialty shops
Bounded by The Bowery, Houston, Clinton, and Canal Sts. Vis. Ctr. at 261 Broome St.
(212) 226-9010

Macy's Herald Square
Famous department store
151 W. 34th St.
(212) 695-4400

SoHo (South of Houston)
Art galleries and boutiques
Between Houston and Canal Sts., between Broadway and 6th Ave.

▶ VISITOR INFORMATION

NYC & Company
810 7th Ave., New York City, NY 10019
(212) 484-1200
www.nycvisit.com

Chinatown Visitor Information Kiosk
Triangle where Canal, Walker, and Baxter Sts. meet

City Hall Visitor Information Kiosk
City Hall Park
Broadway at Park Row

Federal Hall Visitor Information Center
26 Wall St.

Harlem Visitor Information Center
2037 5th Ave.

continued on page 77

Viewing the World Trade Center Site

There is a viewing area at Liberty St. and Church St., near Broadway. NYC & Company operates an Official Visitors Information kiosk in City Hall Park at Broadway and Park Row, only a five-minute walk from the viewing area. For walking tours, call (866) 737-1184.

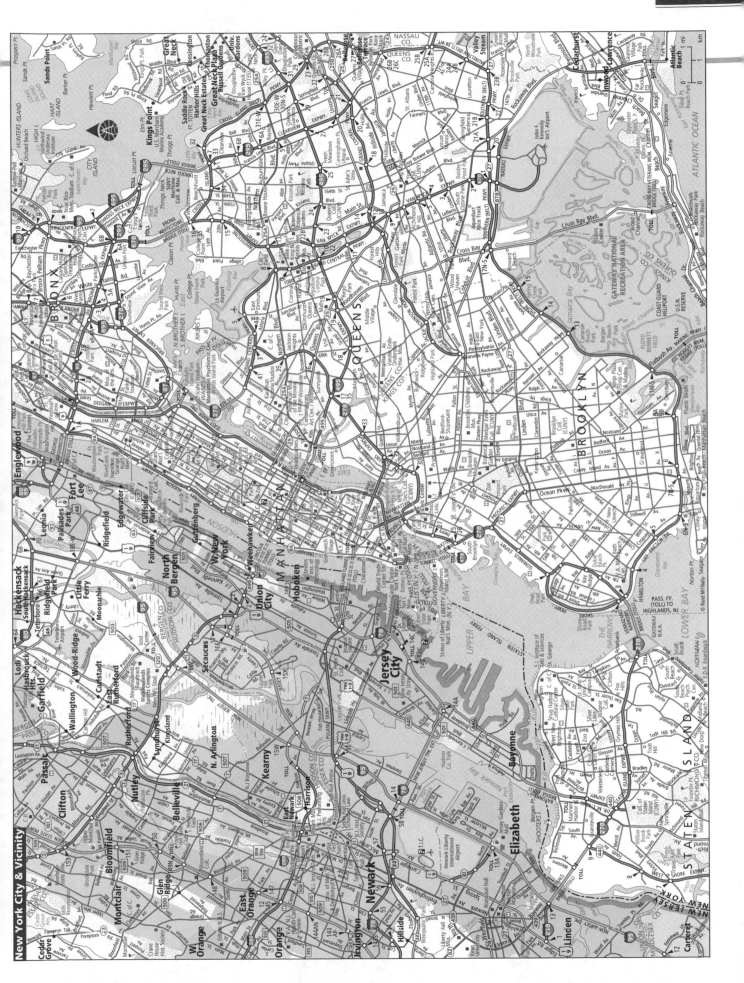

New York City & Vicinity

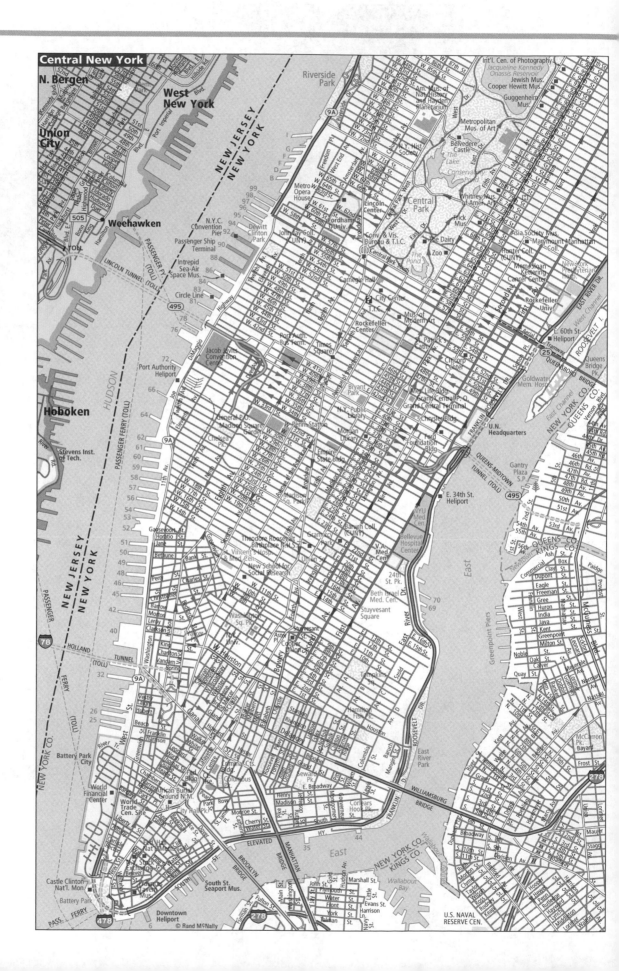

Central New York

"The play's the thing." — *Hamlet/Act II, Scene II*

When in New York, do as tourists and residents do: Take in a play! The New York stage is legendary. It razzles and dazzles like no other.

Box Offices

Al Hirschfeld Theater
302 W. 45th St., between 8th & 9th Aves.

Ambassador Theater
219 W. 49th St.,
between Broadway & 8th Aves.

American Airlines Theater
227 W. 42nd St., between 7th & 8th Aves.

Apollo Theatre
253 W. 125th St. at 8th Ave.
(212) 531-5300

August Wilson Theater
245 W. 52nd St.,
between Broadway & 8th Ave.

Avery Fisher Hall
10 Lincoln Center Plaza,
Columbus Ave. & W. 65th St.
(212) 875-5030

Belasco Theater
111 W. 44th St., between 6th & 7th Aves.

Bernard B. Jacobs Theatre
242 W. 45th St.,
between Broadway & 8th Ave.

Biltmore Theater
261 W. 47th St.
between Broadway & 8th Ave.

Booth Theater
222 W. 45th St.,
between Broadway & 8th Ave.

Broadhurst Theater
235 W. 44th St.,
between Broadway & 8th Ave.

Broadway Theater
1681 Broadway, between 52nd & 53rd Sts.

Brooks Atkinson Theater
256 W. 47th St.,
between Broadway & 8th Ave.

Circle in the Square
235 W. 50th at Broadway

Cort Theater
138 W. 48th St., between 6th & 7th Aves.

Ethel Barrymore Theater
243 W. 47th St.,
between Broadway & 8th Ave.

Eugene O'Neill Theater
230 W. 49th St.,
between Broadway & 8th Ave.

Gerald Schoenfeld Theater
236 W. 45th St.,
between Broadway & 8th Ave.

Gershwin Theater
222 W. 51st St.,
between Broadway & 8th Ave.

Helen Hayes Theater
240 W. 44th St.,
between Broadway & 8th Ave.

Hilton Theatre
213 W. 42nd St.,
between 7th & 8th Aves.

Imperial Theater
249 W. 45th St.,
between Broadway & 8th Ave.

John Golden Theater
252 W. 45th St.,
between Broadway & 8th Ave.

Julliard School
60 Lincoln Center Plaza, Broadway &
W. 65th St.
(212) 799-5000

Longacre Theatre
220 W. 48th St.,
between Broadway & 8th Ave.

Lunt-Fontanne Theater
205 W. 46th St.,
between Broadway & 8th Ave.

Lyceum Theatre
149 W. 45th St.
between 6th & 7th Aves.

Majestic Theater
247 W. 44th St.,
between Broadway & 8th Ave.

Marquis Theatre
1535 Broadway, between 45th & 46th Sts.

Metropolitan Opera House
Lincoln Center Plaza, Columbus Ave.
between 62nd & 65th Sts.
(212) 362-6000

Minskoff Theater
200 W. 45th St. at Broadway

Music Box Theater
239 W. 45th St.,
between Broadway & 8th Ave.

Nederlander Theater
208 W. 41st St., between 7th & 8th Aves.

Neil Simon Theater
250 W. 52nd St.,
between Broadway & 8th Ave.

New Amsterdam Theater
214 W. 42nd St., between 7th & 8th Aves.

Palace Theater
1564 Broadway at 47th St.

Radio City Music Hall
1260 Avenue of the Americas at 50th St.

Richard Rodgers Theater
226 W. 46th St.,
between Broadway & 8th Ave.

Sam S. Shubert Theater
225 W. 44th St.,
between Broadway & 8th Ave.

St. James Theater
246 W. 44th St.,
between Broadway & 8th Ave.

New York City's theater district

Studio 54
254 W. 54th St., between 7th & 8th Aves.

Vivian Beaumont Theater
150 W. 65th St., Lincoln Center

Walter Kerr Theater
219 W. 48th St.,
between Broadway & 8th Ave.

Winter Garden Theater
1634 Broadway, between 50th & 51st Sts.

Line up at a TKTS Ticket Booth for last-minute seats at great prices*:

Times Square Theatre Center at W. 46th St. (Broadway & 8th Ave.)

Lower Manhattan Theatre Center at South Street Seaport, 199 Water St. (Corner of Front & John Sts. near the rear of the Resnick/Prudential Building)

Downtown Brooklyn
1 Metrotech Center
(corner of Jay and Myrtle Sts.)

*TKTS Times Square accepts only cash and travelers' checks; the Lower Manhattan and Downtown Brooklyn locations also accept credit cards.

Tickets by telephone:

Telecharge: (212) 239-6200 or
(800) 545-2559

Ticketmaster: (212) 307-7171

Ticket Central: (212) 279-4200

NORFOLK/VIRGINIA BEACH, Virginia

Tall ships in Norfolk Harbor

Home port of the Atlantic Fleet, Norfolk has transformed itself into more than a Navy town. The *American Rover*, a three-masted schooner, offers narrated harbor cruises. The Chrysler Museum of Art houses 30,000 pieces ranging from antiquities of Africa, Asia, and the Middle East to a renowned Tiffany glass collection. Interactive exhibits at the Nauticus National Maritime Center give visitors a chance to explore life on and under the waves. *Tax: 13% hotel (plus $1 per room occupancy tax per night), 5% sales tax, 11.5% food and beverage.*

Neighboring Virginia Beach has long been a place to find an oceanfront resort, breathe the salt air, and relax. When not lolling about on the beach, visitors can explore the depths of Chesapeake Bay at the Virginia Aquarium and Marine Science Center. High-speed slides, a wave pool, and river floats make for freshwater fun at Ocean Breeze Waterpark. Daring ocean rescues of yore are recounted at the Old Coast Guard Station. *Tax: 13% hotel (plus $1 per room occupancy tax per night), 5% sales, 11.5% food and beverage. For local weather, call (757) 899-4200.*

DON'T MISS DRIVE

Feel suspended over water during the 17.6-mile drive on the Chesapeake Bay Bridge Tunnel, the world's largest bridge-tunnel complex, which connects Norfolk/Virginia Beach to Virginia's Eastern Shore. (757) 331-2960

▶ SELECTED ATTRACTIONS

NORFOLK

American Rover Tall Ship Cruises
Waterside Dr. at Waterside
Festival Marketplace
(757) 627-7245

Attucks Theatre
Historic African American theater
1010 Church St.
(757) 622-4763

Busch Gardens Williamsburg
I-64, exit 243A, Williamsburg
(800) 343-7946

Cannonball Trail
Self-guided walking tour of downtown Norfolk's historic sites
Begins at Freemason Street Reception Center, 401 E. Freemason St.
(757) 441-1526

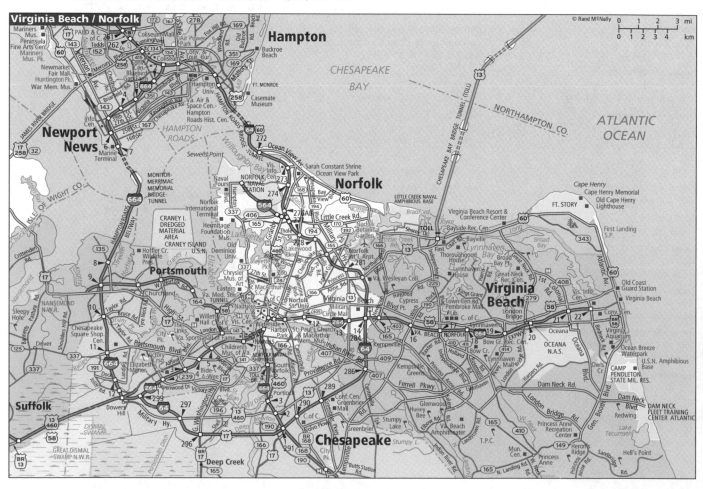

Carrie B. Harbor Tours
Mississippi-style paddle wheeler cruises
Waterside Dr. at Waterside Festival
Marketplace
(757) 393-4735

Children's Museum of Virginia
221 High St., Portsmouth
(757) 393-5258

Chrysler Museum of Art
245 W. Olney Rd. at Mowbray Arch
(757) 664-6200

Douglas MacArthur Memorial
Bounded by Bank St., Plume St., Court St.,
and City Hall Ave. in MacArthur Square
(757) 441-2965

Hampton Roads Naval Museum
1 Waterside Dr. inside Nauticus
(757) 322-2987

Hermitage Foundation Museum
Art museum in Arts & Crafts-style home
7637 N. Shore Rd.
(757) 423-2052

**Nauticus: The National Maritime Center
& Battleship *Wisconsin***
1 Waterside Dr.
(757) 664-1000 or (800) 664-1080

Norfolk Botanical Garden
6700 Azalea Garden Rd.
(757) 441-5830

Norfolk Naval Station
9079 Hampton Blvd., adjacent to Gate 5
(757) 444-7955

Virginia Zoo
3500 Granby St.
(757) 441-2374

▶ **SHOPPING**

NORFOLK

Historic Ghent District
Specialty shops, galleries, and antiques
Bounded by Monticello Ave., 22nd St.,
Brambleton Ave., and Hampton Blvd.

MacArthur Center
Department stores and specialty shops
300 Monticello Ave.
(757) 627-6000

Waterside Festival Marketplace
Specialty boutiques and restaurants
333 Waterside Dr.
(757) 627-3300

▶ **SELECTED ATTRACTIONS**

VIRGINIA BEACH

Adam Thoroughgood House
17th-century hall and parlor house
1636 Parish Rd.
(757) 460-7588

Atlantic Wildfowl Heritage Museum
Wildfowl art and decoys
1113 Atlantic Ave. in de Witt Cottage
(757) 437-8432

Cape Henry Lighthouse
Off US 60 at Fort Story (583 Atlantic Ave.)
(757) 422-9421

**Chesapeake Bay Center/First Landing
State Park**
Interactive historic displays and touch tank
2500 Shore Dr.
(757) 412-2300 or (800) 933-7275

Contemporary Art Center of Virginia
2200 Parks Ave.
(757) 425-0000

Francis Land House Historic Site
*200-year-old plantation home, gardens,
and wooded wetlands trail*
3131 Virginia Beach Blvd.
(757) 431-4000

Lynnhaven House
Early colonial planter's home
4405 Wishart Rd.
(757) 460-7109

Ocean Breeze Waterpark
849 General Booth Blvd.
(757) 422-4444 or (800) 678-9453

Old Coast Guard Station
Museum in former lifesaving station
24th St. and Atlantic Ave.
(757) 422-1587

**Virginia Aquarium & Marine
Science Center**
Exhibits, aquarium, and IMAX theater
717 General Booth Blvd.
(757) 385-3474

Virginia Aquarium and Marine Science Center

Virginia Legends Walk
Self-guided tour honoring famous Virginians
13th St. between Atlantic and Pacific Aves.
(757) 463-4500

▶ **SHOPPING**

VIRGINIA BEACH

Farmers Market
Local produce and food items, gift stores
3640 Dam Neck Rd.
(757) 385-4395

Lynnhaven Mall
Department stores and specialty shops
701 Lynnhaven Pkwy.
(757) 340-9340

Pembroke Mall
*Department stores, specialty shops, and
movie theater*
Virginia Beach and Independence Blvds.
(757) 497-6255

▶ **VISITOR INFORMATION**

Norfolk Convention and Visitors Bureau
232 E. Main St.
Norfolk, VA 23510
(757) 664-6620 or (800) 368-3097
www.norfolkcvb.com

**Virginia Beach Convention and
Visitor Bureau**
2101 Parks Ave., Ste. 500
Virginia Beach, VA 23451
(757) 385-4700 or (800) 700-7702
www.vbfun.com

Norfolk Visitor Information Center
9401 4th View St.
(757) 441-1852

Virginia Beach Visitors Center
2100 Parks Ave.
(800) 822-3224

▶ **DIVERSION**

Experience life before the American Revolution at Colonial Williamsburg, a
301-acre living-history village about 50 miles northwest of Norfolk. Shop at
authentic 18th-century stores and eat in colonial taverns. I-64 west to exit 238,
VA 143. (800) 447-8679

OKLAHOMA CITY, Oklahoma

Bricktown Canal

Born of the 1889 land rush, Oklahoma's state capital thrived with the discovery of oil. Range riders still herd cattle on the surrounding plains; their legendary way of life is celebrated at the National Cowboy & Western Heritage Museum. At the center of the modern downtown of glass and steel, the Myriad Botanical Gardens offer 17 acres of landscaped grounds with the stunning Crystal Bridge Tropical Conservatory at its heart. The Oklahoma City National Memorial, a quiet and powerful tribute to those who lost their lives in the bombing of the Murrah Federal Building, lies a short distance away. *Tax: 13.875% hotel, 8.375% sales. For local weather, call (405) 360-5928.*

DON'T MISS DRIVE

Spend a few hours exploring the Heritage Hills Historic District, just north of downtown between NW 13th St. and NW 23rd St. In this part of Oklahoma City, mansions from the turn of the last century grace tree-lined streets.

SELECTED ATTRACTIONS

Bricktown
Entertainment, shopping, and dining district
Bordered by E. Main St. and Gaylord, Reno, and Byers Aves.
(405) 236-8666

Bricktown Ballpark
Home of the Oklahoma Redhawks
2 S. Mickey Mantle Dr.
(405) 218-1000

Myriad Botanical Gardens & Crystal Bridge
301 W. Reno Ave.
(405) 297-3995

National Cowboy & Western Heritage Museum
1700 NE 63rd St.
(405) 478-2250

Oklahoma City Museum of Art
415 Couch Dr.
(405) 236-3100

Oklahoma State Capitol
NE 23rd St. and Lincoln Blvd.
(405) 521-3356

Oklahoma City National Memorial and Museum
620 N. Harvey Ave.
(405) 235-3313 or (888) 542-4673

Oklahoma City Zoo and Botanical Garden
2101 NE 50th St.
(405) 424-3344

Stockyards City
Livestock auction, shops, and restaurants
Agnew exit off I-40 to Exchange Ave.
(405) 235-7267

SHOPPING

50 Penn Place
Upscale retail shops, restaurants
1900 NW Expwy.
(405) 848-7588

Crossroads Mall
Family shopping destination
7000 Crossroads Blvd.
(405) 631-4422

Paseo Arts District
Galleries, shops, and restaurants
NW 30th St. and Dewey Ave.
(405) 525-2688

Penn Square Mall
Department stores and specialty shops
NW Expwy. and Pennsylvania Ave.
(405) 842-4424

Quail Springs Mall
Department stores and retro food court
2501 W. Memorial Rd.
(405) 755-6530

Western Avenue
Boutiques, clubs, and restaurants
NW 36th St. to Wilshire Blvd.
(405) 412-5990

VISITOR INFORMATION

Oklahoma City Convention and Visitors Bureau
189 W. Sheridan Ave.
Oklahoma City, OK 73102
(405) 297-8912 or (800) 225-5652
www.visitokc.com

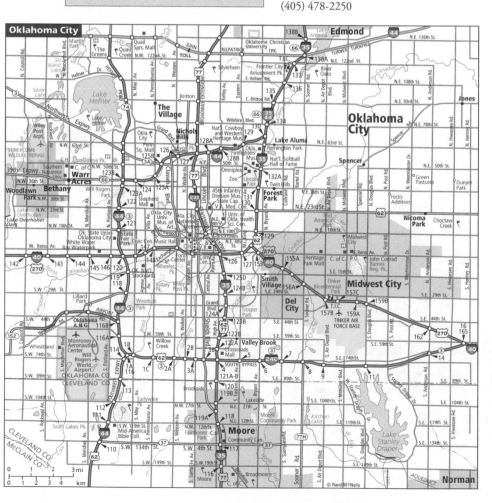

OMAHA, Nebraska

A center for agriculture, insurance, and telecommunications, Omaha got its first big boost when the transcontinental railroad began its western journey here. The Durham Museum in the restored Union Station displays exhibits on the city's railroading past, early settlers, and first inhabitants. The Old Market district offers restaurants, galleries, and shops in a former warehouse area. Recent additions to the outstanding Henry Doorly Zoo include the Hubbard Gorilla Valley, a free-range exhibit where only the spectators are in captivity, and Orangutan Forest, with both outdoor and indoor forest habitats. *Tax: 16.48% hotel, 7% sales. For local weather, call (402) 259-5166.*

Gene Leahy Pedestrian Mall

▶ SELECTED ATTRACTIONS

Boys Town
Historic home for at-risk youth
137th and W. Dodge Rd.
(402) 498-1140 or (800) 625-1400

The Durham Museum
801 S. 10th St.
(402) 444-5071

El Museo Latino
Art and history museum and cultural center
4701 S. 25th St.
(402) 731-1137

Eugene T. Mahoney State Park
28500 W. Park Hwy., Ashland
(402) 944-2523

Gerald R. Ford Birth Site and Gardens
3202 Woolworth Ave.
(402) 444-5955

Henry Doorly Zoo
3701 S. 10th St.
(402) 733-8401

Joslyn Art Museum
2200 Dodge St.
(402) 342-3300

Joslyn Castle
1903 historic home
3902 Davenport St.
(402) 595-2199

Lauritzen Gardens
Botanical garden and center
100 Bancroft St.
(402) 346-4002

Lewis and Clark Landing
515 N. Riverfront Dr.
(402) 444-5900

Mormon Trail Center
Covered wagon, cabin, and pioneer artifacts
3215 State St.
(402) 453-9372

Neale Woods Nature Center
14323 Edith Marie Ave.
(402) 453-5615

Omaha Children's Museum
500 S. 20th St.
(402) 342-6164

Strategic Air & Space Museum
28210 W. Park Hwy., off I-80,
exit 426, Ashland
(402) 944-3100 or (800) 358-5029

Wildlife Safari Park
16406 N. 292nd St., off I-80,
exit 426, Ashland
(402) 944-9453

▶ SHOPPING

Nebraska Crossing Outlet Center
Off I-80, exit 432 (NE 31), Gretna
(402) 332-4940

Old Market
Boutiques, specialty shops, and restaurants
10th to 13th Sts. and Harney to Jackon Sts.
(402) 346-4445

Regency Court
Unique designer shops and boutiques
120 Regency Pkwy.
(402) 393-8474

Westroads Mall
Department stores and specialty shops
10000 California St.
(402) 397-2398

▶ VISITOR INFORMATION

Omaha Convention and Visitors Bureau
1001 Farnam-on-the-Mall, Ste. 200
Omaha, NE 68102
(402) 444-4660 or (866) 937-6624
www.visitomaha.com

▶ DIVERSION

Check out 1,400 acres of forest and 17 miles of trails at the Fontenelle Forest Nature Center. Located on the Missouri River south of Omaha on US 75 to Bellevue. (402) 731-3140

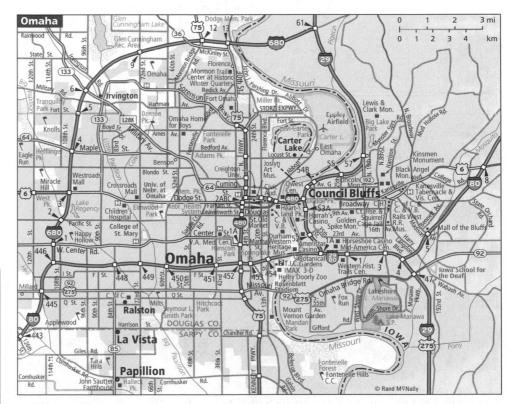

ORLANDO, Florida

Epcot Center, Walt Disney World

At one time little more than a peaceful orange grove, Orlando began its ascendance to theme-park supremacy with the arrival of Walt Disney's Magic Kingdom in 1971. Since then, Disney World has developed into an empire of resorts and multiple amusement parks, and others such as Universal Orlando Resort have brought along their own brand of thrills. For a true immersion experience, Discovery Cove offers lagoons where visitors can swim with playful dolphins and watch sharks and barracuda from a close (but safe) distance. *Tax: 11.5%-12.5% hotel, 6.5% sales. For local weather, call (321) 255-2900.*

▶ SELECTED ATTRACTIONS

Discovery Cove Orlando
Snorkel and swim with dolphins
6000 Discovery Cove Way, adjacent to
SeaWorld off I-4 at FL 528
(407) 370-1280 or (877) 434-7268

Kennedy Space Center Visitor Complex
35 miles east of Orlando off
FL 405, Titusville
(321) 449-4444

Orlando Museum of Art
American and African collections
2416 N. Mills Ave.
(407) 896-4231

**Ripley's Believe It or Not!
Orlando Odditorium**
8201 International Dr.
(407) 345-0501 or (800) 998-4418, ext. 3

SeaWorld Orlando
7007 SeaWorld Dr. off I-4 at FL 528
(407) 351-3600 or (800) 327-2424

Universal Orlando Resort
Theme park and entertainment complex
1000 Universal Studios Plaza, off I-4
(407) 363-8000

Walt Disney World Resort
25 miles southwest of Orlando off I-4,
Lake Buena Vista
(407) 939-6244

Wet 'n Wild Orlando
Water park
6200 International Dr.
(407) 351-1800 or (800) 992-9453

▶ SHOPPING

The Florida Mall
8001 S. Orange Blossom Trail
(407) 851-6255

Lake Buena Vista Factory Stores
Outlet stores
15657 SR 535
(407) 238-9301

The Mall at Millenia
Upscale stores and specialty shops
4200 Conroy Rd.
(407) 363-3555

Pointe Orlando
Specialty shops, entertainment, restaurants
9101 International Dr.
(407) 248-2838

Prime Outlets International Orlando
Upscale and designer outlet stores
4951 International Dr.
(407) 352-9600

▶ VISITOR INFORMATION

**Orlando/Orange County Convention
& Visitors Bureau**
6700 Forum Dr., Ste. 100
Orlando, FL 32821
(407) 363-5872 or (800) 972-3304
www.orlandoinfo.com

The Official Visitor Center
8723 International Dr., Ste. 101
(407) 363-5872 or (800) 643-9492

OTTAWA, Ontario, Canada

With its blend of English and French cultures, New World and Old, Canada's capital city displays cosmopolitan flair while retaining a small-town feel. For a taste of British tradition, tour Rideau Hall, official home of the Queen's representative, and the Parliament buildings, where colorful changing of the guard ceremonies are performed during summer months. One of Ottawa's many museums, the Bytown, traces the city's early history. At the river's edge, the architecturally splendid National Gallery houses a collection of modern, traditional, and aboriginal art. *Tax: 13% hotel, 5% GST, 8% PST.*

Changing of the guard at Parliament Hill

▶ SELECTED ATTRACTIONS

Bytown Museum and Ottawa Locks
History museum and Rideau Canal locks
1 Canal Ln., along the Rideau Canal
(613) 234-4570

Canada Aviation Museum
11 Aviation Pkwy. at Rockcliffe Pkwy.
(613) 993-2010

Canadian Museum of Civilization
100 Laurier St., Gatineau, QC
(819) 776-7000 or (800) 555-5621

Canadian Museum of Contemporary Photography
1 Rideau Canal (entrance on Wellington St.)
(613) 990-8257

Canadian Museum of Nature
240 McLeod St.
(613) 566-4700 or (800) 263-4433

Canadian War Museum
1 Vimy Pl.
(819) 776-8600 or (800) 555-5621

Casino du Lac-Leamy
1 Casino Blvd., Gatineau, QC
(819) 772-2100 or (800) 665-2274

Currency Museum of the Bank of Canada
245 Sparks St.
(613) 782-8914

Gatineau Park
33 Scott Rd. across the Macdonald-Cartier Bridge
(819) 827-2020 or (800) 465-1867

Laurier House
19th-century home and former residence of two Canadian prime ministers
335 Laurier Ave. E. at Chapel St.
(613) 992-8142

National Gallery of Canada
380 Sussex Dr.
(613) 990-1985 or (800) 319-2787

Parliament Hill
Headquarters of the Canadian government
90 Sparks St.
(613) 996-0896

Rideau Hall
Historic residence and workplace of Canada's Governor General
1 Sussex Dr.
(613) 991-4422 or (866) 842-4422

Royal Canadian Mint
320 Sussex Dr.
(613) 993-8990 or (800) 276-7714

▶ SHOPPING

ByWard Market
Fashion boutiques and unique shops
Between Sussex and Cumberland Sts. and Rideau and Cathcart Sts.
(613) 562-3325

Rideau Centre
Department stores and specialty shops
50 Rideau St.
(613) 236-6565

Sparks Street Mall
Department stores and specialty shops
Sparks St. from Elgin to Lyon Sts.
(613) 230-0984

Westboro Village
Antiques and studios
Richmond Rd. at Churchill Ave.
(613) 729-8145

▶ VISITOR INFORMATION

Ottawa Tourism and Convention Authority
130 Albert St., Ste. 1800
Ottawa, ON K1P 5G4, Canada
(613) 237-5150 or (800) 363-4465
www.ottawatourism.ca

▶ DIVERSION

View the world-famous Thousand Islands from a small cruise ship departing from Brockville, 100 kilometers (about 60 miles) from Ottawa, passing spectacular scenery, even castles. Take ON 416 south to ON 401 west. (613) 345-7333

PHILADELPHIA, Pennsylvania

Philadelphia Museum of Art with the city's skyline

Philadelphia, the "Cradle of Liberty," successfully integrates modern growth with its colonial past. The city's centerpiece, Independence National Historical Park, preserves the Liberty Bell, the hall in which the Declaration of Independence was adopted, and other significant sites large and small. Benjamin Franklin's personal effects are at the Franklin Institute Science Museum. The popular Manayunk neighborhood and posh Rittenhouse Square offer boutiques and galleries for a leisurely afternoon (or two) of shopping. For a personal Philly cheese steak taste-off, visitors head to the legendary Geno's Steaks, then across the street to the equally legendary Pat's King of Steaks. *Tax: 14% hotel, 7% sales. For local weather, call (609) 261-6600.*

▶ SELECTED ATTRACTIONS

Academy of Natural Sciences
1900 Benjamin Franklin Pkwy.
(215) 299-1000

Adventure Aquarium
4 miles from downtown across the Benjamin Franklin Bridge
1 Aquarium Dr., Camden, NJ
(856) 365-3300

African American Museum in Philadelphia
701 Arch St.
(215) 574-0380

Atwater Kent Museum of Philadelphia
Museum of Philadelphia history
15 S. 7th St.
(215) 685-4830

Betsy Ross House
18th-century home of American flag designer
239 Arch St.
(215) 686-1252

Christ Church
First U.S. Protestant Episcopal Church and Benjamin Franklin's grave site
2nd St. above Market St.
(215) 922-1695

Franklin Institute Science Museum
222 N. 20th St. at Benjamin Franklin Pkwy.
(215) 448-1200

Franklin Court Underground Museum
Site where Benjamin Franklin's home once stood
Market St. between 3rd and 4th Sts.
(215) 597-2761

Historic Bartram's Garden
Botanic garden, 18th-century coachhouse, and wildflower meadow
54th St. and Lindbergh Blvd.
(215) 729-5281

Independence National Historical Park
Includes the Liberty Bell, Independence Hall, and National Constitution Center
143 S. 3rd St.
(215) 965-2305

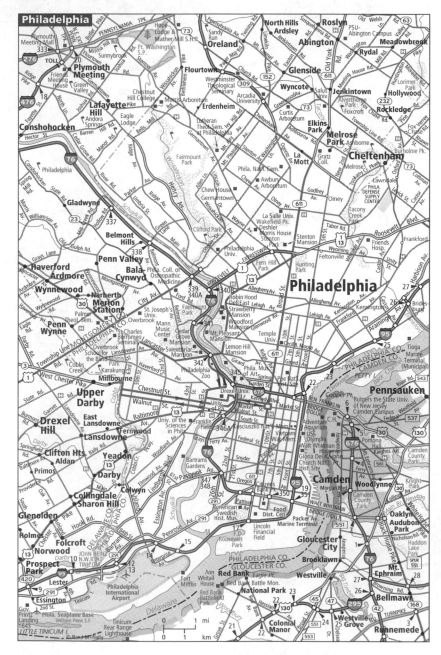

▶ DON'T MISS DRIVE

A drive down Benjamin Franklin Parkway between City Hall and the Philadelphia Art Museum captures the stately and historic aura of Philadelphia. It is replete with cathedrals, fountains, parks, and monuments.

John Heinz National Wildlife Refuge at Tinicum
8601 Lindbergh Blvd.
(215) 365-3118

National Constitution Center
Museum dedicated to the U.S. Constitution
525 Arch St. in Independence Mall
(215) 409-6600

Philadelphia Museum of Art
26th St. and Benjamin Franklin Pkwy.
(215) 763-8100

Philadelphia Zoo
3400 W. Girard Ave. in Fairmount Park
(215) 243-1100

Please Touch Museum
Children's museum
210 N. 21st St.
(215) 963-0667

Valley Forge National Historical Park
Revolutionary War site
18 miles northwest off I-76, exit 328A,
Valley Forge
(610) 783-1077

SHOPPING

Chestnut Hill Shopping District
Boutiques, galleries, antique shops, cafes, and restaurants
Along Germantown Ave.
(215) 247-6696

Franklin Mills Mall
Outlet stores
1455 Franklin Mills Cir., I-95 and
Woodhaven Rd.
(215) 632-1500

Jewelers Row
8th St. between Chestnut and Walnut Sts.
and Sansom St. between 7th and 8th Sts.
(215) 627-1834

Manayunk National Historic District
Boutiques, galleries, and restaurants
7 miles west of Center City off I-76,
exit 338
(215) 668-0164

Rittenhouse Row
Upscale boutiques and galleries
Bounded by the Avenue of the Arts (Broad
St.) and 21st, Pine, and Market Sts.
(215) 668-0164

Shops at Liberty Place
Upscale boutiques and specialty shops
1625 Chestnut St. between 16th
and 17th Sts.
(215) 851-9055

South Street/Headhouse District
Eclectic shops and restaurants
Bounded by Front, 11th, Pine, and
Christian Sts.
(215) 413-3713

VISITOR INFORMATION

Philadelphia Convention and Visitors Bureau
1700 Market St., Ste. 3000
Philadelphia, PA 19103
(215) 636-3300 or (800) 225-5745
www.pcvb.org

Independence Visitor Center
1 N. Independence Mall W.,
6th and Market Sts.
(215) 965-7676 or (800) 537-7676

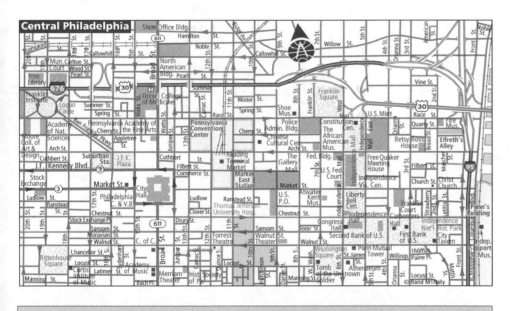

DIVERSION

In nearby Merion, view 4,000 objects of art on display, including a stunning collection of French early Modern and Post-Impressionist paintings, Native American pottery, and Greek, Roman, and Egyptian artifacts at the Barnes Foundation Gallery and Arboretum. Stroll the 12 acres of gardens. Advance reservations are required. Call (610) 667-0290, option 5, or go to www.barnesfoundation.org for reservation forms. Take I-76 west to exit 339 to US 1 south. Turn right onto 54th St. (Old Lancaster Rd.), taking a left onto N. Latch's Lane, then follow signs.

PHOENIX, Arizona

Hot-air balloon race over Phoenix

Baking in the dry Southwestern sun, Phoenix is a busy, growing metropolis surrounded by mountain resorts and fertile, well-irrigated fields. In the heart of the city, Copper Square is filled with restaurants, stores, theaters, and big-time sports venues, plus the Arizona Science Center, a family-oriented exploration arena with more than 350 hands-on activities, a planetarium, and a large-screen theater. The Heard Museum also offers interactive exhibits among its 10 galleries devoted to the art and culture of the Southwest's Native Americans. At the Desert Botanical Garden in Papago Park, visitors can stroll through 145 acres of cacti and other dry-region plants. *Tax: 12.27% hotel, 8.3% sales. For local weather, call (602) 275-0073.*

▶ SELECTED ATTRACTIONS

Arizona Capitol Museum
1700 W. Washington St.
(602) 542-4675

Arizona Mining and Mineral Museum
1502 W. Washington St.
(602) 771-1600

Arizona Science Center
600 E. Washington St.
(602) 716-2000

Deer Valley Rock Art Center
Ancient petroglyphs in a desert preserve
3711 W. Deer Valley Rd.
(623) 582-8007

Desert Botanical Garden
1201 N. Galvin Pkwy.
(480) 941-1225

Dolly Steamboat Excursion
Canyon Lake boat tours
45 miles east off AZ 88 (via US 60),
Canyon Lake
(480) 827-9144

Hall of Flame Museum of Firefighting
6101 E. Van Buren St.
(602) 275-3473

Heard Museum
Native American art
2301 N. Central Ave.
(602) 252-8848

Hot Air Expeditions
Hot-air balloon flights
2243 E. Rose Garden Loop
(480) 502-6999 or (800) 831-7610

Huhugam Heritage Center
Gila River Indians gallery and museum store
4759 N. Maricopa Rd., Chandler
(520) 796-3500

Museo Chicano
Museum of Latino arts, history, and culture
147 E. Adams St.
(602) 257-5536

Oasis Water Park
Arizona Grand Resort
8000 S. Grand Ave.
(602) 438-9000

Phoenix Art Museum
1625 N. Central Ave.
(602) 257-1880

Phoenix Zoo
455 N. Galvin Pkwy.
(602) 273-1341

Pioneer Arizona Living History Village
*95 acres of historic buildings and
Fort Brent Wood*
3901 W. Pioneer Rd., exit 225 off I-17
(623) 465-1052

**Pueblo Grande Museum and
Archaeological Park**
Prehistoric Hohokam Indian ruins
4619 E. Washington St.
(602) 495-0901 or (877) 706-4408

Taliesin West
Frank Lloyd Wright's winter home and studio
Cactus Rd. and Frank Lloyd Wright Blvd.,
Scottsdale
(480) 860-8810 or (480) 860-2700

▶ SHOPPING

Arizona Center
Restaurants and specialty shops
3rd and Van Buren Sts.
(602) 271-4000

Arizona Mills
Factory outlet stores and specialty shops
US 60 and I-10, Tempe
(480) 491-7300

Arrowhead Towne Center
*Department stores, specialty retailers,
and cinema*
75th Ave. and Bell Rd., Glendale
(623) 979-8928

Biltmore Fashion Park
Upscale boutiques
2502 E. Camelback Rd.
(602) 955-8400

The Borgata of Scottsdale
*Unique stores and eateries in an
open-air setting*
6166 N. Scottsdale Rd., Scottsdale
(602) 953-6311

Chandler Fashion Center
Shops, restaurants, and movie theaters
3111 W. Chandler Blvd., Chandler
(480) 812-8488

Scottsdale Fashion Square
7014-590 E. Camelback Rd.
(480) 941-2140

Tlaquepaque
*Spanish colonial village with specialty
galleries and shops*
336 AZ 179, Sedona
(928) 282-4838

▶ VISITOR INFORMATION

**Greater Phoenix Convention and
Visitors Bureau**
400 E. Van Buren St., Ste. 600
Phoenix, AZ 85004
(602) 254-6500 or (877) 225-5749
www.visitphoenix.com

Visitor Center
125 N. 2nd St., Ste. 120

▶ DON'T MISS DRIVE

Cruise downtown Phoenix, especially Copper Square, to see the murals, copper-painted fixtures, and newer architectural icons like Chase Field, home of the city's Major League Baseball team, the Arizona Diamondbacks.

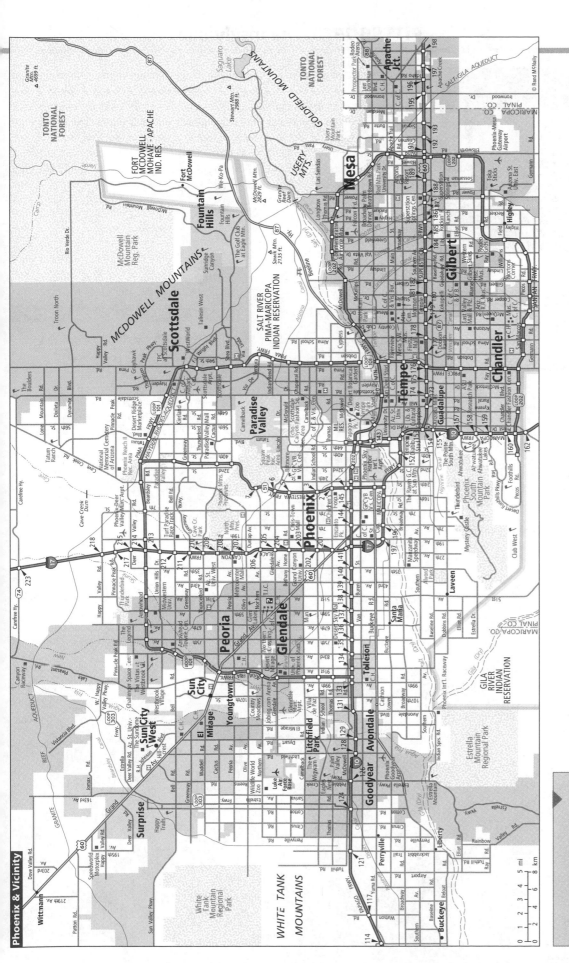

Phoenix & Vicinity

DIVERSION

See the majesty of purple mountains on a day trip to Sedona and Oak Creek Canyon. It's about a 90-minute drive. Take I-17 north to AZ 179 and look for the Sedona exit.

PITTSBURGH, Pennsylvania

Point State Park

Tucked into the steep hills of the Allegheny Plateau, this once-grimy town now sparkles with steel and glass. Barges ply the waters of the Ohio, Allegheny, and Monongahela rivers past Point State Park, where the Fort Pitt Museum interprets Pittsburgh's early history. North of the rivers, the Carnegie Science Center invites visitors to try hundreds of hands-on experiments, and the Andy Warhol Museum displays some 500 works by the most well-known American artist of the late 20th century. For a taste of commuting Pittsburgh-style, ride the century-old Duquesne Incline cable cars. *Tax: 14% hotel, 7% sales. For local weather, call (412) 262-2170.*

▶ SELECTED ATTRACTIONS

Andy Warhol Museum
117 Sandusky St.
(412) 237-8300

Carnegie Museums of Art and Natural History
4400 Forbes Ave.
(412) 622-3131

Carnegie Science Center
Includes planetarium and Omnimax theater
1 Allegheny Ave.
(412) 237-3400

Duquesne Incline
Cable car incline up Mt. Washington
1220 Grandview Ave.
(412) 381-1665

Frick Art & Historical Center
7227 Reynolds St.
(412) 371-0600

Hartwood Acres
Tudor mansion in 629-acre park
200 Hartwood Acres
(412) 767-9200

Kennywood
Amusement park
4800 Kennywood Blvd., West Mifflin
(412) 461-0500

National Aviary
Allegheny Commons West at Ridge and Arch Sts.
(412) 323-7235

Phipps Conservatory and Botanical Gardens
1 Schenley Park
(412) 622-6914

Point State Park
Fort Pitt Blockhouse and Museum
101 Commonwealth Pl., Golden Triangle
(412) 471-0235

▶ SHOPPING

Downtown
Department stores and specialty shops
Bounded by Wood St., Sixth St., Smithfield St., and Forbes Ave.

The Mall at Robinson
Department stores and specialty shops
100 Robinson Centre Dr.
(412) 788-0816

Shadyside
Upscale specialty shops and boutiques
Walnut St. between Aiken and Shady Aves.
(412) 682-1298

The Waterfront
Department store, specialty shops, and entertainment
149 W. Bridge St., Homestead
(412) 461-7820

▶ VISITOR INFORMATION

Greater Pittsburgh Convention and Visitors Bureau
425 6th Ave., 30th Fl.
Pittsburgh, PA 15219
(412) 281-7711 or (800) 359-0758
www.visitpittsburgh.com

Downtown Visitor Center
On Liberty Ave. at Stanwix St., adjacent to Gateway Center

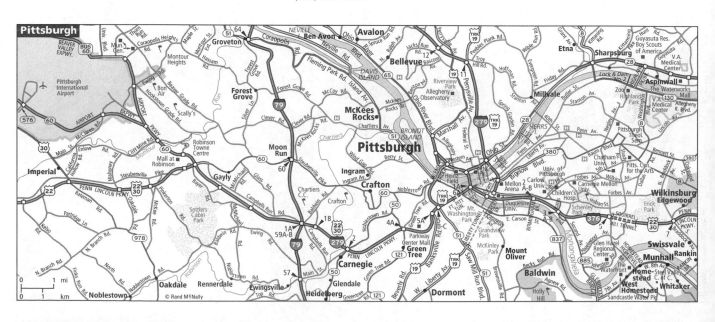

PORTLAND, Oregon

Under the gaze of Mount Hood, Portland takes pride in citywide environmental consciousness. The transportation system, much of it free, connects neighborhoods, suburbs, and attractions. The International Rose Test Gardens in Washington Park help the city earn its title as the "City of Roses." Anchoring the Culture District, the Oregon Historical Society brings the story of the Northwest alive through artifacts and multimedia presentations. The reinvented Pearl District finds shoppers looking through boutiques and tasting daring cuisines in what was once an area of heavy industry. *Tax: 12.5% hotel, no sales tax. For local weather, call (503) 261-9246.*

Portland skyline with Mount Hood

▶ SELECTED ATTRACTIONS

The Grotto: National Sanctuary of Our Sorrowful Mother
Catholic shrine and botanical garden
NE 85th Ave. and Sandy Blvd.
(503) 254-7371

Hoyt Arboretum
4000 SW Fairview Blvd. in Washington Park
(503) 865-8733

International Rose Test Garden
400 SW Kingston Ave. in Washington Park
(503) 823-3636

Oregon Historical Society Museum
1200 SW Park Ave.
(503) 222-1741

Oregon Museum of Science and Industry
1945 SE Water Ave.
(503) 797-4000

Oregon Zoo
4001 SW Canyon Rd. in Washington Park
(503) 226-1561

Pittock Mansion
1914 mansion of the founder of The Oregonian *newspaper*
3229 NW Pittock Dr.
(503) 823-3624

Portland Art Museum
1219 SW Park Ave.
(503) 226-2811

Portland Children's Museum
4015 SW Canyon Rd. in Washington Park
(503) 223-6500

Portland Classical Chinese Garden
239 NW Everett St.
(503) 228-8131

World Forestry Center
4033 SW Canyon Rd. in Washington Park
(503) 228-1367

▶ SHOPPING

Lloyd Center
Department stores and specialty shops
NE Multnomah St. and 9th Ave.
(503) 282-2511

Nob Hill/Northwest Portland
Trendy shops, restaurants, and cafés
Along NW 23rd and 21st Aves.
(503) 706-6532

Pearl District
Industrial-chic architecture, galleries and restaurants
Bounded by NW Broadway Ave., I-405, NW Naito-Parkway, and W. Burnside Ave.
(503) 227-8519

Pioneer Place
Department stores and specialty shops
700 SW 5th Ave.
(503) 228-5800

▶ VISITOR INFORMATION

Travel Portland
1000 SW Broadway, Ste. 2300
Portland, OR 97205
(503) 275-9750 or (800) 962-3700
www.travelportland.com

Travel Portland Information Center
701 SW 6th Ave.
Pioneer Square
(503) 275-8355 or (877) 678-5263

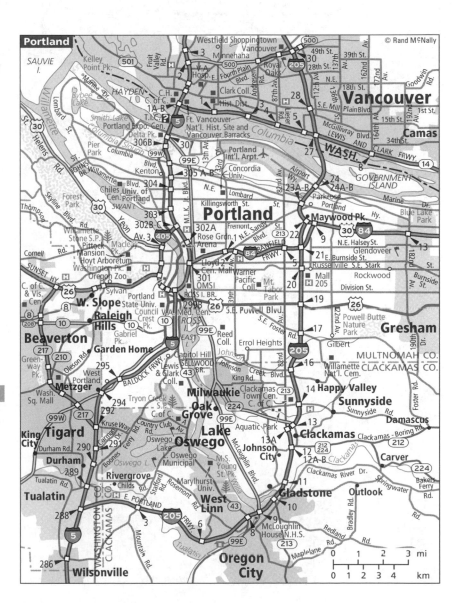

PROVIDENCE, Rhode Island

Morning in Providence

Founded on principles of religious freedom by Roger Williams, Providence is still regarded as a bastion of liberal idealism. Home to Brown University, the city displays its Colonial-era roots along Benefit Street. The collections at the RISD Museum touch upon all eras of human endeavor. Five thousand years of cooking and hospitality are the focus of the Culinary Archives and Museum. Bargain hunters head to The Arcade, reputedly the nation's first enclosed shopping area. *Tax: 13% hotel, 7% sales. For local weather, call (508) 822-0634.*

▶ SELECTED ATTRACTIONS

Culinary Archives & Museum at Johnson & Wales University
315 Harborside Blvd.
(401) 598-2805

DePasquale Plaza/Federal Hill
Historic Italian neighborhood
Atwells Ave.

John Brown House
Historic home of 18th-century merchant
52 Power St.
(401) 273-7507

The Meeting House
America's first Baptist church
75 N. Main St.
(401) 454-3418

Providence Children's Museum
100 South St.
(401) 273-5437

The RISD Museum
Fine and decorative arts
224 Benefit St.
(401) 454-6500

Roger Williams National Memorial
Tribute to Rhode Island's founder
282 N. Main St.
(401) 521-7266

▶ SHOPPING

The Arcade
Specialty shops
65 Weybosset St.
(401) 861-9150

Providence Place Mall
One Providence Pl.
(401) 270-1000

Thayer Street
Galleries and boutiques
Between Lloyd Ave. and George St.

Wickenden Street
Antiques, galleries, and coffeehouses
Between Benefit and Hope Sts.

▶ VISITOR INFORMATION

The Providence Warwick Convention and Visitors Bureau
144 Westminster St.
Providence, RI 02903
(401) 456-0200 or (800) 233-1636
www.goprovidence.com

Providence Visitors Center
1 Sabin St. (in the Rhode Island Convention Center)
(401) 751-1177 or (800) 233-1636

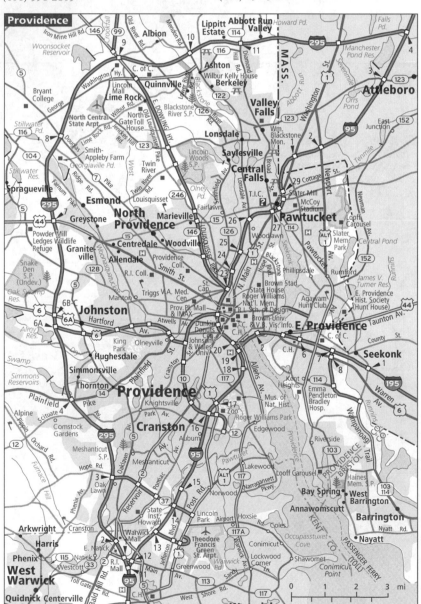

DIVERSION

Relive Gilded Age glamour on a tour of Newport, where historic, opulent mansions were built as summer homes by some of America's wealthiest families at the turn of the 20th century. Take I-195 east to RI 24 south, then RI 114 south into downtown Newport and to Bellevue Ave. (800) 976-5122

RALEIGH/DURHAM/CHAPEL HILL, North Carolina

The three cities that make up the Research Triangle region are unusually well endowed with institutions of higher learning. Raleigh is home to North Carolina State University as well as many fine museums. The Museum of History features displays on the Civil War, health and healing, and a sports hall of fame. Interactive exhibits at Marbles Kids Museum encourage visitors to connect with other cultures of the world. *Tax: 13% hotel, 7% sales, 1% prepared food and beverage. For local weather, call (919) 515-8209.*

Durham first came to prominence thanks to bright leaf tobacco. Duke University was founded through the largess of tobacco's wealthiest families. The rough existence of the first tobacco farmers is retold by costumed interpreters at the Duke Homestead historic site. Downtown, former tobacco warehouses now house galleries, restaurants, and shops in the redeveloped Brightleaf Square. *Tax: 12.75% hotel, 6.75% sales (retail and restaurants), 2% sales (groceries), car rental: 16% in Durham, 25.61% at RDU International Airport.*

The original University of North Carolina was chartered at Chapel Hill in 1789. Budding stargazers can travel to the edge of the universe through the Star Theatre at the campus's Morehead Planetarium. The Collection Gallery displays diverse artifacts, including items from the Sir Walter Raleigh collection. Lovers of flowers and trees can stop at the Coker Arboretum on campus or head to the 600-acre North Carolina Botanical Garden. *Tax: 12.75% hotel, 6.75% sales.*

Raleigh skyline

Marbles Kids Museum
Interactive world cultures and children's museum
201 E. Hargett St.
(919) 834-4040

North Carolina Museum of History
5 E. Edenton St.
(919) 807-7900

North Carolina State Capitol
1 E. Edenton St. in Capitol Square
(919) 733-4994

continued on the next page

▶ SELECTED ATTRACTIONS

RALEIGH

African American Cultural Complex
Exhibits, performances, and outdoor drama
119 Sunnybrook Rd.
(919) 250-9336

Artspace
Art gallery
201 E. Davie St. in City Market
(919) 821-2787

Raleigh continued

► SHOPPING

RALEIGH

Cameron Village Shopping Center
Upscale boutiques, salons, and antiques
1900 Cameron St.
(919) 821-1350

City Market
Art galleries, specialty shops, and restaurants
Blake St. at Martin and Blount Sts.
(919) 821-8023

Crabtree Valley Mall
Department stores and specialty shops
4325 Glenwood Ave.
(919) 787-8993

Triangle Town Center
Department stores and specialty shops
5959 Triangle Town Blvd. at Capital Blvd.
and Old Wake Forest Rd.
(919) 792-2222

Butterfly house at the North Carolina Museum of Life and Science in Durham

► SELECTED ATTRACTIONS

DURHAM

Bennett Place State Historic Site
Site of Confederate surrender
4409 Bennett Memorial Rd.
(919) 383-4345

Duke Homestead State Historic Site and Tobacco Museum
2828 Duke Homestead Rd.
(919) 477-5498

Duke University Chapel
Chapel Dr. on the Duke University
West campus
(919) 684-2572

Hayti Heritage Center
African American artifacts and performances
804 Old Fayetteville St.
(919) 683-1709

Museum of Life and Science
Butterfly house and insectarium
433 Murray Ave.
(919) 220-5429

Sarah P. Duke Gardens
426 Anderson St. on the Duke
University West campus
(919) 684-3698

► DON'T MISS DRIVE

Visit Raleigh's Historic Oakwood District, a Victorian neighborhood listed on the National Register of Historic Places. The restored homes in this 20-block enclave, bordered by Franklin, Watauga, Linden, Jones and Person Sts., date from 1870 to 1912. The Oakwood Cemetery (701 Oakwood Ave.) is the burial site of 1,500 Confederate soldiers and five Civil War generals.

► SHOPPING

DURHAM

Brightleaf Square
Art galleries and specialty shops
905 W. Main St.
(919) 682-9229

Ninth Street Shopping District
Shops, boutiques, and restaurants
Between Main St. and Club Blvd., near
Duke University's East campus

Northgate Mall
Department stores and specialty shops
1058 W. Club Blvd. off I-85, exit 176-A
(919) 286-4400

The Streets at Southpoint
Department stores and specialty shops
6910 Fayetteville Rd.
(919) 572-8808

► SELECTED ATTRACTIONS

CHAPEL HILL

Ackland Art Museum
E. Franklin St. at S. Columbia St. on the
UNC campus
(919) 966-5736

Chapel Hill Museum
523 E. Franklin St.
(919) 967-1400

Horace Williams House
19th-century home and art gallery
610 E. Rosemary St.
(919) 962-1236

Morehead Planetarium and Science Center
250 E. Franklin St. on the UNC campus
(919) 962-1236

North Carolina Botanical Garden
US 15-501/NC 54 Bypass (Fordham Blvd.)
to Old Mason Farm Rd.
(919) 962-0522

North Carolina Collection Gallery
Sir Walter Raleigh rooms and North Carolina history
Wilson Library on the
UNC campus
(919) 962-1172

► SHOPPING

CHAPEL HILL

Downtown Shopping District
Boutiques and specialty shops
Franklin and Rosemary Sts. at Columbia St.

University Mall
Department stores and specialty shops
201 S. Estes Dr.
(919) 967-6934

► VISITOR INFORMATION

Greater Raleigh Convention and Visitors Bureau
421 Fayetteville Street, Ste. 1505
Raleigh, NC 27601
(919) 834-5900 or (800) 849-8499
www.visitraleigh.com

Durham Convention and Visitors Bureau and Information Center
101 E. Morgan St.
Durham, NC 27701
(919) 687-0288 or (800) 446-8604
www.durham-nc.com

Chapel Hill/Orange County Visitors Bureau
501 W. Franklin St.
Chapel Hill, NC 27516
(919) 968-2060 or (888) 968-2060
www.chocvb.org

Capital Area Visitor Center
Lobby of Museum of History
5 E. Edenton St., Raleigh
(919) 807-7950

UNC Visitors Center at Morehead Planetarium
250 E. Franklin St., Chapel Hill
(919) 962-1630

North Carolina Botanical Garden in Chapel Hill

RENO, Nevada

Self-tagged "The Biggest Little City in the World," Reno is expanding beyond its image as a glittery gambler's oasis. While casinos and top-name musical acts are still the main draw, the city's newer attractions stress the arts and outdoors activities. The Nevada Museum of Art collection focuses on land and the environment. The Truckee River Whitewater Park runs straight through downtown, offering class II and III rapids over a half-mile course. *Tax: 13.5% hotel, 7.375% sales. For local weather, call (775) 673-8130.*

Nightlife in Reno

▶ SELECTED ATTRACTIONS

Brüka Theater
Live theater
99 N. Virginia St.
(775) 323-3221

Eldorado Hotel and Casino
345 N. Virginia St.
(775) 786-5700 or (800) 648-5966

Fleischmann Planetarium and Science Center
Off N. Virginia St., north of Lawlor Events Center
(775) 784-4812

Magic Underground
Live theatrical illusions
148 Greenridge Dr.
(775) 770-2176

National Automobile Museum
Vintage, classic, and special-interest vehicles
10 S. Lake St.
(775) 333-9300

Nevada Museum of Art
160 W. Liberty St.
(775) 329-3333

Sierra Safari Zoo
Seasonal wildlife park
10200 N. Virginia St.
(775) 677-1101

Truckee River Whitewater Park
Wingfield Park, First St. and Arlington Ave.
(775) 334-2262

Wilbur D. May Center/Great Basin Adventure
Museum, arboretum, and seasonal children's park
Rancho San Rafael Park, 1595 N. Sierra
(775) 785-5961

Wild Island Family Adventure Park
Water park
250 Wild Island Ct.
I-80 and Sparks Blvd., Sparks
(775) 359-2927

W.M. Keck Museum
Nevada mineral exhibits
Center and 9th Sts. in the Mackay School of Mines, University of Nevada
(775) 784-4528

▶ SHOPPING

Meadowood Mall
Department and specialty stores
5000 Meadowood Mall Cir.
S. Virginia St. and McCarran Blvd.
(775) 827-8450

The Riverwalk District
Art galleries and upscale boutiques
Along Truckee River between Arlington Ave. and Lake St.
(775) 825-9255

The Summit
Department stores and specialty shops
13925 S. Virginia St.
(775) 853-7800

▶ VISITOR INFORMATION

Reno-Sparks Convention and Visitors Assocation
4001 S. Virginia
Reno, NV 89502
(775) 827-7600 or (800) 367-7366
www.visitrenotahoe.com

Sparks Chamber of Commerce Visitor Center
634 Pyramid Way
Sparks, NV 89431

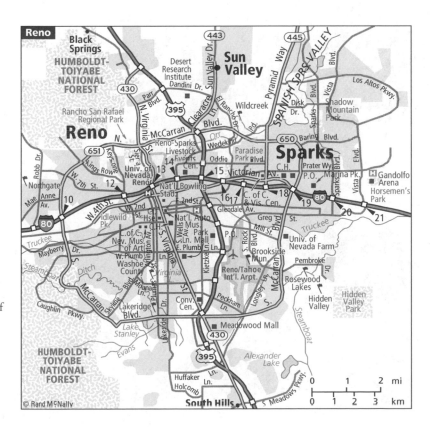

RICHMOND, Virginia

Sunken Garden at Agecroft Hall

Bristling with history, the capital of Virginia has witnessed much modern development even as it has successfully preserved its past. The Canal Walk offers an attractive stroll along the historic banks of the James River. Hipsters head to Shockoe Slip and Shockoe Bottom—areas once ravaged by floods and now reborn as headquarters for nightclubs, restaurants, and artists' lofts. A tour of the state capitol offers a view of its surprising hidden dome. *Tax: 13% hotel, 5% sales, 11% meal. For local weather, call (757) 899-4200.*

▶ SELECTED ATTRACTIONS

Agecroft Hall and Gardens
15th-century mansion moved from England
4305 Sulgrave Rd.
(804) 353-4241

Edgar Allen Poe Museum
1914 E. Main St.
(804) 648-5523

Kings Dominion
Theme park
20 miles north off I-95, Doswell
(804) 876-5000

Lewis Ginter Botanical Garden
1800 Lakeside Ave.
(804) 262-9887

Maymont
House museum, children's farm, and nature/visitor center
2201 Shields Lake Dr.
(804) 358-7166

Museum and White House of the Confederacy
1201 E. Clay St.
(804) 649-1861

St. John's Church
Site of Patrick Henry speech
2401 E. Broad St.
(804) 648-5015

State Capitol
1000 Bank St.
(804) 698-1788

Three Lakes Nature Center and Aquarium
400 Sausiluta Dr.
(804) 262-5055

Virginia Historical Society Museum
428 N. Boulevard
(804) 358-4901

Virginia Museum of Fine Arts
200 N. Boulevard
(804) 340-1400

▶ SHOPPING

Carytown
Unique shops and boutiques
Cary St. from Thompson St. to the Boulevard
(804) 422-2279

Chesterfield Towne Center
Department stores and specialty shops
11500 Midlothian Tpk.
(804) 794-4662

Regency Square Mall
Department stores and specialty shops
1420 Parham Rd.
(804) 740-7467

Short Pump Town Center
Department stores and high-end shops
11800 W. Broad St.
(804) 364-9500

▶ VISITOR INFORMATION

Richmond Metropolitan Convention and Visitors Bureau
401 N. 3rd St., Richmond, VA 23219
(804) 782-2777, (800) 370-9004, or (888) 742-4666
www.visit.richmond.com

Richmond Region Visitor Center
405 N. 3rd St.
(804) 783-7450

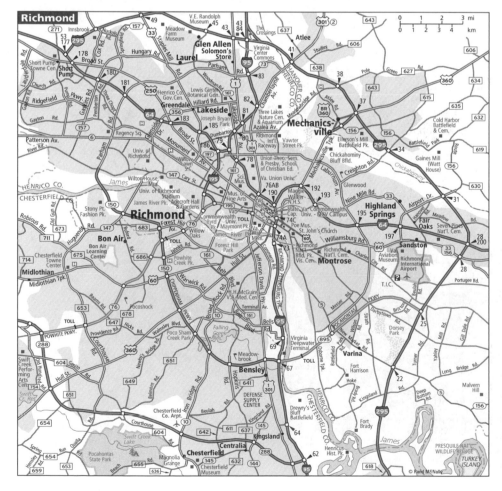

DON'T MISS DRIVE

Tree-lined Monument Avenue commemorates Richmondites in statues of figures such as Confederate General Robert E. Lee, Confederate President Jefferson Davis, scientist/oceanographer Matthew Fontaine Maury, and tennis legend Arthur Ashe.

SACRAMENTO, California

California's state capital, where the gold rush began in 1849, is a major commercial center and inland port thanks to a deep water channel to San Francisco Bay. The city enjoys a wealth of historic sites including Sutter's Fort, the area's first European outpost, and the Governor's Mansion, which includes period furnishings of the 19th century. The clapboard buildings and cobblestone streets of Old Sacramento give visitors a taste of pioneer days. The many museums found here include the State Railroad Museum and its collection of painstakingly restored engines, coaches, dining, and work cars. *Tax: 12% hotel, 7.75% sales. For local weather, call (916) 646-2000.*

Paddlewheelers on the Sacramento River

▶ SELECTED ATTRACTIONS

California Museum for History, Women and the Arts
1020 O St.
(916) 653-7524

California State Capitol Museum
10th and L Sts.
(916) 324-0333

California State Indian Museum
2618 K St.
(916) 324-0971

California State Railroad Museum
111 I St., Old Sacramento
(916) 445-6645

Crocker Art Museum
216 O St.
(916) 264-5423

Discovery Museum Gold Rush History Center
History exhibits
101 I St., Old Sacramento
(916) 264-7057

Discovery Museum Science and Space Center
Science and technology museum
3615 Auburn Blvd.
(916) 575-3941

Governor's Mansion State Historic Park
16th and H Sts.
(916) 323-3047

Old Sacramento Historic District
Museums and entertainment district
1002 2nd St.
(916) 442-7644

Sutter's Fort State Historic Park
2701 L St.
(916) 445-4422

Towe Auto Museum
2200 Front St.
(916) 442-6802

Wells Fargo History Museum
Commercial history exhibits
400 Capitol Mall
(916) 440-4161

Wells Fargo Pavilion
Home to Music Circus
1419 H St.
(916) 557-1999

▶ SHOPPING

Arden Fair
Department stores and specialty shops
Capital City Frwy. at Arden Way
(916) 920-1167

Pavilions
Upscale fashion boutiques and specialty shops
563 Pavilions Ln.
(916) 925-4463

Downtown Plaza
Department stores and specialty shops
547 L St.
(916) 442-4000

▶ VISITOR INFORMATION

Sacramento Convention and Visitors Bureau
1608 I St.
Sacramento, CA 95814
(916) 808-7777 or (800) 292-2334
www.sacramentocvb.org

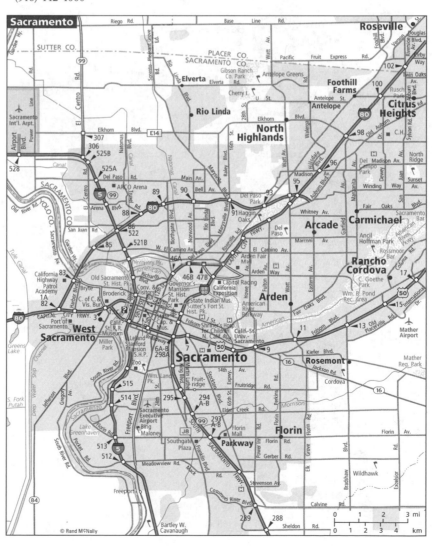

ST. LOUIS, Missouri

Downtown St. Louis and the Gateway Arch

Rolling westward from the banks of the Mississippi River, St. Louis offers a vision of national expansion symbolized in the city's most prominent landmark, the Gateway Arch. A ride to the top of this engineering marvel yields far-flung views of city, rivers, and plains. The green expanse of Forest Park is home to the top-rated St. Louis Zoo and the wide-ranging collections of the St. Louis Art Museum. Fine dining establishments line the quiet streets of the Central West End.

Tax: 15.491% hotel, 8.241% sales. For local weather, call (314) 321-2222 or (636) 441-8467.

▶ SELECTED ATTRACTIONS

Anheuser-Busch Brewery Tour
Clydesdale horse paddock/stable, historic brew house, and hospitality center
12th and Lynch Sts.
(314) 577-2626

Gateway Arch-Jefferson National Expansion Memorial
St. Louis Riverfront
(314) 655-1700

Laumeier Sculpture Park
Monumental contemporary sculpture
12580 Rott Rd.
(314) 821-1209

Magic House: St. Louis Children's Museum
516 S. Kirkwood Rd.
(314) 822-8900

Missouri Botanical Garden
4344 Shaw Blvd.
(314) 577-9400

St. Louis Art Museum
1 Fine Arts Dr. in Forest Park
(314) 721-0072

St. Louis Zoo
1 Government Dr. in Forest Park
(314) 781-0900

▶ SHOPPING

Cherokee Antique Row
Fine antiques to funky collectibles
Cherokee St. from Indiana to Lemp Sts.
(314) 772-9177

St. Louis Union Station
Specialty shops and restaurants
1820 Market St.
(314) 421-6655

St. Louis Galleria
Upscale boutiques and department stores
1155 St. Louis Galleria
(314) 863-5500

▶ VISITOR INFORMATION

St. Louis Convention and Visitors Commission
701 Convention Plaza, Ste. 300
St. Louis, MO 63101
(314) 421-1023 or (800) 888-3861
www.explorestlouis.com

▶ DON'T MISS DRIVE

Relive the glory days of Route 66. Markers along Chippewa and Manchester Roads will guide you. Follow it west through St. Louis County to see roadside motels and diners scattered among busy modern areas.

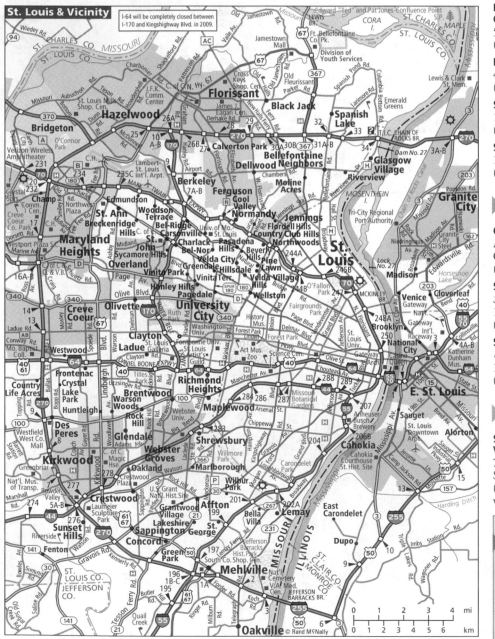

St. Louis & Vicinity

I-64 will be completely closed between I-170 and Kingshighway Blvd. in 2009.

© Rand McNally

SALT LAKE CITY, Utah

Founded as a haven for the Mormon church in 1847, Salt Lake City has become a magnet for outdoor enthusiasts who find plenty of mountain resort areas within a few miles of downtown. Temple Square and the Beehive House once occupied by early Mormon leader Brigham Young are two of the historic sites related to the Latter-day Saints. Of more recent vintage, Olympic Park, where the 2002 Winter Games were held, is now a training site for the U.S. Olympic team; tours are available. *Tax: 12.67% hotel, 6.8% goods and services, 7.8% restaurants. For local weather, call (801) 524-5133.*

Beehive House

▶ SELECTED ATTRACTIONS

Beehive House
Restored residence of Brigham Young
67 E. South Temple St.
(801) 240-2671

Clark Planetarium and IMAX Theatre
Star shows, science exhibits, and theater
110 S. 400 West St.
(801) 456-7827

Family History Library
World's largest genealogical research library
35 N. West Temple St.
(801) 240-2584 or (866) 406-1830

Historic Temple Square
Mormon Tabernacle, museums, and choir
Bounded by N., S., and W. Temple Sts. and Main St.
(801) 240-4872 or (800) 537-9703

Utah's Hogle Zoo
2600 E. Sunnyside Ave.
(801) 582-1631

▶ SHOPPING

Fashion Place Mall
Department stores and specialty shops
6191 S. State St., Murray
(801) 262-9447

Gardner Village
Specialty shops in historic area
1100 W. 7800 S., West Jordan
(801) 566-8903

The Gateway
Specialty shops, restaurants, and entertainment
90 South 400 West
(801) 456-0000

Trolley Square
Shops, dining, and entertainment marketplace
Corner of 600 South and 700 East
(801) 521-9877

▶ VISITOR INFORMATION

Salt Lake City Convention and Visitors Bureau
90 S. West Temple St.
Salt Lake City, UT 84101
(801) 534-4900 or (800) 541-4955
www.visitsaltlake.com

▶ DIVERSION

Swoosh! Site of the 2002 Olympic Winter Games, Utah Olympic Park is located 28 miles east of Salt Lake City on I-80, off exit 145. Tours include competition sites plus an opportunity to see future Olympians in training. You can even ride a bobsled at 70 mph. (435) 658-4200

SAN ANTONIO, Texas

Entrance to the Spanish Governor's Palace

Although it has earned a place among the top 10 largest cities in the country, San Antonio retains a laidback atmosphere amid the singular charms of its Spanish colonial past. A nine-mile walking and biking path connects the mission churches preserved along the Mission National Historic District. Shops, hotels, and restaurants line three miles of riverwalk along the San Antonio River. Tour boats ply the water here, too. First and foremost, the city will always be known for the Alamo, the most enduring symbol of Texas's independent frame of mind. *Tax: 16.75% hotel, 8.125% sales. For local weather, call (830) 606-3617 or (830) 609-2029.*

DON'T MISS DRIVE

Relive history along the Mission Trail. Pick up a map and start at the visitor center for the San Antonio Missions National Historical Park, 6701 San Jose Dr. (210) 932-1001

SELECTED ATTRACTIONS

The Alamo
Site of Texan holdout in 1836
300 Alamo Plaza
(210) 225-1391

Buckhorn Saloon and Museum
Texas history artifacts
318 E. Houston St.
(210) 247-4000

Casa Navarro State Historic Site
Texas history preserved in a circa-1800 house
228 S. Laredo St.
(210) 226-4801

IMAX Theatre at Rivercenter
849 E. Commerce, Rivercenter Mall
(800) 354-4629

Japanese Tea Garden
3853 N. St. Mary's St.
(210) 207-7275

King William Historic District
Shopping and entertainment district
King William St. and surrounding area
(210) 227-8786

Majestic Theater
Historic vaudeville movie palace and home of the San Antonio Symphony
224 E. Houston
(210) 226-3333

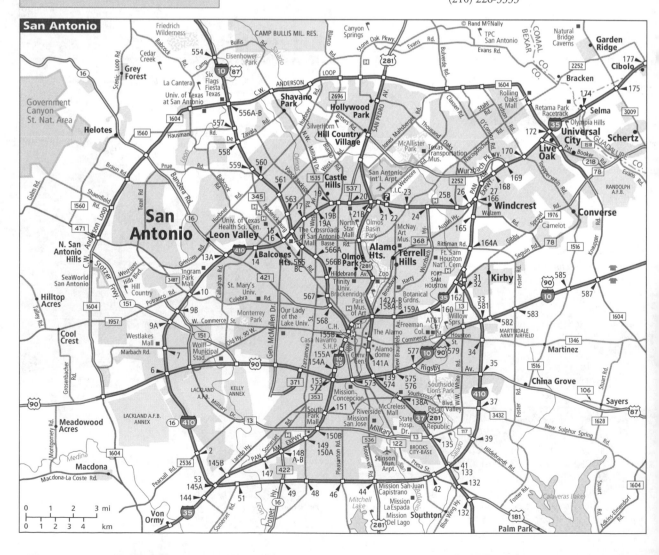

McNay Art Museum
6000 N. New Braunfels St.
(210) 824-5368

Natural Bridge Wildlife Ranch
26515 Natural Bridge Caverns Rd.
(830) 438-7400

San Antonio Botanical Gardens
555 Funston Pl.
(210) 207-3250

San Antonio Missions National Historic Park
2202 Roosevelt Ave.
(210) 534-8833

San Antonio Museum of Art
200 W. Jones Ave.
(210) 978-8100

San Antonio Zoo
3903 N. St. Mary's St.
(210) 734-7184

SeaWorld San Antonio
10500 SeaWorld Dr.
(800) 700-7786

Six Flags Fiesta Texas
15 miles west off I-10
(210) 697-5050

Spanish Governor's Palace
105 Plaza de Armas, behind City Hall
(210) 224-0601

Tower of the Americas
Panoramic views and restaurant
600 HemisFair Park
(210) 223-3101

UTSA's Institute of Texan Cultures
Texas history and culture
801 S. Bowie St. at HemisFair Park
(210) 458-2330

Witte Museum
Museum of history, science, and culture
3801 Broadway St. in Brackenridge Park
(210) 357-1900

SHOPPING

Artisans Alley
Handcrafted pottery and folk art
555 W. Bitters Rd.
(210) 494-3226

El Mercado—Market Square
Farmers' market and specialty shops
514 W. Commerce St.
(210) 207-8600

La Villita
Arts and crafts shops
S. Alamo St. at Nueva St.
(210) 207-8610

North Star Mall
Fine shops and the world's largest cowboy boots
7400 San Pedro
(210) 342-2325

River Walk
Specialty shops, restaurants, and nightlife
Downtown along the San Antonio River
(210) 227-4262

VISITOR INFORMATION

San Antonio Convention and Visitors Bureau
203 S. St. Mary's St., 2nd Floor
San Antonio, TX 78205
(210) 207-6700 or (800) 447-3372
www.visitsanantonio.com

The Alamo

DIVERSION

Mission San Juan Capistrano, established along the banks of the San Antonio River in 1731, has a bell tower still in operation and self-guided nature trails. 9101 Graf Rd. (210) 534-0749

The Ursuline Campus of the Southwest School of Art & Craft

is located within walking distance of the Riverwalk. The convent was established in 1851 and the complex expanded throughout the 1800s under the architectural direction of Francois Giraud. In 1971, it came into the hands of the Southwest School of Art & Craft, which continues to restore the buildings and grounds. The facility is now on the National Register of Historic Places. Visitors are taken aback by the elegant architecture, the serenity of the chapel with some original stained glass windows, and the gardens. Parking, tours, a restaurant, museum, and retail shop are located at 300 Augusta in San Antonio. (210) 224-1848

SAN DIEGO, California

Gaslamp Quarter National Historic District

With sunshine and mild temperatures year-round, San Diego enjoys an ideal climate few cities can match. Balboa Park—part urban wilderness, part cultural domain—houses a dozen museums and the world-famous San Diego Zoo. The city's original settlement is preserved at Old Town Park, now filled with specialty shops and restaurants. Trendy nightspots are found downtown in the Gaslamp Quarter. Animals and people cavort at Mission Bay Park on the north side, where SeaWorld's manatees, dolphins, and other sea creatures reside. *Tax: 10.5% hotel, 7.75% sales. For local weather, call (858) 297-2107.*

▶ SELECTED ATTRACTIONS

Balboa Park
Zoo, museums, theaters, and gardens
1549 El Prado
(619) 239-0512

DON'T MISS DRIVE

Prospect Street in San Diego's La Jolla neighborhood is lined with boutiques and art galleries and offers some of the finest seaside dining around.

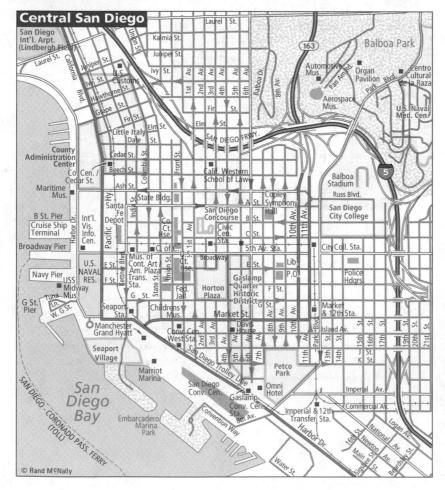

Birch Aquarium at Scripps Institute
2300 Expedition Way, La Jolla
(858) 534-3474

Cabrillo National Monument
Museum, historic lighthouse, and trails
At the end of Cabrillo Memorial Dr.
(619) 557-5450

Hotel del Coronado
Historic lodging featuring Victorian architecture and design
1500 Orange Ave., Coronado
(619) 435-6611

LEGOLAND California
Amusement park, rides, and games
1 Legoland Dr., Carlsbad
(760) 918-5346

Mission San Luis Rey de Francia
California's largest mission
4050 Mission Ave., Oceanside
(760) 757-3651

Museum of Contemporary Art San Diego
1001 Kettner Blvd.
(858) 454-3541
700 Prospect St., La Jolla
(858) 454-3541

Old Town San Diego State Historic Park
4002 Wallace St.
(619) 220-5422

Reuben H. Fleet Science Center
1875 El Prado in Balboa Park
(619) 238-1233

San Diego Air & Space Museum
2001 Pan American Plaza in Balboa Park
(619) 234-8291

San Diego Museum of Man
1350 El Prado in Balboa Park
(619) 239-2001

San Diego Zoo's Wild Animal Park
15500 San Pasqual Valley Rd., Escondido
(760) 747-8702

San Diego Zoo
2920 Zoo Dr. in Balboa Park
(619) 231-1515

SeaWorld San Diego
500 SeaWorld Dr. in Mission Bay Park
(619) 226-3900 or (800) 257-4268

▶ SHOPPING

Gaslamp Quarter National Historic District
Shops, restaurants, clubs, and theaters
Between Broadway and W. Harbor Dr. and 4th and 6th Aves.
(619) 233-4692

Seaport Village
Waterfront shops, dining, and entertainment
Kettner Blvd. and W. Harbor Dr.
(619) 235-4014

Horton Plaza
Shops, dining, and entertainment
Between Broadway and G St. and 1st and
4th Aves.
(619) 239-8180

▶ **VISITOR INFORMATION**

**San Diego Convention and
Visitors Bureau**
2215 India St.
San Diego, CA 92101
(619) 232-3101
www.sandiego.org

International Visitor Information Center
1040 1/3 W. Broadway
(619) 236-1212

La Jolla Visitor Information Center
7966 Herschel Ave.
(619) 236-1212

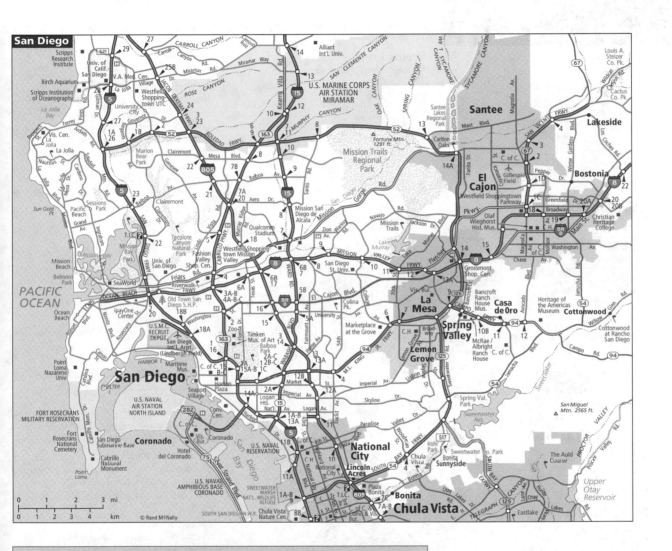

DIVERSION

Only 17 miles south of San Diego in Baja California, Mexico, Tijuana offers duty-free shopping, great food, and authentic Mexican folk art. Take I-5 or I-805 south to the border. For more on Tijuana, see page 111. For tips on border crossing, see page 177.

SAN FRANCISCO, California

Alcatraz Island, part of Golden Gate National Recreation Area

Cable cars, Chinatown, and the Golden Gate Bridge are just a few of the symbols by which the world recognizes this, the most romantic of American cities. Restaurants and souvenir shops swarm the waterfront at places like The Cannery and Fisherman's Wharf. Tours of Alcatraz Island show visitors life at the former prison, which lies within earshot of the city. For a bit of quiet time, sit and sip at the Japanese Tea Garden, one of many pleasures found within enormous Golden Gate Park. Silver dollar pancakes at the famous 70-year-old Sears Fine Foods restaurant satisfy hungry breakfast patrons. *Tax: 14% hotel, 8.75% sales. For local weather, call (831) 656-1725.*

▶ SELECTED ATTRACTIONS

Alcatraz Island
Historic federal prison, now part of a national recreation area
Ferry leaves from Pier 33 on
The Embarcadero
(415) 981-7625

Aquarium of the Bay
Embarcadero at Beach St. near Pier 39
(415) 623-5300 or (888) 732-3483

Asian Art Museum of San Francisco
200 Larkin St.
(415) 581-3500

Chinatown
Largest Chinatown in the U.S.
Bounded by Bush, Stockton, Jackson, and Kearney Sts.
(415) 982-3000

Coit Tower on Telegraph Hill
Said to be a memorial to San Francisco's firefighters
Kearny & Filbert Sts.
(415) 362-0808

Exploratorium
Hands-on science and art museum
3601 Lyon St.
(415) 561-0360

Fisherman's Wharf
Waterfront marketplace and entertainment district
Jefferson St. between Hyde and Powell Sts.

Golden Gate Bridge
Spans the entrance to San Francisco Bay on US 101
(415) 921-5858

Golden Gate National Recreation Area
Recreation and nearly 60 miles of coastline in and near San Francisco
Presidio Visitor Center
102 Montgomery & Lincoln Blvd.
(415) 561-4323

Golden Gate Park
Museums, arboretum, and Japanese garden
Bounded by the Great Highway, Lincoln Way, and Stanyan and Fulton Sts.
(415) 831-2700

Grace Cathedral
Third-largest Episcopal cathedral in the country and a re-creation of Notre Dame
1100 California St.
(415) 749-6300

Legion of Honor
European fine art museum
34th Ave. and Clement St. in Lincoln Park
(415) 750-3600

continued on page 104

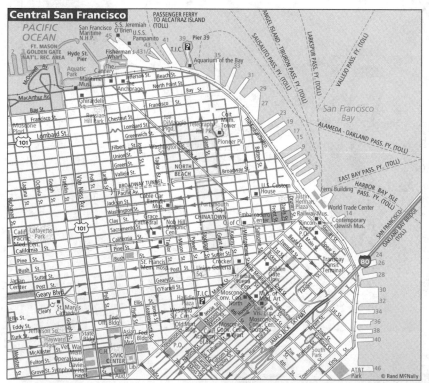

Central San Francisco

▶ DON'T MISS DRIVE

Drive the "crookedest street in the world" in San Francisco: Lombard Street between Hyde and Leavenworth Streets. It zigzags down steep Russian Hill, passing beautiful homes and affording views of Coit Tower and North Beach.

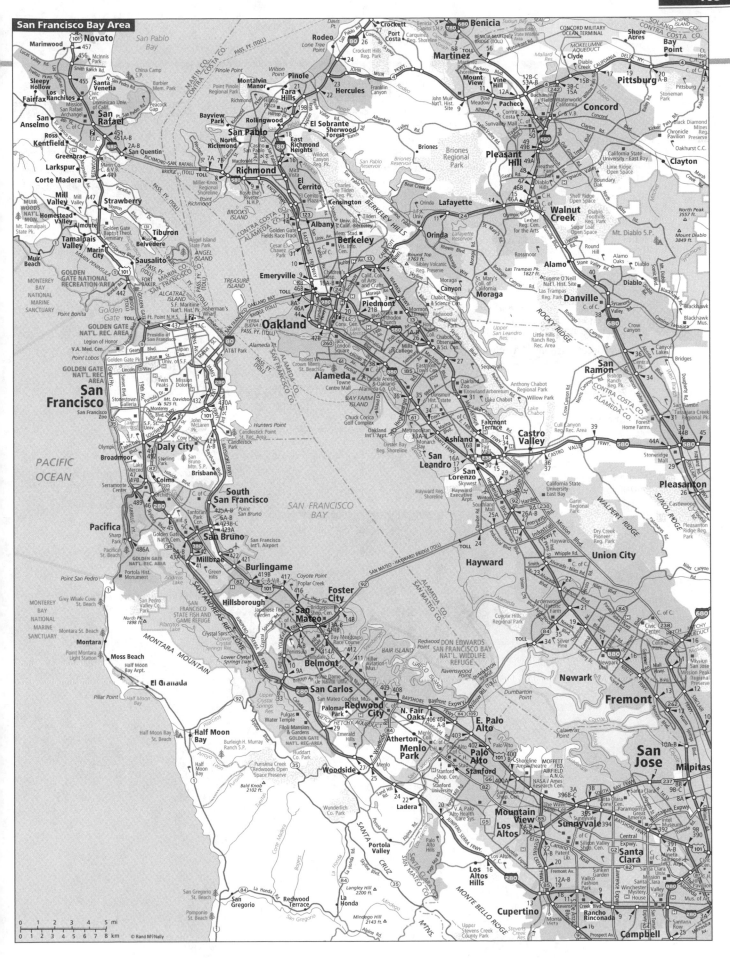

San Francisco Bay Area

San Francisco attractions continued

North Beach/Little Italy
Italian neighborhood and nightlife area
Along Columbus Ave.

Pacific Heights
Stately Victorian mansions
Jackson Street near the northwest corner of
Alta Plaza Park

San Francisco Art Institute
800 Chestnut St.
(415) 771-7020

San Francisco Cable Car Museum
1201 Mason St.
(415) 474-1887

**San Francisco Maritime National
Historical Park**
Historical ships and maritime museum
Visitors Center at Hyde and Jefferson Sts.
(415) 447-5000

San Francisco Museum of Modern Art
151 3rd St.
(415) 357-4000

San Francisco Zoo
Sloat Blvd. and 47th Ave.
(415) 753-7080

Wax Museum at Fisherman's Wharf
145 Jefferson St.
(415) 202-0400 or (800) 439-4305

Yerba Buena Center for the Arts
Visual and performing arts complex
701 Mission St.
(415) 978-2787

SHOPPING

Anchorage Square
Specialty shops, dining, and entertainment
2800 Leavenworth St. at Fisherman's Wharf
(415) 775-6000

The Cannery
Waterfront marketplace
2801 Leavenworth St.
(415) 771-3112

Crocker Galleria
Restaurants, shops, and services
50 Post St.
(415) 393-1505

Embarcadero Center
*Specialty stores, shops, restaurants, and
movie theater*
Bounded by Clay, Sacramento, Drumm, and
Battery Sts.
(415) 772-0700

Ferry Building Marketplace
Culinary-themed shops and eateries
On the Embarcadero at Market St.
(415) 983-8000

Ghirardelli Square
*Specialty stores, restaurants, landscaped
gardens, and great views of the bay*
N. Point St. just west of Fisherman's Wharf
(415) 775-5500

DIVERSION

Visit Sonoma County's coastal and historic towns, heirloom produce farms, and state parks as well as its many vineyards and wineries. Only 35 miles north of the Golden Gate Bridge on US 101. (800) 380-5392

Pier 39
*Shops, restaurants, cinema, aquarium, bay
cruises, and other attractions*
Beach St. and Embarcadero
Two blocks east of Fisherman's Wharf
(415) 705-5500

San Francisco Centre
Multi-story mall with spiral escalators
865 Market St.
(415) 495-5656

Stonestown Galleria
*Department stores, specialty shops,
and cinema*
3251 20th Ave.
(415) 564-8848

VISITOR INFORMATION

**San Francisco Convention and
Visitors Bureau**
Convention Plaza
201 3rd St., Ste. 900
San Francisco, CA 94103
(415) 974-6900
www.onlyinsanfrancisco.com

Visitor Information Center
900 Market St.
(415) 391-2000

Golden Gate Bridge

SAN JOSE, California

San Jose boomed when the computer revolution changed a thriving agricultural center into the heart of Silicon Valley. Through interactive exhibits, the Tech Museum of Innovation demonstrates how everyday lives are affected by advances in communications and information sharing. Area theme parks range from the high-tech thrills at Great America to the horticultural wonders and old-fashioned rides found at Gilroy Gardens. Another older attraction still well worth a look is the Winchester Mystery House; its nonsensical design was meant to keep evil spirits at bay. *Tax: 10% hotel, 8.25% sales. For local weather, call (831) 656-1725.*

Downtown San Jose

► SELECTED ATTRACTIONS

Children's Discovery Museum of San Jose
180 Woz Way
(408) 298-5437

Gilroy Gardens Family Theme Park
3050 Hecker Pass Hwy., Gilroy
(408) 840-7100

Great America
Theme park
3 miles north off US 101, Santa Clara
(408) 988-1776

Guadalupe River Park and Gardens
438 Coleman Ave.
(408) 298-7657

Happy Hollow Park and Zoo
Children's rides and amusements
1300 Senter Rd.
(408) 277-3000

History Park at Kelley Park
Original and replica buildings c.1890
1650 Senter Rd.
(408) 287-2290

Monopoly in the Park
Discovery Meadow, Guadalupe Park
(408) 995-6487

Peralta Adobe and Fallon House
Historic Spanish and Victorian homes
175 W. St. John St.
(408) 993-8300

Raging Waters
Water park
2333 S. White Rd.
(408) 238-9900

Roaring Camp Railroads
5500 Graham Hill Rd., Felton
(831) 335-4484

Rosicrucian Egyptian Museum & Planetarium
1342 Naglee Ave.
(408) 947-3636

San Jose Museum of Art
110 S. Market St.
(408) 271-6840

San Jose Museum of Quilts and Textiles
520 S. 1st St.
(408) 971-0323

Tech Museum of Innovation
Technology museum and IMAX theater
201 S. Market St.
(408) 294-8324

Winchester Mystery House
525 S. Winchester Blvd.
(408) 247-2101

► SHOPPING

Great Mall
Manufacturers and retail outlets
447 Great Mall Dr., Milpitas
(408) 956-2033

Santana Row
Unique stores and specialty shops
368 Santana Row
(408) 551-4611

Westfield Oakridge Mall
Department stores and specialty shops
925 Blossom Hill Rd. at CA 85 and CA 87
(408) 578-2912

Valley Fair
Department stores and specialty shops
2855 Stevens Creek Blvd., Santa Clara
(408) 248-4450

► VISITOR INFORMATION

San Jose Convention and Visitors Bureau
408 Almaden Blvd.
San Jose, CA 95110
(408) 295-9600 or (800) 726-5673
www.sanjose.org

► DON'T MISS DRIVE

Proceed west on Heading St. to see the full diversity of the city. Take in varied architecture, from industrial nouveau to traditional estate-style homes. The drive also passes elaborate rose gardens and is a good way to enjoy fall foliage.

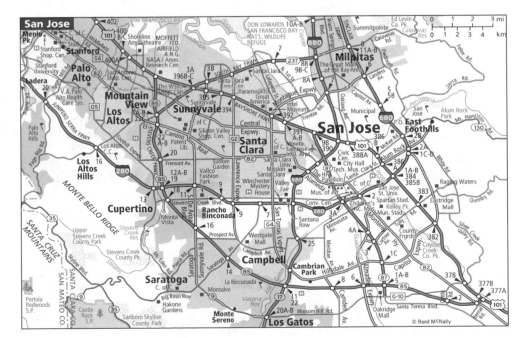

SANTA FE, New Mexico

Artists' colony, state capital, and repository of Spanish and Native American culture, Santa Fe attracts both art and history buffs. Adobe architecture abounds; it's the signature style of public buildings including the state capitol. The four facilities of the Museum of New Mexico include the Palace of the Governors, which dates from 1610, and the New Mexico Museum of Art, where works by American painters and sculptors are displayed. More art can be found at the Georgia O'Keeffe Museum and at the many galleries and studios of the working artists living along Canyon Road. *Tax: 14.938% hotel, 7.938% sales. For local weather, call (505) 988-5151.*

El Rancho de las Golondrinas

DIVERSION

Steep, narrow canyons and acres of backcountry form a dramatic backdrop at Bandelier National Monument. Just 40 miles north of Santa Fe, via US 84 to NM 502 and then NM 4, Bandelier provides spectacular views, especially of the ancestral dwellings of the Anasazi people. (505) 672-3861

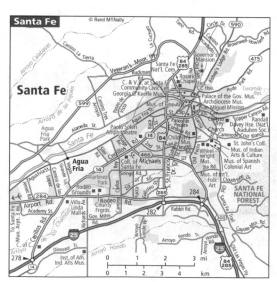

▶ SELECTED ATTRACTIONS

Canyon Road
Gallery district
Canyon Rd. between Paseo de Peralta and Camino Cabra

Cathedral Basilica of St. Francis of Assisi
213 Cathedral Pl.
(505) 982-5619

Chapel of Our Lady of Guadalupe
Oldest U.S. shrine to patron saint of Mexico
Agua Fria St.
(505) 988-2027

Chapel of San Miguel
Oldest active U.S. church
401 Old Santa Fe Trail
(505) 983-3974

El Rancho de las Golondrinas
Spanish Colonial living history museum
334 Los Pinos Rd.
(505) 471-2261

Georgia O'Keeffe Museum
217 Johnson St.
(505) 946-1000

Institute of American Indian Arts Museum
Contemporary Native American art
108 Cathedral Pl.
(505) 983-1777

Loretto Chapel/Miraculous Staircase
207 Old Santa Fe Trail
(505) 982-0092

Museum Hill
Includes the Museum of International Folk Art, Museum of Indian Arts and Culture, Museum of Spanish Colonial Art, and Wheelwright Museum of the American Indian
Camino Lejo off Old Santa Fe Trail
(505) 476-1203

New Mexico Museum of Art
107 W. Palace Ave.
(505) 476-5072

Palace of the Governors
Regional history museum
100 W. Palace Ave.
(505) 476-5100

Santa Fe Children's Museum
1050 Old Pecos Trail
(505) 989-8359

Santa Fe Opera
7 miles north on US 84/285
(505) 986-5955

SITE Santa Fe
Contemporary art museum
1606 Paseo de Peralta
(505) 989-1199

▶ SHOPPING

Fashion Outlets Santa Fe
Designer factory outlet shops
8380 Cerrillos Rd.
(505) 474-4000

Guadalupe Street/Historic Railyard District
Boutiques, galleries, and specialty shops
Guadalupe St. and Cerrillos Rd.
(505) 982-3373

Santa Fe Place
Department stores, upscale shops, and restaurants
4250 Cerrillos Rd.
(505) 473-4253

Santa Fe Plaza
Boutiques, galleries, and specialty shops
Bounded by Palace Ave., Washington Ave., San Francisco St., and Lincoln Ave. in the downtown area

▶ VISITOR INFORMATION

Santa Fe Convention and Visitors Bureau
Santa Fe Community Convention Center
Brant & Marcy Sts.
Santa Fe, NM 87504
(505) 955-6200 or (800) 777-2489
www.santafe.org

New Mexico Visitors Center
491 Old Santa Fe Trail
(505) 827-7336 or (800) 545-2070

SEATTLE, Washington

Bounded by Puget Sound and Lake Washington, Seattle is surrounded by four national parks and a wealth of outdoor adventures. Above the harbor, Pike Place Market entertains with its vendors of fish, flowers, and vegetables. Head to Chittenden Locks for a close-up look at salmon climbing from the ocean to the lakes above. A four-hour tour across Puget Sound to Tillicum Village includes a salmon dinner and lively stage show celebrating Native American life. High-tech wizardry gives the unique Experience Music Project—a museum where visitors can explore their inner rock stars—an energy all its own. *Tax: 15.7% hotel, 9% sales, 0.5% food and beverage. For local weather, call (206) 526-6087.*

Pike Place Market and Puget Sound

▶ SELECTED ATTRACTIONS

The Children's Museum
305 Harrison St. at Seattle Center
(206) 441-1768

Experience Music Project (EMP)
Interactive music museum
325 5th Ave. N. at Seattle Center
(206) 770-2700

Hiram M. Chittenden Locks
Canal locks, botanical garden, and fish ladder
3015 NW 54th St.
(206) 783-7059

Museum of Flight
9404 E. Marginal Way S.
(206) 764-5720

Pacific Science Center
200 2nd Ave. N. at Seattle Center
(206) 443-2001

Seattle Aquarium
1483 Alaskan Way on Pier 59
(206) 386-4300

Seattle Art Museum
1300 1st Ave.
(206) 654-3100

Seattle Monorail
Runs between downtown and Seattle Center
370 Thomas St., Ste. 200
(206) 905-2600

Seattle Underground Tours
19th-century Seattle storefronts now 10 feet below city streets
608 1st Ave.
(206) 682-4646

Space Needle
400 Broad St. in Seattle Center
(206) 905-2100

Tillicum Village
Native American village tour
Tour leaves from Pier 55
(206) 933-8600 or (800) 426-1205

Washington State Ferries
20 Terminals
(206) 464-6400

Woodland Park Zoo
N. 50th St. and Fremont Ave.
(206) 684-4800

▶ SHOPPING

Fremont Neighborhood
Artsy, one-of-a-kind shops
N. 34th St. and Fremont Ave.
(206) 632-1500

Pacific Place
Department stores and upscale boutiques
600 Pine St.
(206) 405-2655

Pike Place Market
Fresh produce and unique shops
1st Ave. and Pike St.
(206) 682-7453

continued on the next page

▶ DON'T MISS DRIVE

Take Highland Drive up steep Queen Ann Hill to see Seattle with spectacular Mount Rainier in the background. Continue west on Highland to Parsons Gardens for super views of Puget Sound and the Olympic Mountains, too.

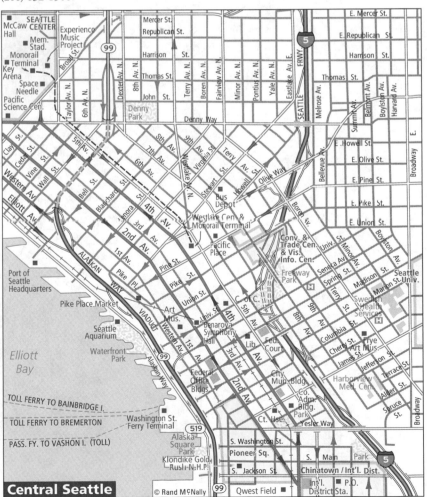

Central Seattle
© Rand McNally

Seattle shopping continued

Rainier Square
Upscale boutiques and specialty shops
5th Ave. between Union and University Sts.
(206) 628-5050

Westlake Center
Specialty stores
400 Pine St.
(206) 467-1600

▶ **VISITOR INFORMATION**

Seattle Convention and Visitors Bureau
701 Pike St., Ste. 800
Seattle, WA 98101
(206) 461-5800
www.visitseattle.org

Seattle Visitor Center
Washington State Convention and
Trade Center
7th and Pike, Main Floor
(206) 461-5888 or (866) 732-2695

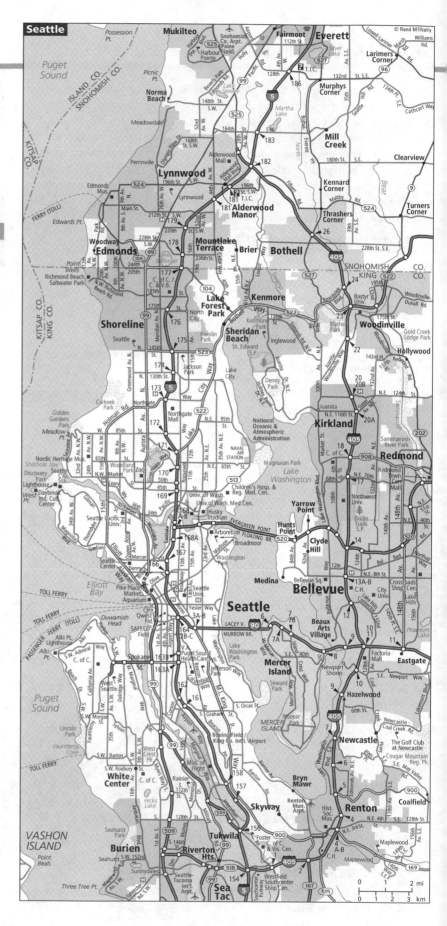

TAMPA/ST. PETERSBURG, Florida

The business, technology, and shipping center for southwest Florida, Tampa also claims its share of attractions with family appeal. Water parks such as Buccaneer Bay and Adventure Island help cool kids down. And at Busch Gardens, thrill rides overlook African jungles patrolled by elephants, lions, and tropical predators. *Tax: 12% hotel, 7% sales tax. For local weather, call (813) 645-2507.*

St. Petersburg—all sunshine and sparkling blue waters—has outgrown its image as an icon of retirement living. Miles of white-sand beaches and waterfront parks attract sunseekers and kayakers. Families enjoy attractions such as Great Explorations, a museum with hands-on science exhibits, and the Children's Art Museum, where exhibits are designed to stimulate young creativity. Works by the 20th-century surrealist Salvador Dali are on display at the eponymous museum. *Tax: 12% hotel, 7% sales. For local weather, call (813) 645-2506.*

The Florida Aquarium

▶ SELECTED ATTRACTIONS

TAMPA

Adventure Island
Water park
10001 McKinley Dr.
(888) 800-5447

Busch Gardens Tampa Bay
Amusement and wild animal park
10001 McKinley Dr.
(888) 800-5447

The Florida Aquarium
701 Channelside Dr.
(813) 273-4000

Glazer Children's Museum
1107 E. Jackson St.
(813) 277-3199

Museum of Science and Industry
4801 E. Fowler Ave.
(813) 987-6100

Tampa Bay History Center
Regional history museum
801 St. Pete Times Forum Dr.
(813) 228-0097

Tampa Museum of Art
Greek and Roman antiquities to contemporary art
600 N. Ashley Dr.
(813) 274-8130

Tampa's Lowry Park Zoo
Natural habitats, children's zoo, shows, rides
1101 W. Sligh Ave.
(813) 935-8552

University of South Florida Botanical Gardens
Pine and Alumni Dr. on USF campus
(813) 974-2329

Weeki Wachee Springs/Buccaneer Bay
Mermaid shows and water park
6131 Commercial Way, Weeki Wachee
(352) 596-2062

Ybor City Museum State Park
History of cigar-making and local culture
1818 E. 9th Ave.
(813) 247-6323

continued on the next page

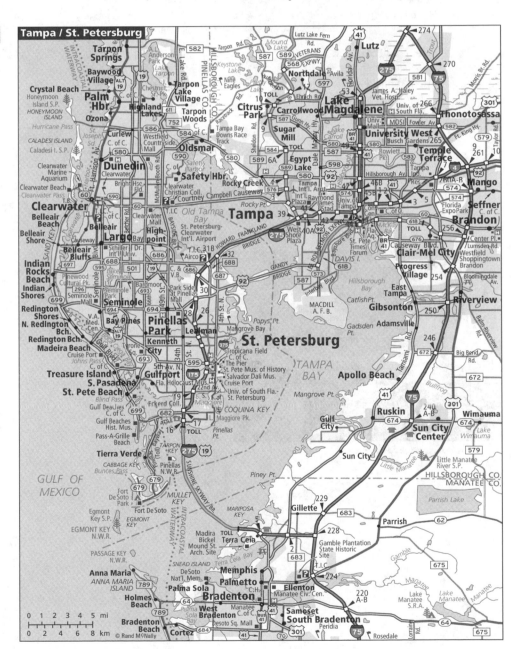

Tampa continued

► SHOPPING

TAMPA

Centro Ybor
Shopping and nightlife
1600 E. 8th Ave.
(813) 242-4660

Citrus Park
*Department stores, upscale shops,
and restaurants*
8021 Citrus Park Town Center
(813) 926-4644

Hyde Park Village
*Old-world setting of upscale shops, dining,
and theaters*
Swann and Dakota Aves.
(813) 251-3500

International Plaza and Bay Street
*Department stores, boutiques, and
outdoor restaurants*
2223 N. Westshore Blvd.
(813) 342-3790

WestShore Plaza
*Department stores, specialty shops, theaters,
and dining*
250 WestShore Pl.
(813) 286-0790

The Pier shopping area in St. Petersburg

► DON'T MISS DRIVE

In St. Petersburg, cruise down Coffee Pot Blvd. in the Granada Terrace Historic District among beautiful plazas and parkways. The drive parallels the waterfront, and the southern portion takes drivers through Granada Park.

► SELECTED ATTRACTIONS

ST. PETERSBURG

Boyd Hill Nature Preserve
1101 Country Club Way S.
(727) 893-7326

Captain Memo's Pirate Cruise
Family-friendly scenic cruise
25 Causeway Blvd., Dock 3
(727) 446-2587

Celebration Station
Go-karts, bumper boats, mini-golf, and shows
24546 US 19 North, Clearwater
(727) 791-1799

**Dunedin Fine Art Center and David L.
Mason Children's Art Museum**
1143 Michigan Blvd., Dunedin
(727) 298-3322

Florida International Museum
*Smithsonian affiliate with changing
cultural exhibits*
244 2nd Ave. N.
(727) 341-7900

Fort DeSoto Park
*Five connected islands with beaches, camping,
trails, and boat docks*
3500 Pinellas Bayway S., Tierra Verde
(727) 582-2267

**Great Explorations: The
Children's Museum**
1925 4th St. N.
(727) 821-8992

Heritage Village
Restored homes, pioneer museum
11909 125th St. N., Largo
(727) 582-2123

Museum of Fine Arts
255 Beach Dr. NE
(727) 896-2667

The Pier Aquarium
800 2nd Ave. NE
(727) 895-7437

Salvador Dali Museum
1000 3rd St. S.
(727) 823-3767

St. Petersburg Museum of History
335 2nd Ave. NE
(727) 894-1052

► SHOPPING

ST. PETERSBURG

BayWalk
*Open-air plaza with shopping, restaurants,
and nightlife*
153 2nd Ave. N.
(727) 895-9277

Beach Drive
Specialty shops, art galleries, and museums
Downtown waterfront

John's Pass Village & Boardwalk
Shops along the waterfront
150 John's Pass Boardwalk, Madeira Beach
(727) 394-0756

The Pier
Shops, dining, and entertainment
800 2nd Ave. NE
(727) 821-6443

Tyrone Square Mall
Department stores and specialty shops
6901 22nd Ave. N.
(727) 347-3889

► VISITOR INFORMATION

Tampa Bay & Company
401 E. Jackson St., Ste. 2100
Tampa, FL 33602
(813) 223-1111 or (800) 448-2672
www.visittampabay.com

Tampa Visitor Center
615 Channelside Dr., Ste 108A
(813) 223-2752

**St. Petersburg/Clearwater Area
Convention and Visitors Bureau**
13805 58th St. N., Ste. 2-200
Clearwater, FL 33760
(727) 464-7200 or (877) 352-3224
www.floridasbeach.com

Clearwater Chamber Welcome Center
3350 Gulf to Bay Blvd. (SR 60)
(727) 726-1547
www.visitclearwaterflorida.com

TIJUANA, Baja California, Mexico

Bumping against the border, Tijuana draws thousands of immigrant hopefuls from the south and hordes of American citizens from the north. Southern Californians have long enjoyed making quick excursions for shopping, dining, and partying all night at the clubs and discotheques along Avenida Revolucion. For a more in-depth take, the Centro Cultural Tijuana offers outstanding performances, an Omnimax theater, and a museum devoted to Mexican identities. Exhibits on the area's cultural and natural history are featured at the Museo de las Californias. *Tax: 10% hotel, 10% value-added sales tax is usually included in the retail price.*

Tijuana Cultural Center

▶ SELECTED ATTRACTIONS

Bullfighting Ring of Tijuana (Plaza de Toros Monumental de Tijuana)
Playas de Tijuana, Baja California
(664) 680-1808

Caliente Racetrack
Greyhound races and bingo saloon
Blvd. Agua Caliente and Tapachula 12027, Col. Hipódromo
011-52-664-633-7300*

El Trompo
Interactive museum
Libramiento de los Insurgentes S/N
Rio Tijuana 3ra Etapa
011-52-664-634-3446
www.eltrompo.org

Fun World (Mundo Divertido La Mesa)
Amusement park and children's games
Via Rapida, Poniente 15035 Fracc. San Jose
011-52-664-701-7133*

L.A. Cetto Winery
Ave. Cañón Johnson 2108, Col. Hidalgo
011-52-664-685-3031 or
011-52-664-685-1644*

Museum of the Californias (Museo de las Californias)
Missions, petroglyphs, historical exhibits
Paseo de los Heroes at Javier Mina Zona Rio
in the Tijuana Cultural Center
011-52-664-687-9600 or
011-52-664-687-9635*

Tijuana Brewery (Cerveceria Tijuana)
Blvd. Fundadores 2951 Colonia Juarez
011-52-664-638-8662 or
011-52-664-638-8663*

Tijuana Cultural Center (Centro Cultural Tijuana)
Museum, Omnimax theater, and performing arts theater
Paseo de los Heroes at Javier Mina
Zona Rio
011-52-664-687-9600*

Wax Museum (Museo de Cera)
Calle 1a 8281, Zona Centro
011-52-664-688-2478*

▶ SHOPPING

Av. Revolución
Jewelry, clothing, pottery, arts and crafts
Between 1st and 10th Sts.

Mercado de Artesanías
Handmade crafts and leather goods
Calle 1 between Ave. Negrete and Ave. Ocampo

Mercado Hidalgo
Authentic Mexican market
Av. Independencia at Av. Sánchez Taboada
(664) 684-0485

Plaza Río Tijuana
Shops, movie theaters, and restaurants
Paseo de los Héroes #96 and 98, Zona Rio
011-52-664-684-0402*

Pueblo Amigo
Restaurants, shops, and nightlife
Via Oriente # 9211, Zona Rio
011-52-664-684-2711*

Shopping is also found at these local markets:
- Centro Comercial Viva Tijuana
  Via de la Juventud Norte #8800
- Plaza Carrusel
  Blvd. Diaz Ordaz #15602, Las Brisas
- Plaza Mundo Divertido La Mesa
  Via Rapida, La Mesa

▶ VISITOR INFORMATION

Tijuana Convention and Visitors Bureau
Paseo de los Héroes No. 9365-201
Tijuana, BC, Mexico
011-52-664-684-0537 or
011-52-664-684-0538
www.tijuanaonline.org

Tijuana Tourism Board
Blvd. Agua Caliente 4558, 11th Floor
Tijuana, BC, Mexico
011-52-664-686-1103,
011-52-664-686-1345, or
(888) 775-2417 (U.S. only)
www.seetijuana.com

Mexico Tourism Board (U.S.)
(800) 446-3942
www.visitmexico.com

Baja California State's Secretariat of Tourism
Juan Ruiz de Alarcon, No. 1572 Edif. Rio
3rd Fl, Zona Rio
Tijuana, BC
(664) 682-3367
www.discoverbajacalifornia.com

Pedestrian Border Crossing International Visitor Information Center
Across the pedestrian border crossing ramp
011-52-664-607-3097 (Spanish and English spoken)

*Number listed may or may not have an English-speaking person available.

DIVERSION

Rosarito is 30 kilometers (about 18 miles) south of Tijuana on Federal Highway 10. It has one of Baja California's largest beaches and decent waves for surfing, and has been featured in many Hollywood films. Don't pass up the lobster Puerto Nuevo—the town is famous for it.

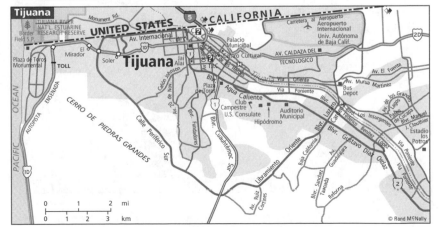

TORONTO, Ontario, Canada

Ontario Place theme park

Lying at the western edge of Lake Ontario, Canada's most international city fairly bursts with ethnic diversity. This is a city with no fewer than three Chinatowns as well as a Greektown, Little Italy, and other cultural enclaves. Many popular attractions line the lakeside. Ontario Place offers rides, attractions and live entertainment for each member of the family. For shopping, recreation, and a year-round lineup of events with a cultural flair, visitors head to Harbourfront Centre. Overlooking all is the impressive view from the observation deck of the CN Tower, the city's most familiar landmark. Its glass floor gives visitors a 1,122-foot view straight down. *Tax: 13% hotel, 5% GST, 8% PST.*

▶ SELECTED ATTRACTIONS

Art Gallery of Ontario
317 Dundas St. W.
(416) 979-6648

The Bata Shoe Museum
327 Bloor St. W.
(416) 979-7799

Canada's Wonderland
Theme park
20 miles north off ON 400 at Rutherford Rd. exit, Vaughn
(905) 832-7000

Casa Loma
Historic castle
1 Austin Terr.
(416) 923-1171

CN Tower
World's tallest free-standing structure
301 Front St. W.
(416) 868-6937

The Distillery Historic District
Arts, culture, food, and entertainment
55 Mill St.
(416) 364-1177

Harbourfront Centre
Theaters, galleries, marina, ice skating
235 Queen's Quay W.
(416) 973-4000

Hockey Hall of Fame
30 Yonge St. in Brookfield Place
(416) 360-7735

Ontario Place
Theme park
955 Lakeshore Blvd. W.
(416) 314-9900

Royal Botanical Gardens
680 Plains Road W., Burlington
(905) 527-1158

Royal Ontario Museum
Nature and history museum
100 Queen's Park
(416) 586-8000

Rogers Centre (SkyDome)
Tours of the home of Blue Jays baseball
1 Blue Jays Way
(416) 341-2770

Toronto Zoo
Meadowvale Rd. off ON 401, Scarborough
(416) 392-5929

▶ SHOPPING

Toronto Antiques on King
Antiques and collectibles
276 King St. W.
(416) 345-9941

Queen's Quay Terminal
Specialty shops on the waterfront
207 Queen's Quay W.
(416) 203-0510

St. Lawrence Market
Fresh produce and specialty foods
Front and Jarvis Sts.
(416) 392-7120

Toronto Eaton Centre
Department stores and specialty shops
220 Yonge St.
(416) 598-8560

▶ VISITOR INFORMATION

Toronto Convention & Visitors Association
207 Queen's Quay W.
Toronto, ON M5J 1A7 Canada
(416) 203-2600 or (800) 499-2514
www.torontotourism.com

DON'T MISS DRIVE

Bloor Street W. at the southern edge of Yorkville is known as the "Mink Mile" because it is home to designer boutiques such as Tiffany, Chanel, Hermes, and Giorgio Armani.

Toronto

LAKE ONTARIO

© Rand McNally

0 1 2 3 mi
0 1 2 3 4 km

TUCSON, Arizona

Surrounded by five mountain ranges and the cactus-speckled expanse of the upper Sonoran Desert, Arizona's second-largest metropolis combines resort community living with college-town amenities. The Flandrau Science Center has interactive exhibits and a large collection of gems and minerals. For a first-hand look at the wonders of the surrounding landscape, the Arizona-Sonora Desert Museum combines features of a zoo, natural history museum, and botanical garden. South of the city, Mission San Xavier del Bac is beautiful. *Tax: 12.05% hotel, 6.1% state sales, 2% city sales. For local weather, call (520) 670-6526.*

Mural in historic downtown Tucson

► SELECTED ATTRACTIONS

Arizona-Sonora Desert Museum
Zoo, natural history museum, and botanical garden
2021 N. Kinney Rd.
(520) 883-1380

Center for Creative Photography at the University of Arizona
1030 N. Olive Rd.
(520) 621-7968

Colossal Cave Mountain Park
Cave, ranch, and museum
20 miles east off I-10 on Old Spanish Trail, Vail
(520) 647-7275

Flandrau: The University of Arizona Science Center
1601 E. University Blvd.
(520) 621-7827

International Wildlife Museum
Taxidermy exhibits
4800 W. Gates Pass Rd.
(520) 629-0100

Kartchner Caverns State Park
9 miles south of I-10, exit 302 off State Hwy. 90, Benson
(520) 586-4100 or (520) 586-2283

Mission San Xavier del Bac
"White Dove of the Desert"
1950 W. San Xavier Rd.
(520) 294-2624

Old Tucson Studios
Movie studio and Old West replica town
201 S. Kinney Rd.
(520) 883-0100

Pima Air and Space Museum
6000 E. Valencia Rd.
(520) 574-0462

Sabino Canyon Tours
5900 N. Sabino Canyon Rd.
Coronado National Forest
(520) 749-2327

Saguaro National Park
3693 S. Old Spanish Trail
(520) 733-5153

Tucson Botanical Gardens
2150 N. Alvernon Way
(520) 326-9686

► SHOPPING

Foothills Mall
Outlet stores and cinemas
7401 N. La Cholla Blvd.
(520) 219-0650

4th Avenue Shopping District
Antiques, galleries, and unique shops
4th Ave. near E. University Blvd.
(520) 624-5004

La Encantada
Upscale stores and restaurants
2905 E. Skyline Dr.
(520) 299-3556

Old Town Artisans
Regional and Native American art and jewelry
201 N. Court Ave.
(520) 623-6024

Park Place Mall
Department stores and specialty shops
5870 E. Broadway Blvd.
(520) 748-1222

Tucson Mall
Department stores and specialty shops
4500 N. Oracle Rd. at Wetmore Rd.
(520) 293-7330

► VISITOR INFORMATION

Metropolitan Tucson Convention and Visitors Bureau
100 S. Church Ave.
Tucson, AZ 85701
(520) 624-1817 or (800) 638-8350
www.visittucson.org

► DIVERSION

Tubac, Arizona's oldest European settlement and once the site of a Spanish *presidio*, or fort, is now a thriving arts community. Only 45 minutes south of Tucson via I-10 east to I-19, exit 34. (520) 398-0007

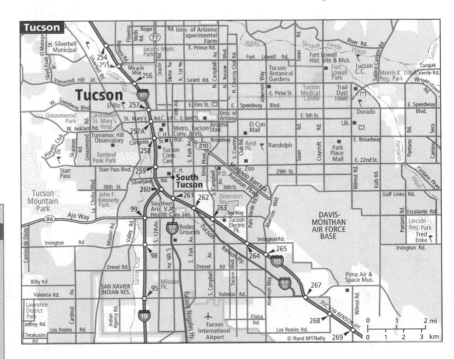

TULSA, Oklahoma

Philbrook Museum of Art

The cultural heart of the prairie, Tulsa has turned its oil wealth into fine arts museums and outstanding architecture. Enhanced gardens at the Philbrook Museum provide a lush setting for this Italianate villa and its collections of art. The art of the American West is the focus of the Gilcrease Museum. At the new home of the Oklahoma Jazz Hall of Fame, visitors recapture the days when artists such as Louis Armstrong and Dizzy Gillespie performed here. Music lovers also can thrill to classical performances by the city's two symphony orchestras.
Tax: 13.517% hotel, 8.517% sales. For local weather, call (918) 743-3311.

DON'T MISS DRIVE

For 10 miles, take Riverside Drive as it follows along the Arkansas River past flowering trees that were present before the city was built and along Zink Lake, where drivers might catch a glimpse of crew teams practicing and fishermen casting.

▶ SELECTED ATTRACTIONS

Discoveryland!
Outdoor amphitheater
19501 W. 41st St., Sand Springs
(918) 245-6552

Gilcrease Museum
Art, artifacts, and archives of the American West
1400 Gilcrease Museum Rd.
(918) 596-2700 or (888) 655-2278

Mary K. Oxley Nature Center
6700 Mohawk Blvd.
(918) 669-6644

Oklahoma Aquarium
300 Aquarium Dr., Jenks
(918) 296-3474

Oklahoma Jazz Hall of Fame
111 E. 1st St.
(918) 596-1001 or (800) 348-9336

Philbrook Museum of Art
2727 S. Rockford Rd.
(918) 749-7941 or (800) 324-7941

Sherwin Miller Museum of Jewish Art
2021 E. 71st St.
(918) 492-1818

Tulsa Air & Space Museum and Planetarium
3624 N. 74th E. Ave.
(918) 834-9900

Tulsa Zoo and Living Museum
6421 E. 36th St. N., Mohawk Park
(918) 669-6600

Will Rogers Memorial
Tribute to great roper, pundit, actor, and writer
1720 W. Will Rogers Blvd., Claremore
(918) 341-0719

Woolaroc Museum and Wildlife Preserve
Art and artifacts of the Southwest
45 miles north off US 75, Bartlesville
(918) 336-0307

▶ SHOPPING

Cherry Street District
Quaint shops in historic neighborhood
E. 15th St. between Peoria and Utica Aves.

The Farm Shopping Center
Uptown shopping in village square setting
51st St. and S. Sheridan Rd.
(918) 622-3860

Tulsa Promenade
Eclectic mix of retailers
41st and S. Yale in midtown Tulsa
(918) 627-9282

Utica Square Shopping Center
Upscale shops and restaurants
21st and S. Utica Ave.

Woodland Hills Mall
Department stores and specialty shops
71st St. and S. Memorial Dr.
(918) 250-1449

▶ VISITOR INFORMATION

Tulsa Convention and Visitors Bureau
2 W. 2nd St., Williams Tower II, Ste. 150
Tulsa, OK 74103
(918) 585-1201 or (800) 558-3311
www.visittulsa.com

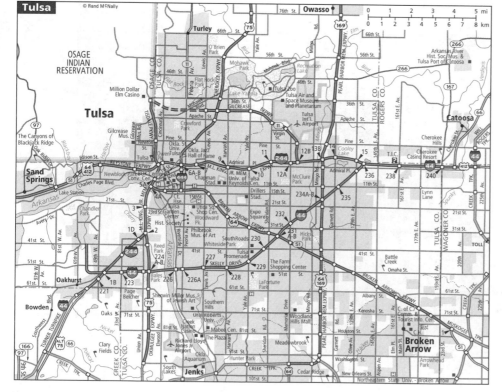

VANCOUVER, British Columbia, Canada

Tucked between ocean waters and steep mountainsides, Vancouver's natural beauty makes it the jewel of western Canada. The city's recreational heart is Stanley Park, a vast playground with formal gardens, miniature train, barnyard, athletics fields, seawall walk, and a forest wilderness easy to get lost in. Vancouver is also rich in fine cuisine, such as the seafood on offer at C Restaurant, where diners can enjoy 180-degree views of the water. Nightclubbers head to the newly trendy Yaletown neighborhood near False Creek. Ferries and water taxis make it easy to get around —this city is surrounded by water on three sides. *Tax: 16.5% hotel, 10% liquor, 5% GST, 7% PST. For local weather, call (604) 664-9010.*

Vancouver skyline

▶ SELECTED ATTRACTIONS

Bloedel Floral Conservatory
Indoor botanical garden
33rd Ave. and Cambie St. in Queen Elizabeth Park
(604) 257-8584

Chinese Cultural Centre
Exhibits and Chinatown walking tours
50 E. Pender St.
(604) 658-8850

Dr. Sun Yat-Sen Classical Chinese Garden
578 Carrall St.
(604) 662-3207

Gastown
1880s district and steam clock
Bounded by Water, Seymour, Cordova, and Columbia Sts.
(604) 683-5650

Grouse Mountain
Skiing and year-round recreation
6400 Nancy Greene Way, North Vancouver
(604) 984-0661

H. R. MacMillan Space Centre
1100 Chestnut St.
(604) 738-7827

Minter Gardens
52892 Bunker Rd., Rosedale
(604) 794-7191 or (888) 646-8377

Museum of Anthropology
6393 NW Marine Dr. at the University of British Columbia
(604) 822-5087

Stanley Park
Gardens, seawall walk, and beaches
2099 Beach Ave.
(604) 257-8400

Vancouver Aquarium
845 Avison Way in Stanley Park
(604) 659-3474

Vancouver Maritime Museum
1905 Ogden Ave. in Vanier Park
(604) 257-8300

▶ SHOPPING

Granville Island
Public market and unique shops
1661 Duranleau St.
(604) 666-5784

Metropolis at Metrotown
Department stores and specialty shops
4800 Kingsway, Burnaby
(604) 438-4700

Pacific Centre Mall
Department stores and specialty shops
910–609 Granville St.
(604) 688-7235

Robson Street
Specialty shops, restaurants, and services
Robson St. from Howe St. to Jervis St.
(604) 669-8132

▶ VISITOR INFORMATION

Greater Vancouver Convention and Visitors Bureau
200 Burrard St., Ste. 210
Vancouver, BC V6C 3L6 Canada
(604) 682-2222
www.tourismvancouver.com

▶ DIVERSION

Drive out to Whistler in the breathtaking Blackcomb Mountains for great downhill skiing. Off the slopes, visit a spa, shop, or gallery hop. Less than 100 miles north off BC 99. (604) 932-5922

▶ DON'T MISS DRIVE

Slip into the soothing waters of Harrison Hot Springs, which bubble all year long. Take Trans-Canada Hwy. 1 east to Rosedale, then BC 9 to Harrison. (604) 796-2244

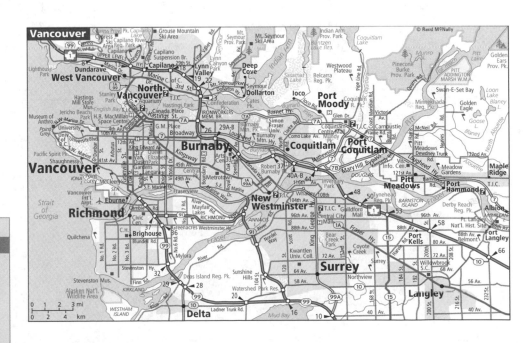

WASHINGTON, D.C.

Smithsonian Institute Building (The Castle)

The great monuments and museums of the nation's capital serve as a welcome reminder of the great American purpose: liberty and justice for all. The National Mall, the greensward stretching from the Lincoln Memorial to the Capitol, is edged by fine institutions including the National Air and Space Museum and the National Gallery of Art, as well as moving tributes to the nation's past such as the Jefferson and Vietnam Veterans memorials. Free tours of the White House can be arranged in advance through members of Congress. Increased security measures may slow down or restrict general access to some public buildings. *Tax: 14.5% hotel, 5.75% sales, 10% food and beverage. For local weather, call (703) 260-0107.*

▶ SELECTED ATTRACTIONS

Arlington National Cemetery
Arlington, VA
(703) 607-8000

Corcoran Gallery of Art
500 17th St. NW
(202) 639-1700

Franklin Delano Roosevelt Memorial
Tidal Basin West
(202) 426-6841

International Spy Museum
Exhibits on the craft, practice, history, and role of espionage
800 F St. NW
(202) 393-7798

Jefferson Memorial
Tidal Basin in E. Potomac Park
(202) 426-6841

Korean War Veterans Memorial
French Dr. SW at the Lincoln Memorial
(202) 426-6841

Library of Congress
Largest library in the world
101 Independence Ave. SE
(202) 707-5000

Lincoln Memorial
23rd St. NW and Constitution Ave.
(202) 426-6841

Mount Vernon
Home of George Washington
8 miles south of Alexandria, VA on George Washington Memorial Pkwy.
(703) 780-2000

National Air and Space Museum
6th St. and Independence Ave. SW
(202) 633-1000

National Gallery of Art
4th St. and Constitution Ave. NW
(202) 737-4215

continued on page 119

▶ DON'T MISS DRIVE

Independence Avenue and Constitution Avenue border the National Mall, with its plethora of monuments and museums. They also pass by the U.S. Capitol.

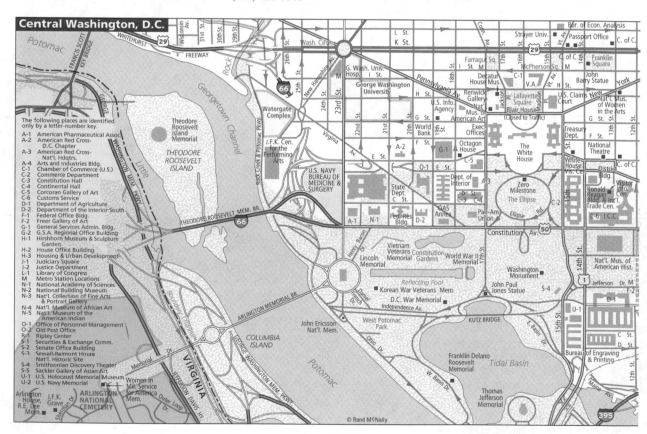

Central Washington, D.C.

The following places are identified only by a letter-number key.

A-1 American Pharmaceutical Assoc.
A-2 American Red Cross-D.C. Chapter
A-3 American Red Cross-Nat'l. Hdqtrs.
A-4 Arts and Industries Bldg.
C-1 Chamber of Commerce (U.S.)
C-2 Commerce Department
C-3 Constitution Hall
C-4 Continental Hall
C-5 Corcoran Gallery of Art
C-6 Customs Service
D-1 Department of Agriculture
D-2 Department of the Interior South
F-1 Federal Office Bldg.
F-2 Freer Gallery of Art
G-1 General Services Admin. Bldg.
G-2 G.S.A. Regional Office Building
H-1 Hirshhorn Museum & Sculpture Garden
H-2 House Office Building
H-3 Housing & Urban Development
J-1 Judiciary Square
J-2 Justice Department
L-1 Library of Congress
M Metro Station Locations
N-1 National Academy of Sciences
N-2 National Building Museum
N-3 Nat'l. Collection of Fine Arts & Portrait Gallery
N-4 Nat'l. Museum of African Art
N-5 Nat'l. Museum of the American Indian
O-1 Office of Personnel Management
O-2 Old Post Office
R-1 Ripley Center
S-1 Securities & Exchange Comm.
S-2 Senate Office Building
S-3 Sewall-Belmont House Nat'l. Historic Site
S-4 Smithsonian Discovery Theater
S-5 Sackler Gallery of Asian Art
U-1 U.S. Holocaust Memorial Museum
U-2 U.S. Navy Memorial

© Rand McNally

When in D.C., do as the tourists do—visit the monuments

Tributes to moments of American history and to those who have led the country are depicted in monuments and memorials in and around the capital. These include:

African American Civil War Memorial
Sculpture commemorating more than 208,000 African American Civil War soldiers.
1200 U St. NW
(202) 667-2667
www.afroamcivilwar.org

FDR Memorial
Multi-acre site that explores the 12 years of Franklin Delano Roosevelt's presidency.
1850 W. Basin Dr. SW
(202) 426-6841
www.nps.gov/fdrm

Jefferson Memorial
Statue of Thomas Jefferson in a rotunda encircled by passages of his writings, including the Declaration of Independence.
E. Basin Dr. SW
(202) 426-6841
www.nps.gov/thje

Korean War Veterans Memorial
Wall etched with 2,500 photographic images of military support personnel flanking a sculpture of foot soldiers.
French Dr. SW at the Lincoln Memorial
(202) 426-6841
www.nps.gov/kowa

Lincoln Memorial
19-foot marble statue of Abraham Lincoln that overlooks the Reflecting Pool, Washington Monument, and U.S. Capitol.
West Potomac Park at 23rd St. NW
(202) 426-6841
www.nps.gov/linc

National Law Enforcement Officers Memorial
Marble walls show the names of officers killed in the line of duty dating back to 1792.
Judiciary Square, E and 4th Sts. NW
(202) 737-3400
www.nleomf.com

National World War II Memorial
First national memorial dedicated to all who served during World War II.
East end of the Reflecting Pool between the Lincoln Memorial and Washington Monument
(202) 426-6841
www.nps.gov/nwwm

Theodore Roosevelt Island
Island of forest and wetlands that honors President Roosevelt's vision as an early champion of conservation (accessible by footbridge).
Off northbound lane of George Washington Memorial Parkway
(703) 289-2500
www.nps.gov/this

Vietnam Veterans Memorial
Black granite walls display the 58,260 names of Americans missing or killed in the Vietnam conflict (Frederick Hart's life-size bronze sculpture of three servicemen is adjacent to the Wall).
Constitution Ave. and Henry Bacon Dr. NW
(202) 426-6841
www.nps.gov/vive

Vietnam Women's Memorial
Glenna Goodacre's bronze statue of three servicewomen and a wounded soldier.
21st St. and Constitution Ave. NW
(202) 426-6841

Washington Monument
Obelisk dedicated in 1885 to George Washington (one of the tallest masonry structures in the world).
15th St. and Constitution Ave. NW
(202) 426-6841
www.nps.gov/wamo

DIVERSION

Drive out to 800-acre Great Falls Park, part of the George Washington Memorial Parkway. Great Falls is known for its scenic beauty. Cross the Potomac River on Arlington Memorial Bridge to connect with the parkway.
(703) 285-2965

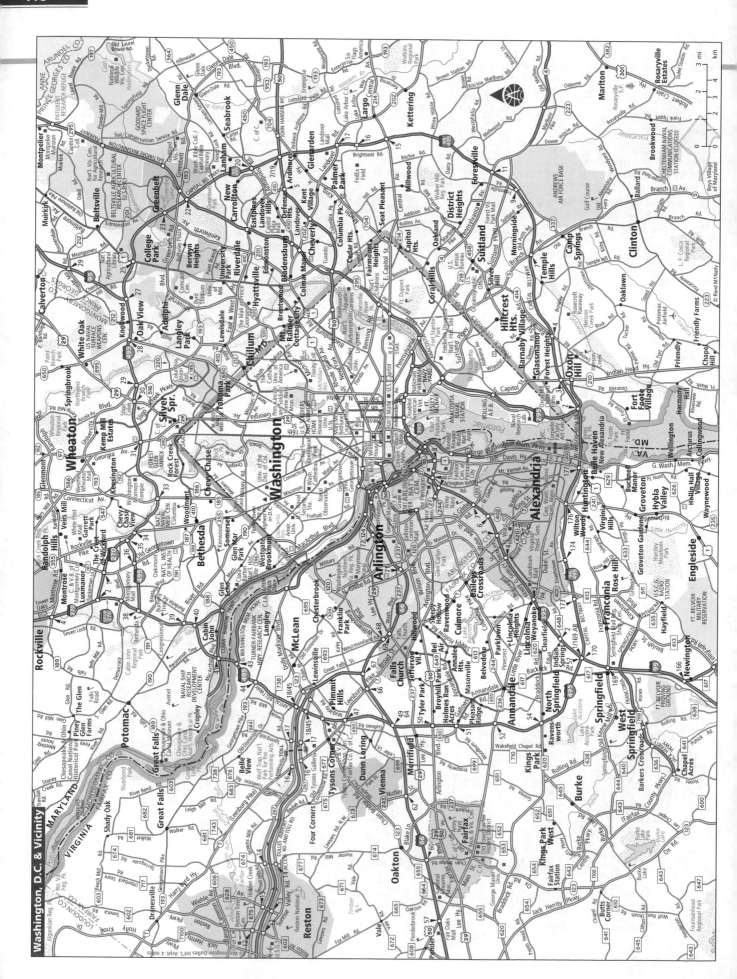

Washington, D.C. attractions continued

National Museum of the American Indian
4th St. & Independence Ave. SW
(202) 633-1000

National Museum of Natural History
10th St. and Constitution Ave. NW
(202) 633-1000

National Zoological Park
3001 Connecticut Ave. NW
(202) 633-4800

Smithsonian Institution Building
"The Castle"
1000 Jefferson Dr. SW
(202) 633-1000

United States Capitol
National Mall at 1st St. NW
(202) 225-6827

United States Holocaust Memorial Museum
100 Raoul Wallenberg Pl. SW at
Independence Ave.
(202) 488-0400

Vietnam Veterans Memorial
Constitution Ave. at Henry Bacon Dr. NW
(202) 426-6841

Washington Monument
National Mall at 15th St. NW and
Constitution Ave.
(202) 426-6841

White House
*Tours available on a limited basis for groups of
10 or more through members of Congress*
1600 Pennsylvania Ave. NW
(202) 456-7041

▶ **SHOPPING**

Fashion Centre at Pentagon City
1100 S. Hayes St., Arlington, VA
(703) 415-2400

Mazza Gallerie
Neiman Marcus and other specialty stores
5300 Wisconsin Ave. NW
(202) 966-6114

Old Post Office Pavilion
Unique shops and boutiques
1100 Pennsylvania Ave. NW
(202) 289-4224

The Shops at Georgetown Park
Specialty shops and galleries
3222 M St. NW
(202) 342-8190

Tysons Corner Center
Department stores and specialty shops
1961 Chain Bridge Rd., McLean
(703) 847-7300

▶ **VISITOR INFORMATION**

**Washington, D.C. Convention and
Tourism Corporation**
901 7th St. NW, 4th Floor
Washington, D.C. 20001
(202) 789-7000
www.washington.org

Photo Credits

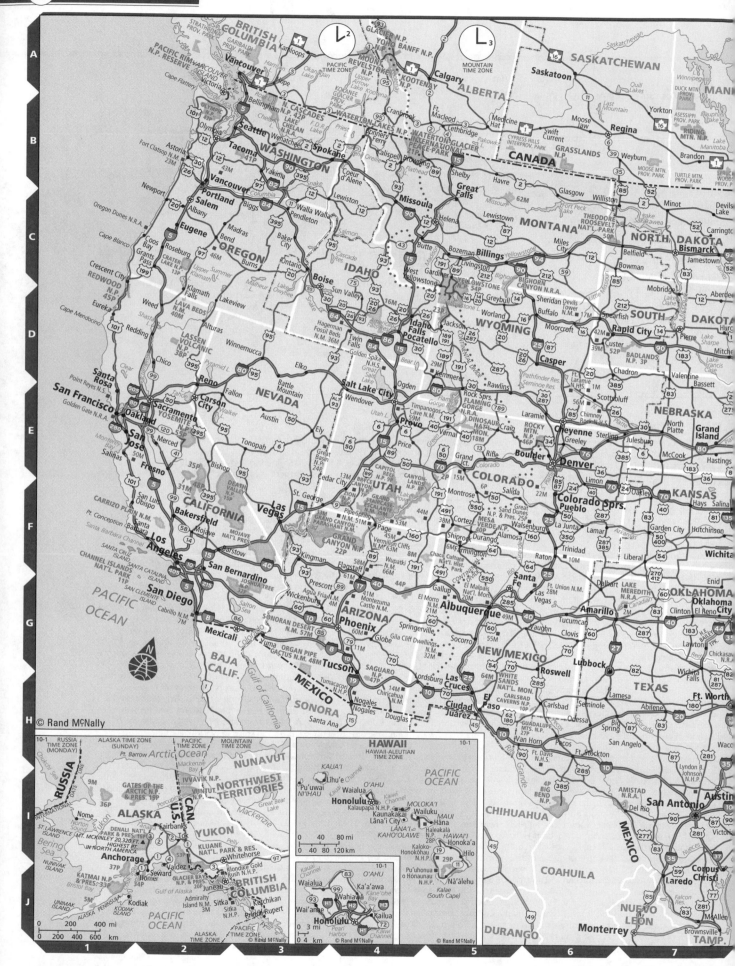

© Rand McNally

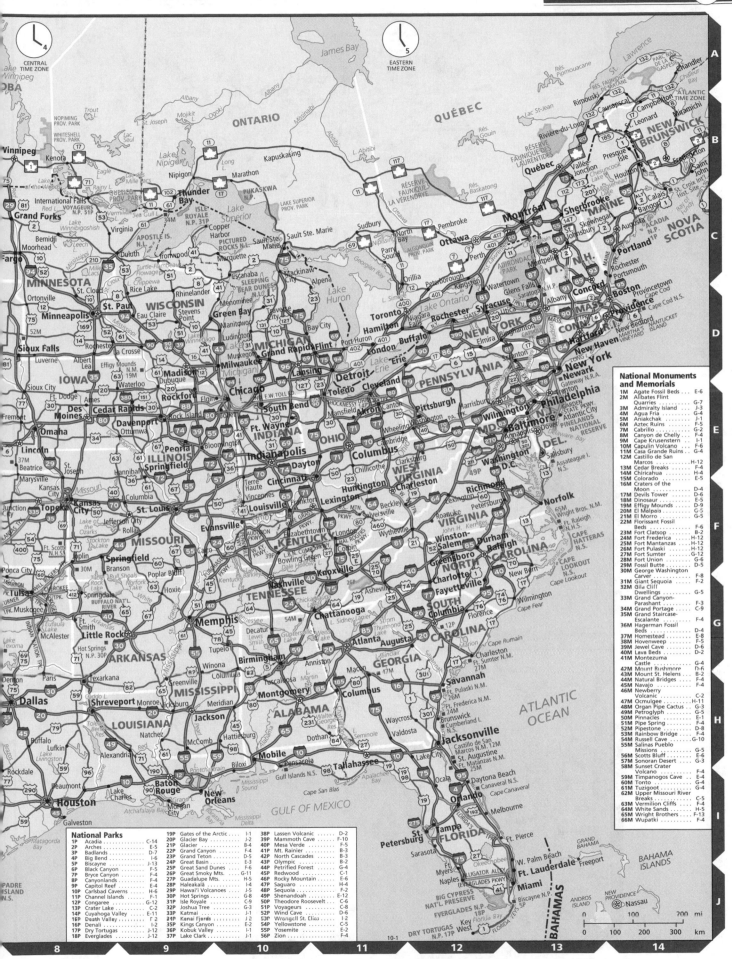

National Monuments and Memorials

1M Agate Fossil Beds . . . E-6
2M Albates Flint Quarries G-7
3M Admiralty Island . . . J-3
4M Agua Fria G-4
5M Aniakchak J-1
6M Aztec Ruins F-5
7M Cabrillo G-2
8M Canyon de Chelly . . . F-4
9M Cape Krusenstern . . . I-1
10M Capulin Volcano F-6
11M Casa Grande Ruins . . G-4
12M Castillo de San Marcos H-12
13M Cedar Breaks F-4
14M Chiricahua H-4
15M Colorado E-5
16M Craters of the Moon D-4
17M Devils Tower D-6
18M Dinosaur E-5
19M Effigy Mounds D-9
20M El Malpais G-5
21M El Morro G-5
22M Florissant Fossil Beds F-6
23M Fort Clatsop B-2
24M Fort Frederica H-12
25M Fort Matanzas H-12
26M Fort Pulaski H-12
27M Fort Sumter G-12
28M Fort Union F-6
29M Fossil Butte D-5
30M George Washington Carver F-8
31M Giant Sequoia F-2
32M Gila Cliff Dwellings G-5
33M Grand Canyon-Parashant F-3
34M Grand Portage C-9
35M Grand Staircase-Escalante F-4
36M Hagerman Fossil Beds D-4
37M Homestead E-8
38M Hovenweep F-5
39M Jewel Cave D-6
40M Lava Beds D-2
41M Montezuma Castle G-4
42M Mount Rushmore D-6
43M Mount St. Helens . . . B-2
44M Natural Bridges F-4
45M Navajo F-4
46M Newberry Volcanic C-2
47M Ocmulgee H-11
48M Organ Pipe Cactus . . G-3
49M Petroglyph G-5
50M Pinnacles F-2
51M Pipe Spring F-4
52M Pipestone D-8
53M Rainbow Bridge F-4
54M Russell Cave G-10
55M Salinas Pueblo Missions G-5
56M Scotts Bluff E-6
57M Sonoran Desert G-3
58M Sunset Crater Volcano F-4
59M Timpanogos Cave . . . E-4
60M Tonto G-4
61M Tuzigoot F-4
62M Upper Missouri River Breaks C-5
63M Vermilion Cliffs F-4
64M White Sands H-5
65M Wright Brothers F-13
66M Wupatki F-4

National Parks

1P Acadia C-14
2P Arches E-5
3P Badlands D-7
4P Big Bend I-6
5P Biscayne J-13
6P Black Canyon F-5
7P Bryce Canyon F-4
8P Canyonlands E-4
9P Capitol Reef H-6
10P Carlsbad Caverns . . . H-6
11P Channel Islands F-1
12P Congaree G-12
13P Crater Lake C-2
14P Cuyahoga Valley E-11
15P Death Valley T-2
16P Denali I-2
17P Dry Tortugas J-12
18P Everglades J-12
19P Gates of the Arctic . . I-1
20P Glacier Bay J-2
21P Glacier B-4
22P Grand Canyon F-4
23P Grand Teton D-5
24P Great Basin E-3
25P Great Sand Dunes . . . F-6
26P Great Smoky Mts. . . . G-11
27P Guadalupe Mts. H-5
28P Haleakalā I-4
29P Hawai'i Volcanoes . . . J-5
30P Hot Springs G-8
31P Isle Royale C-9
32P Joshua Tree G-3
33P Katmai J-1
34P Kenai Fjords J-2
35P Kings Canyon E-2
36P Kobuk Valley I-1
37P Lake Clark J-1
38P Lassen Volcanic D-2
39P Mammoth Cave F-10
40P Mesa Verde F-5
41P Mt. Rainier B-3
42P North Cascades B-3
43P Olympic B-2
44P Petrified Forest G-4
45P Redwood C-1
46P Rocky Mountain E-6
47P Saguaro H-4
48P Sequoia F-2
49P Shenandoah E-12
50P Theodore Roosevelt . . C-6
51P Voyageurs C-8
52P Wind Cave D-6
53P Wrangell St. Elias . . . I-2
54P Yellowstone C-5
55P Yosemite E-2
56P Zion F-4

Alabama

Population: 4,627,851
Land area: 50,744 sq. mi.
Capital: Montgomery

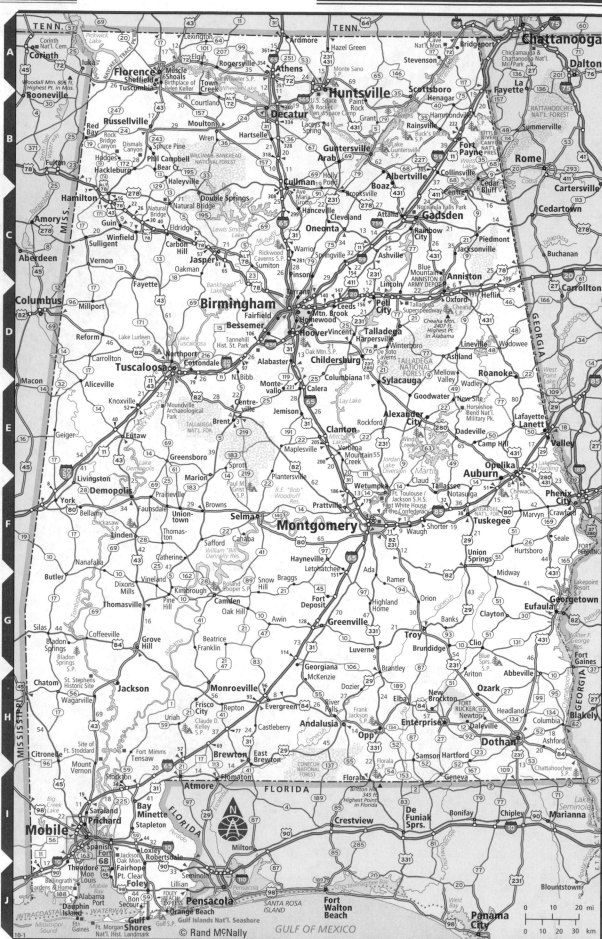

© Rand McNally

© Rand McNally

For continuation see map at right

For border crossing information, please see p. 177.

For border crossing information, please see p. 177.

Get more Arizona info at go.randmcnally.com/AZ

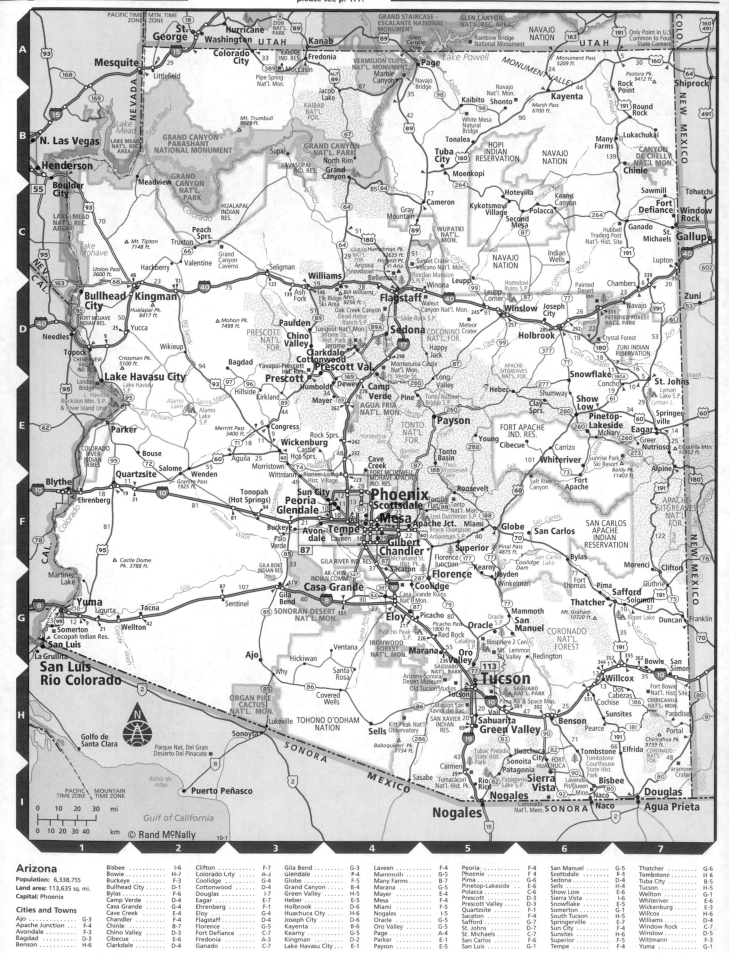

Arizona

Population: 6,338,755
Land area: 113,635 sq. mi.
Capital: Phoenix

Cities and Towns

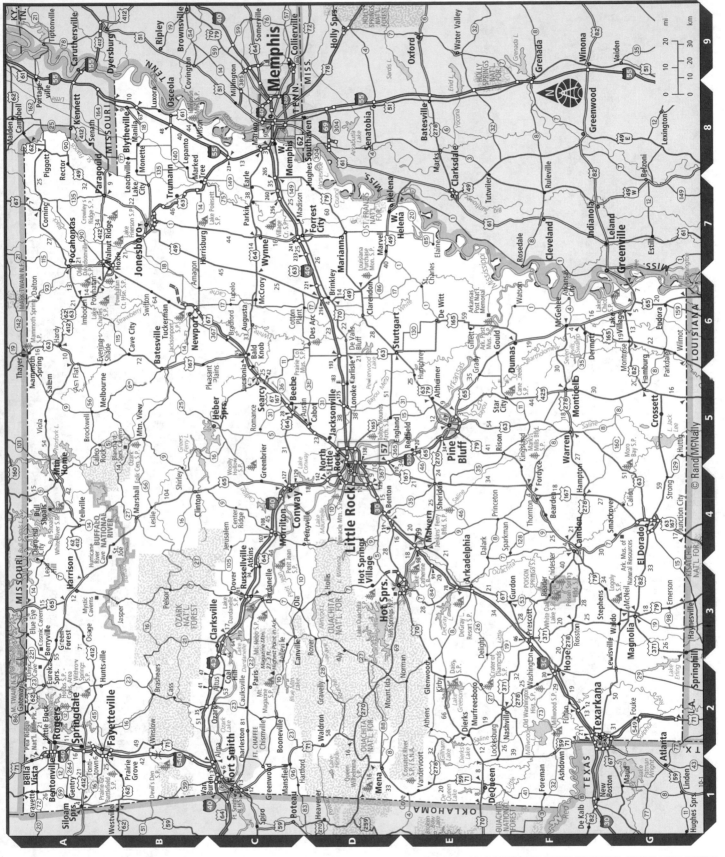

Arkansas

Population: 2,834,797
Land area: 52,068 sq. mi.
Capital: Little Rock

© Rand McNally

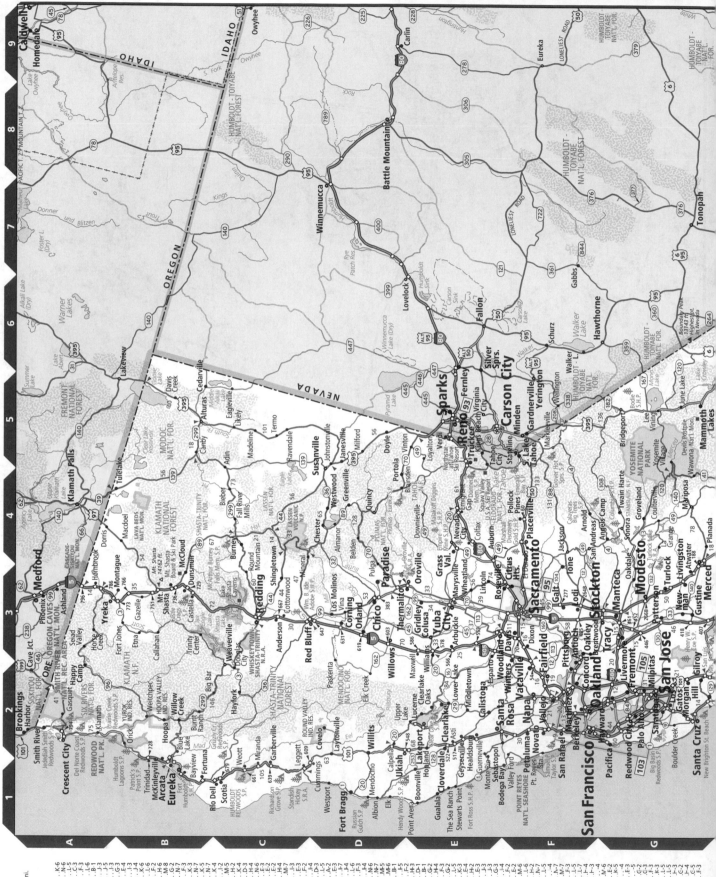

For border crossing information, please see p. 177.

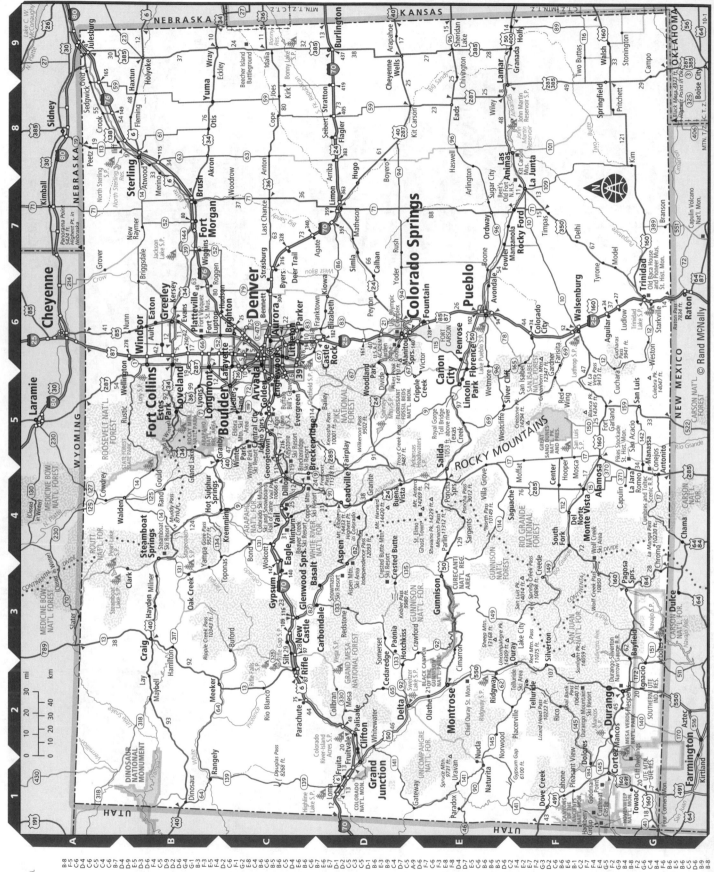

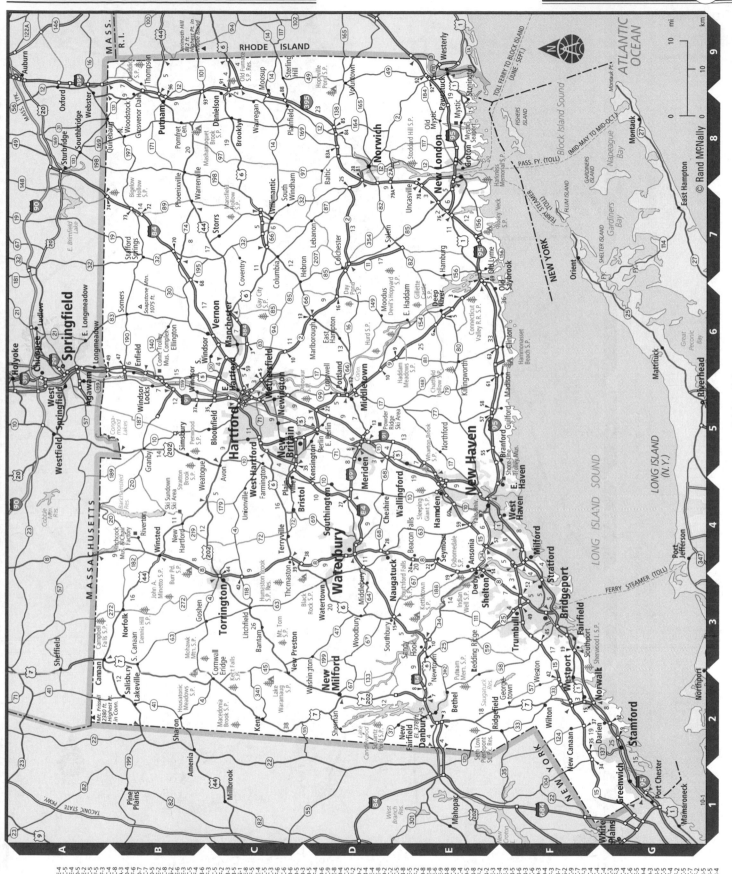

Delaware

Population: 864,764
Land area: 1,954 sq. mi.
Capital: Dover

Cities and Towns

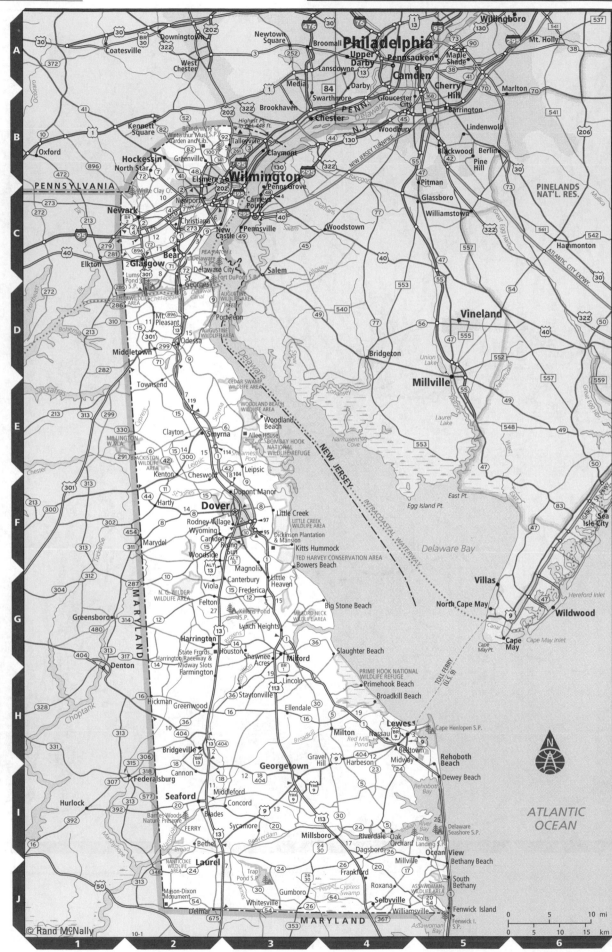

Florida

Population: 18,251,243
Land area: 53,927 sq. mi.
Capital: Tallahassee

Cities and Towns

Altamonte Sprs.	D-4
Apalachicola	J-4
Arcadia	F-4
Atlantic Beach	B-4
Avon Park	F-4
Bartow	E-4
Belle Glade	G-5
Big Pine Key	J-5
Blountstown	I-4
Boca Raton	G-6
Bonifay	I-3
Bradenton	F-3
Brandon	D-3
Brooksville	D-3
Bunnell	C-5
Bushnell	D-4
Cape Canaveral	E-5
Cape Coral	G-4
Chipley	I-3
Clearwater	E-3
Clermont	D-4
Cocoa Beach	E-5
Coral Gables	H-6
Crawfordville	B-1
Crestview	I-2
Cross City	C-2
Dade City	E-3
Dania Beach	H-6
Daytona Beach	D-5
Debary	D-4
De Funiak Springs	I-2
DeLand	D-4
Deerfield Beach	G-6
Delray Beach	G-6
Dunedin	E-3
East Naples	H-4
Edgewater	D-5
Englewood	F-3
Eustis	D-4
Fort Lauderdale	H-6
Fort Myers	G-4
Fort Myers Beach	G-4
Fort Pierce	F-6
Fort Walton Beach	I-2
Gainesville	C-3
Green Cove Sprs.	C-4
Haines City	E-4
Hallandale Beach	H-6
Hialeah	H-6
Holly Hill	C-5
Hollywood	H-6
Homestead	H-6
Hudson	E-3
Immokalee	G-4
Inverness	D-3
Jacksonville	B-4
Jacksonville Bch.	B-4
Jasper	B-3
Jensen Beach	F-6
Jupiter	F-6
Key Largo	I-6
Key West	J-4
Kissimmee	E-4
La Belle	G-4
Lady Lake	D-4
Lake Butler	B-3
Lake City	B-3
Lake Wales	E-4
Lake Worth	G-6
Lakeland	E-4
Largo	E-3
Leesburg	D-4
Lehigh Acres	G-4
Live Oak	B-3
Lutz	E-3
Macclenny	B-4
Madeira Beach	E-3
Madison	B-2
Marathon	I-5
Marco	H-4
Marianna	I-3
Mayo	B-2
Melbourne	E-5
Miami	H-6
Miami Beach	H-6
Milton	I-1
Monticello	B-2
Moore Haven	G-5
Mount Dora	D-4
Naples	H-4
New Port Richey	E-3
New Smyrna Bch.	D-5
North Palm Beach	G-6
Ocala	D-4
Okeechobee	F-5
Orlando	D-4
Ormond Beach	C-5
Palatka	C-4
Palm Bay	E-5
Palm Beach	G-6
Palmetto	F-3
Panama City	J-3
Pensacola	I-1
Perrine	H-6
Perry	B-2
Plant City	E-4
Pompano Beach	G-6
Port Charlotte	F-4
Port Orange	D-5
Port St. Joe	J-3
Port St. Lucie	F-6
Punta Gorda	G-4
Quincy	B-1
St. Augustine	C-4
St. Cloud	E-5
St. Petersburg	E-3
St. Petersburg Bch.	E-3
Sanford	D-5
Sanibel	G-4
Sarasota	F-3
Sebastian	E-5
Sebring	F-4
Starke	C-4
Stuart	F-6
Tallahassee	B-1
Tampa	E-3
Tarpon Springs	E-3
Tavares	D-4
The Villages	D-4
Titusville	D-5
Treasure Island	E-3
Trenton	C-3
Venice	F-3
Vero Beach	F-6
Warrington	I-1
Wauchula	F-4
West Palm Beach	G-6
Winter Garden	D-4
Winter Haven	E-3
Yulee	B-4
Zephyrhills	E-3

© Rand McNally

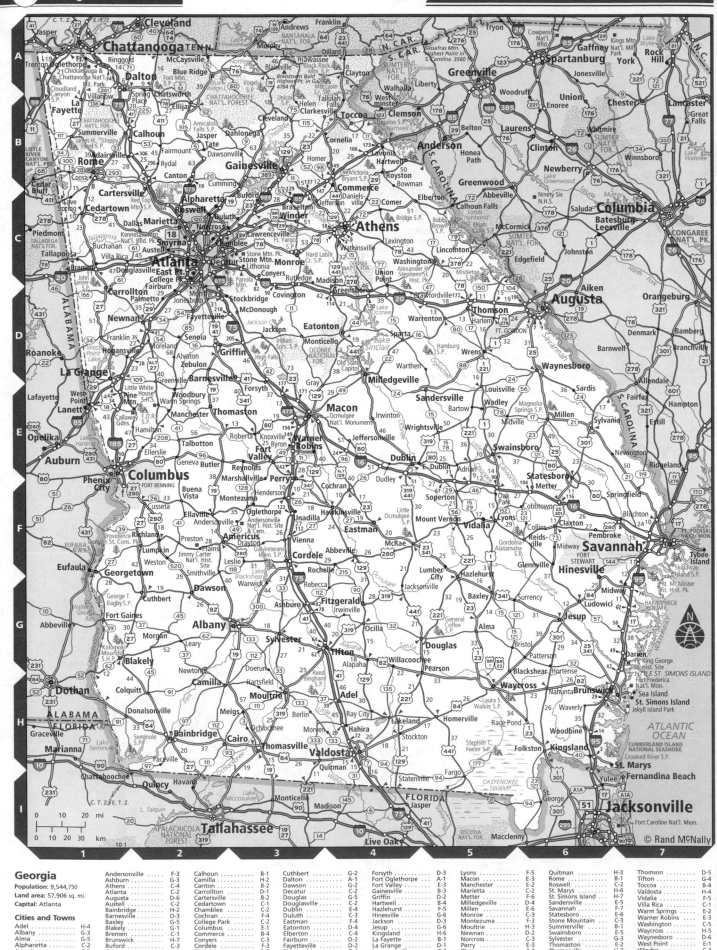

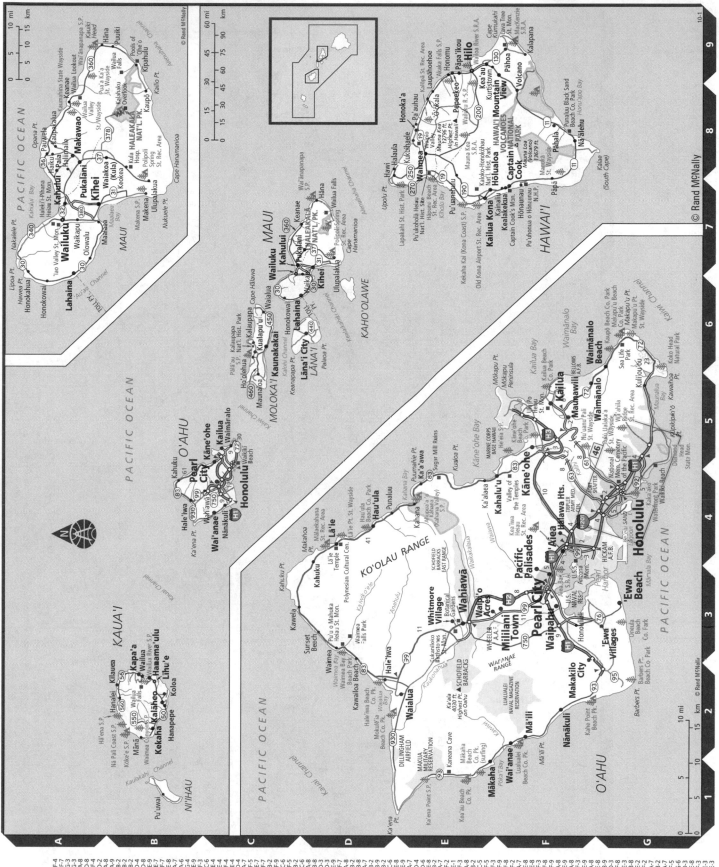

© Rand McNally

For border crossing information, please see p. 177.

Get more Idaho info at go.randmcnally.com/ID

Idaho

Population: 1,499,402
Land area: 82,747 sq. mi.
Capital: Boise

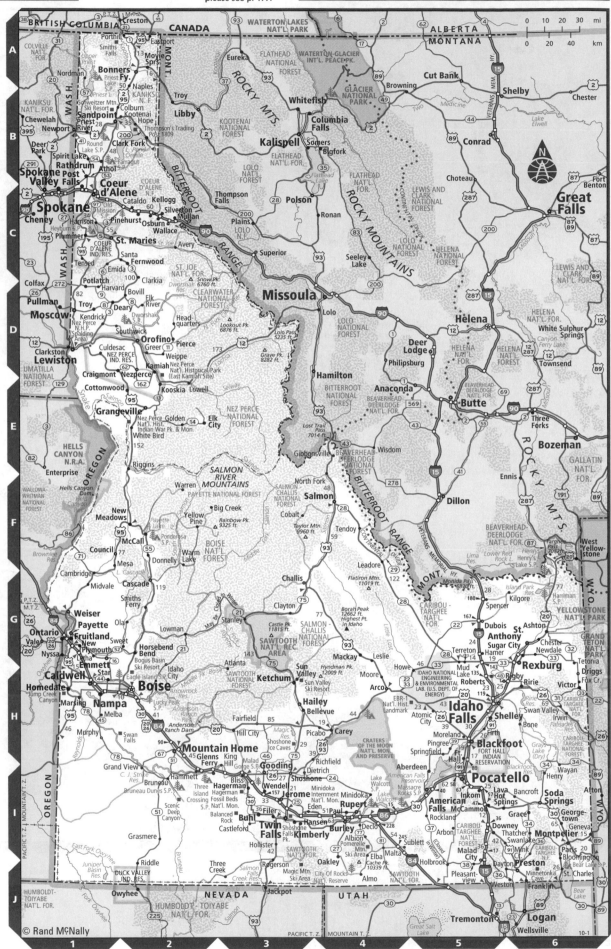

© Rand McNally

10-1

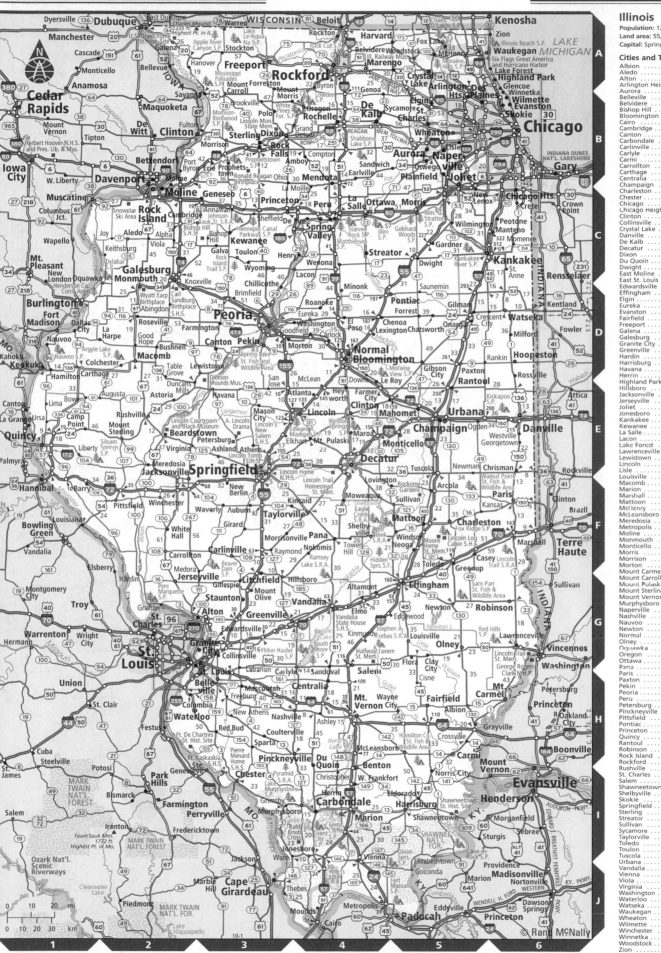

Illinois

Population: 12,852,548
Land area: 55,584 sq. mi.
Capital: Springfield

© Rand McNally

Indiana

Population: 6,345,289
Land area: 35,867 sq. mi.
Capital: Indianapolis

Cities and Towns

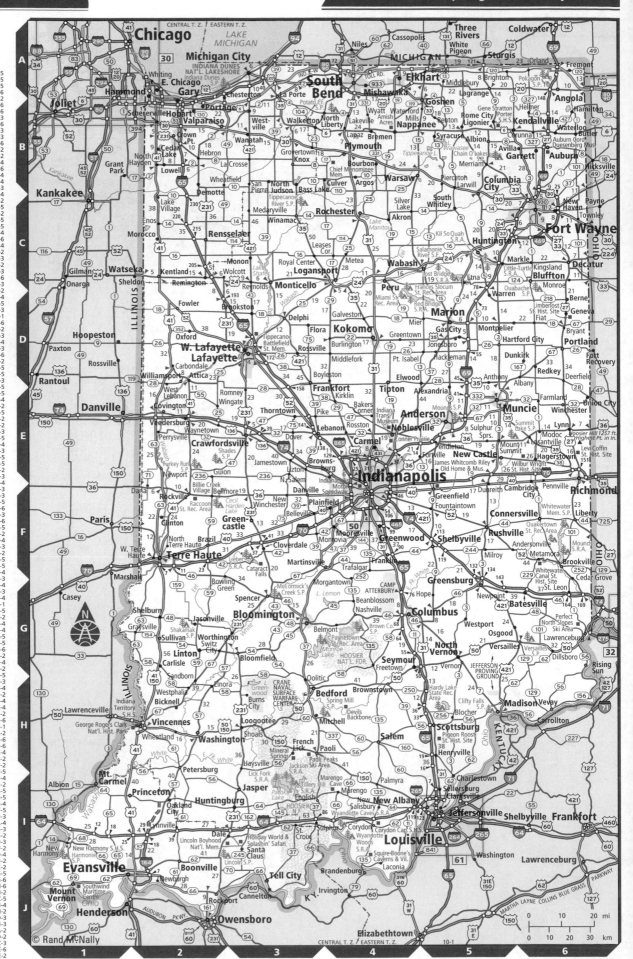

Get more Iowa info at go.randmcnally.com/IA

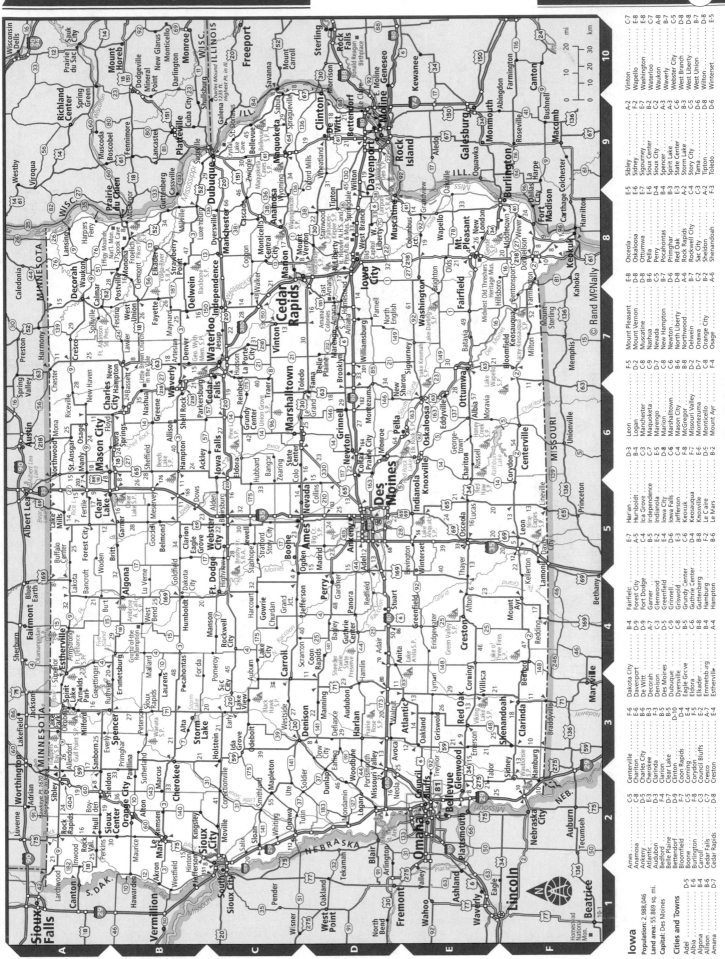

© Rand McNally

Kansas

Population: 2,775,997
Land area: 81,815 sq. mi.
Capital: Topeka

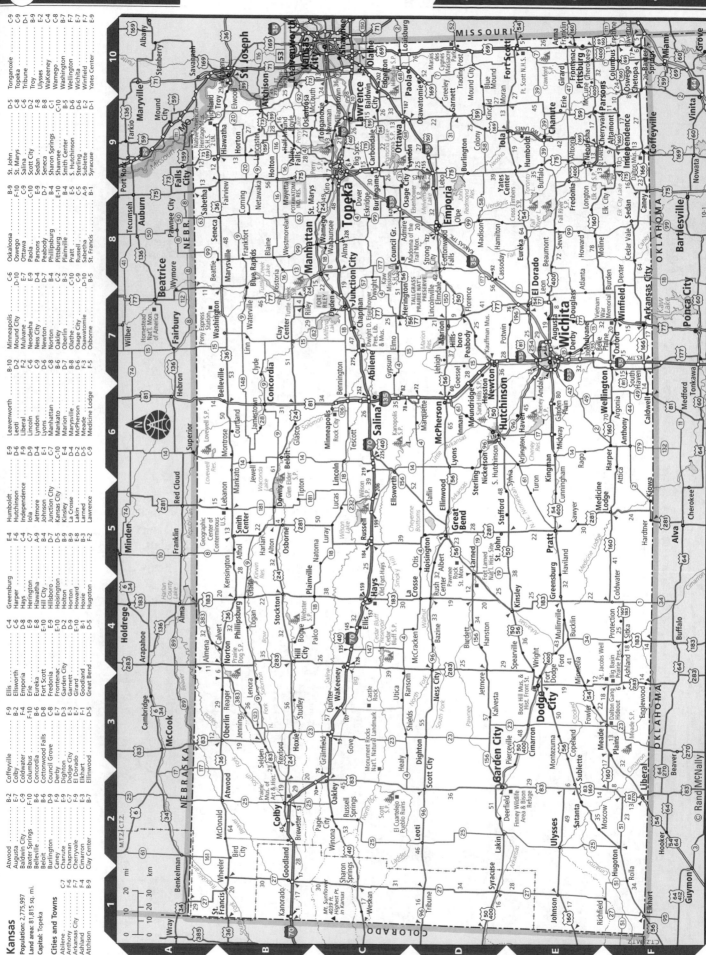

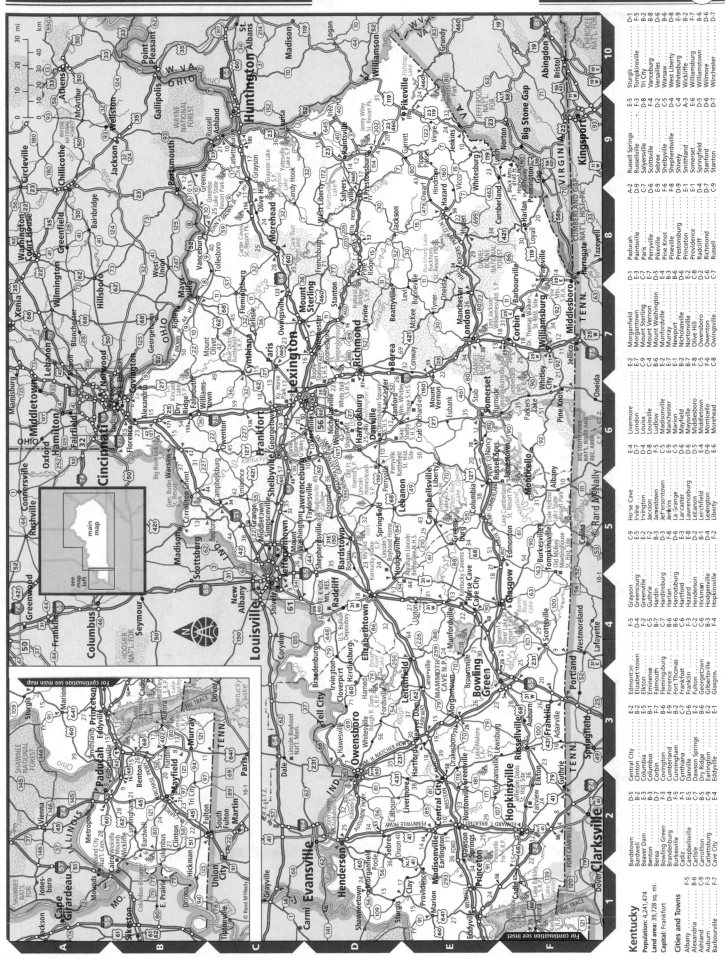

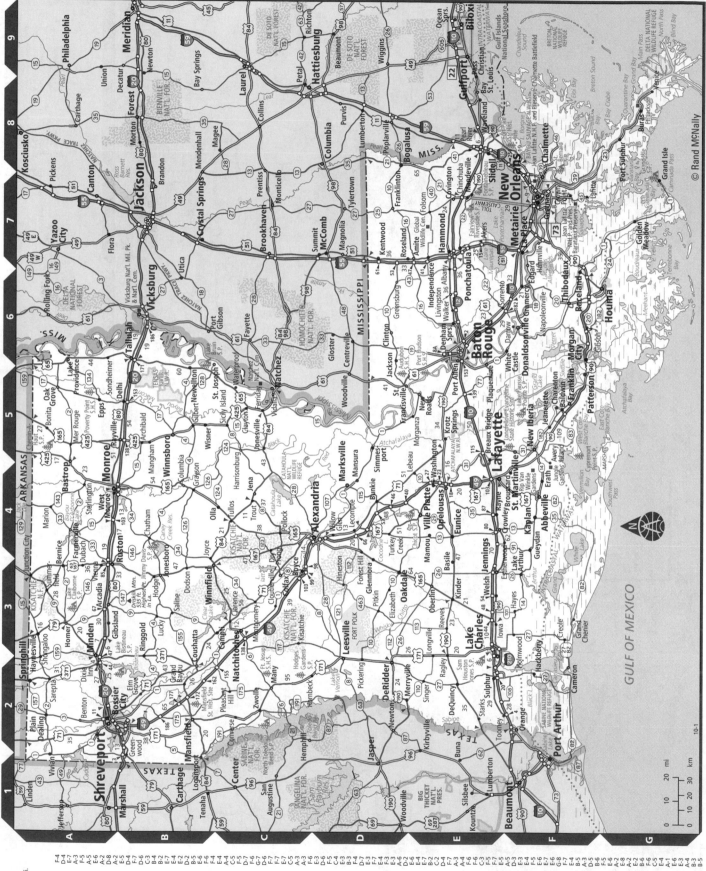

Louisiana

Population: 4,293,204
Land area: 43,562 sq. mi.
Capital: Baton Rouge

Cities and Towns

© Rand McNally

Maine
Population: 1,317,207
Land area: 30,862 sq. mi.
Capital: Augusta

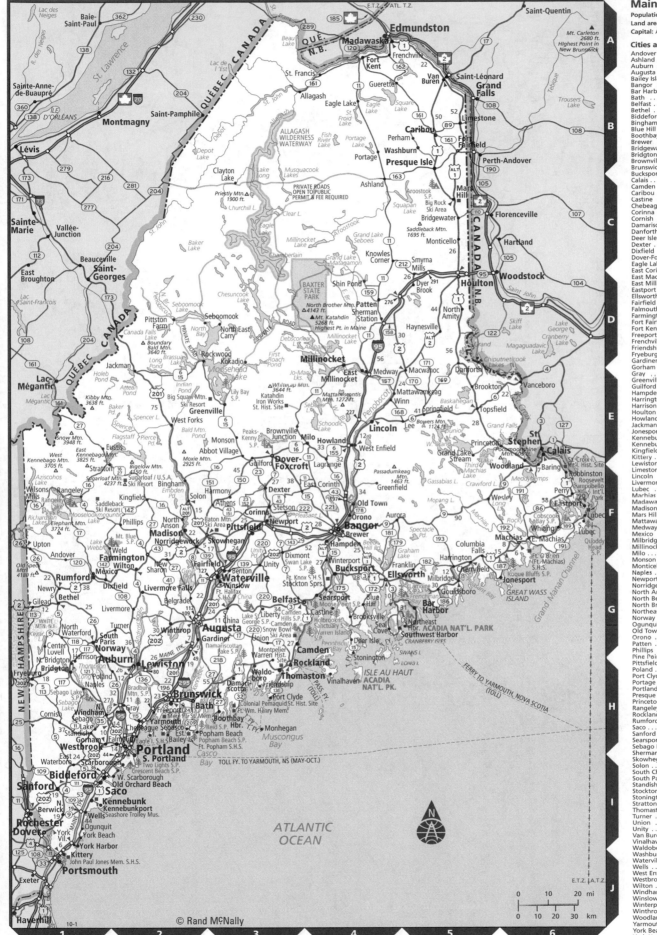

Maryland

Population: 5,618,344
Land area: 9,774 sq. mi.
Capital: Annapolis

Cities and Towns

Aberdeen	B-8
Annapolis	C-7
Baltimore	B-7
Bel Air	B-7

Bel Alton	E-6
Berlin	E-10
Bethesda	C-6
Boonsboro	B-5
Bowie	C-7
Cambridge	D-8
Centreville	C-8
Chesapeake City	B-9
Chestertown	C-7
Church Hill	C-8
Churchville	B-7

Clear Spring	A-4
Cockeysville	B-7
College Park	C-6
Cooksville	C-7
Cornersville	D-8
Corriganville	A-2
Crisfield	F-8
Crocheron	E-8
Cumberland	A-2
Darlington	B-8

Denton	A-4
Easton	B-7
Edgewood	C-6
Elkridge	A-8
Elkton	B-6
Ellicott City	D-8
Emmitsburg	A-2
Fair Hill	F-8
Fairbank	E-8
Flintstone	A-2
Frederick	A-8

Frostburg	A-2
Gaithersburg	C-6
Galena	B-8
Germantown	A-8
Grantsville	A-2
Grasonville	C-8
Hagerstown	A-5
Hampstead	F-8
Hancock	A-4
Havre de Grace	A-3
Honga	B-5

Ingleside	C-8
James	C-6
Keysers Ridge	B-8
La Plata	A-2
Laurel	A-5
Leonardtown	E-7
Level	B-8
Lexington Park	E-7
Libertytown	B-6
Lothian	D-7

Mount Airy	C-8
Nanticoke	D-8
Newburg	A-1
Oakland	B-7
Ocean City	E-9
Olney	C-6
Oxford	C-8
Pocomoke City	E-8
Point Lookout	F-7
Prince Frederick	D-7
Princess Anne	D-7

Queenstown	C-8
Reisterstown	B-6
Ridge	F-7
Riverside	E-6
Rock Hall	C-8
Rockville	C-6
Romancoke	D-7
St. Marys City	E-7
Salisbury	D-8
Scotland	F-7

Shawsville	C-8
Silesia	B-6
Silver Spring	F-7
Snow Hill	E-6
Solomons	E-7
Sudlersville	C-8
Suitland	D-7
Sunderland	E-7
Taneytown	A-6
Taylors Island	E-8
Thurmont	F-7

Tilghman	D-7
Towson	B-7
Tuscarora	C-5
Upper Marlboro	D-6
Waldorf	D-6
Wenona	B-2
Westernport	B-6
Westminster	B-6
White Plains	B-4
Williamsport	B-5
Woodsboro	C-6

District of Columbia

Population:
588,292
Land area: 61 sq. mi.

City

Washington	C-6

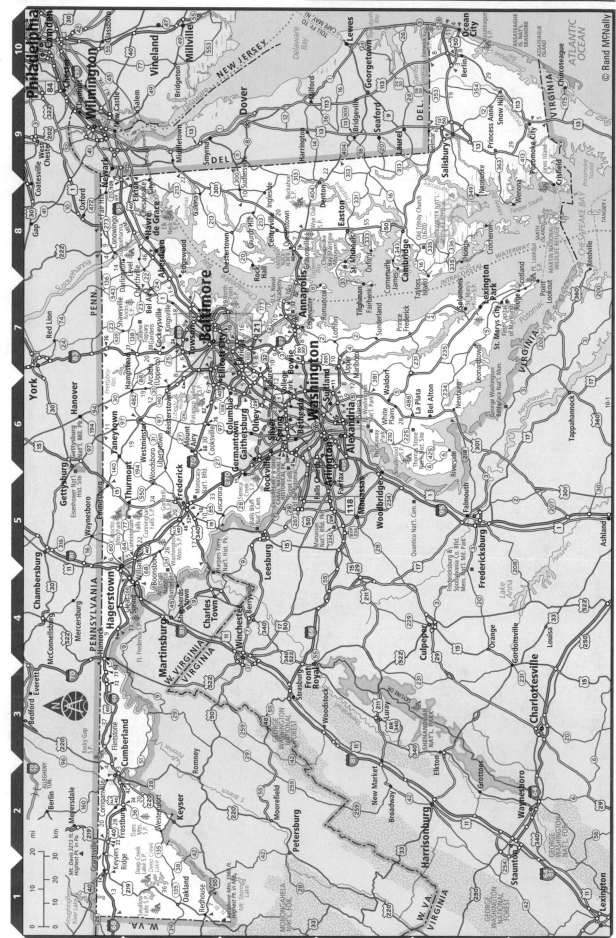

© Rand McNally

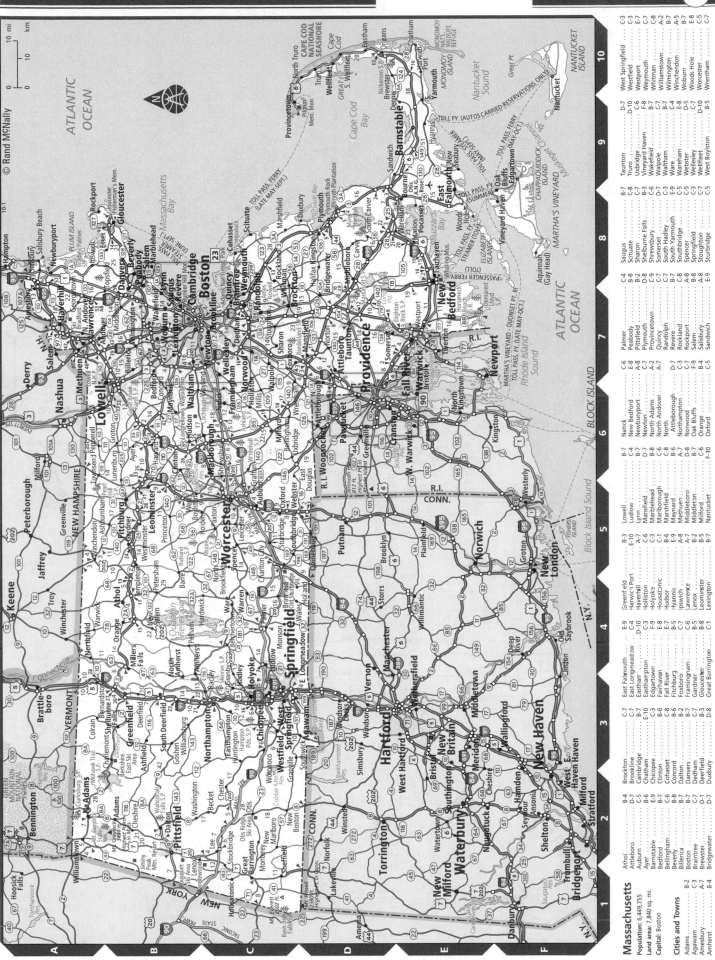

For border crossing information, please see p. 177.

Explore Michigan at go.randmcnally.com/MI

Michigan

Population: 10,071,822
Land area: 56,804 sq. mi.
Capital: Lansing

Cities and Towns

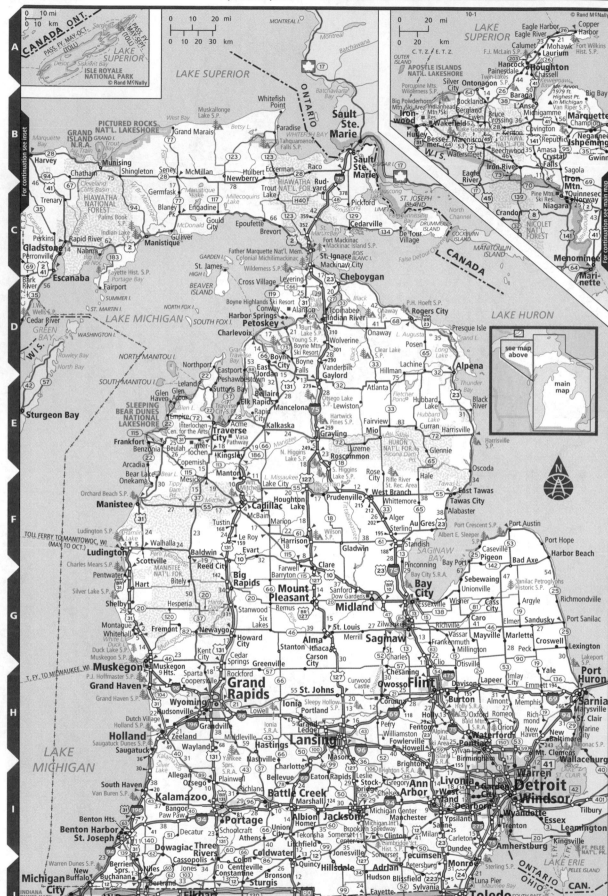

© Rand McNally

Plan a Minnesota trip at go.randmcnally.com/MN

For border crossing information, please see p. 177.

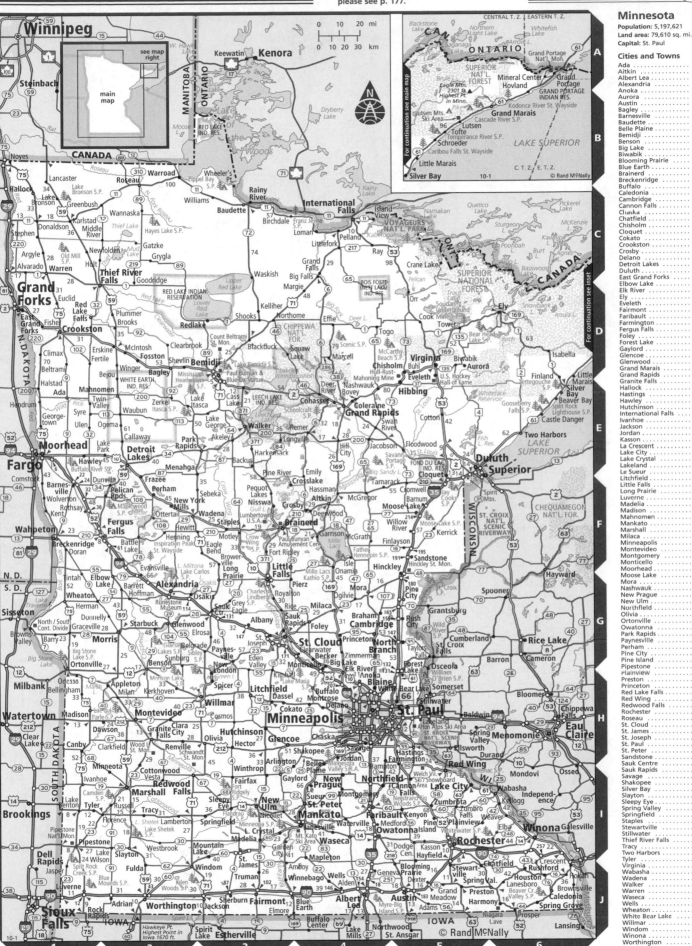

Minnesota

Population: 5,197,621
Land area: 79,610 sq. mi.
Capital: St. Paul

Cities and Towns

Mississippi

Population: 2,918,785
Land area: 46,907 sq. mi.
Capital: Jackson

Cities and Towns

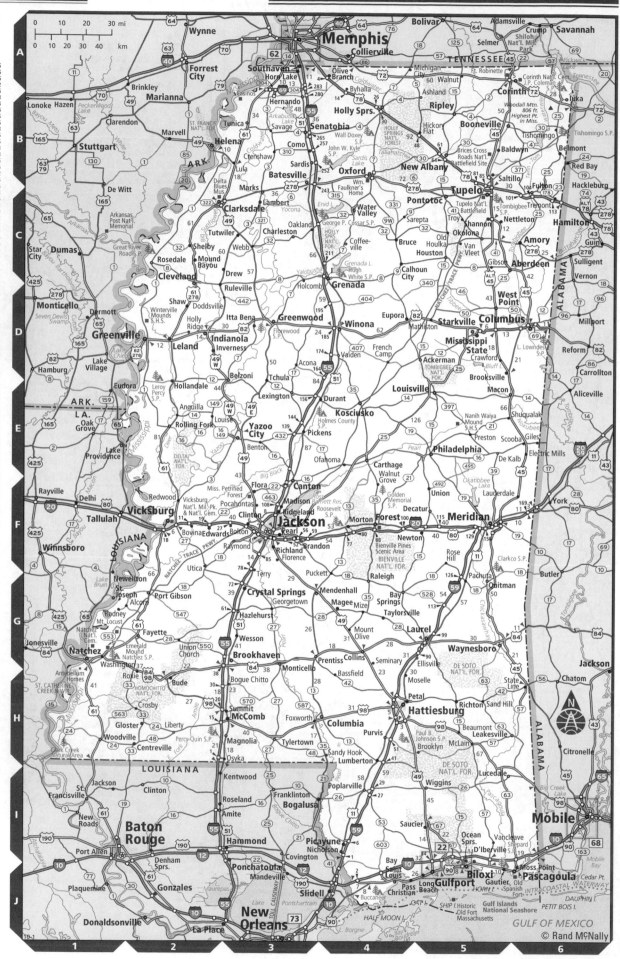

For border crossing information, please see p. 177.

Plan a Montana trip at go.randmcnally.com/MT

Montana

Population: 957,861
Land area: 145,552 sq. mi.
Capital: Helena

Cities and Towns

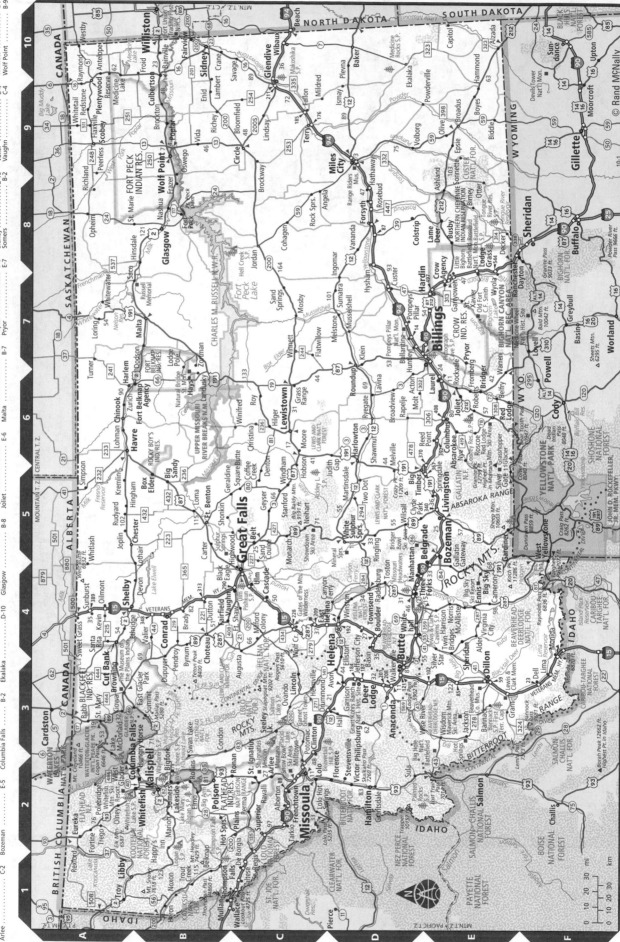

© Rand McNally

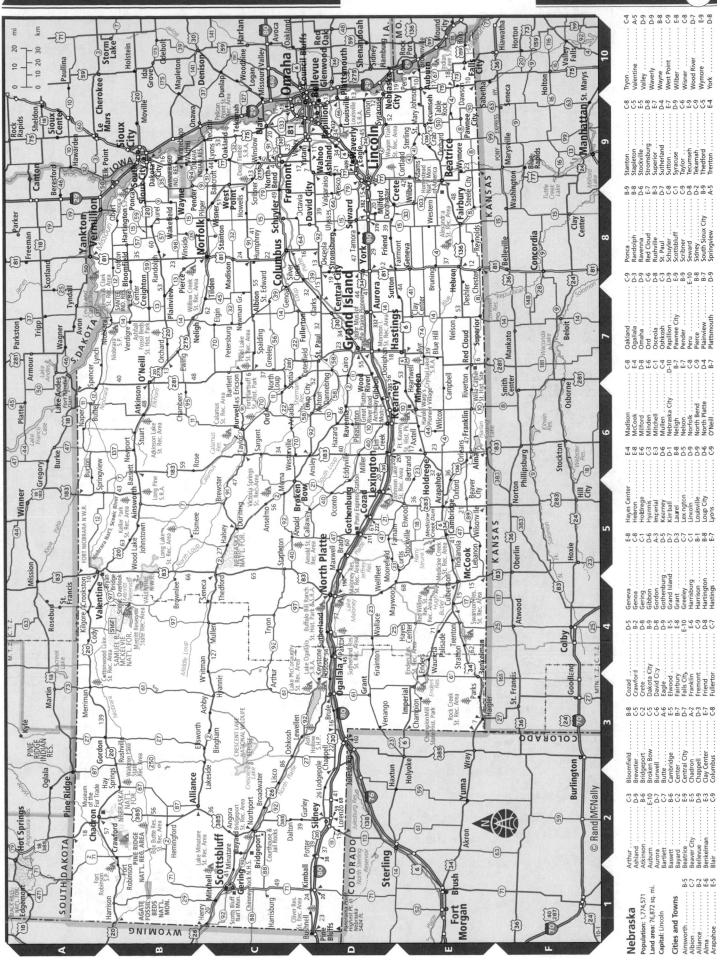

Nevada

Population: 2,565,382
Land area: 109,826 sq. mi.
Capital: Carson City

Cities and Towns

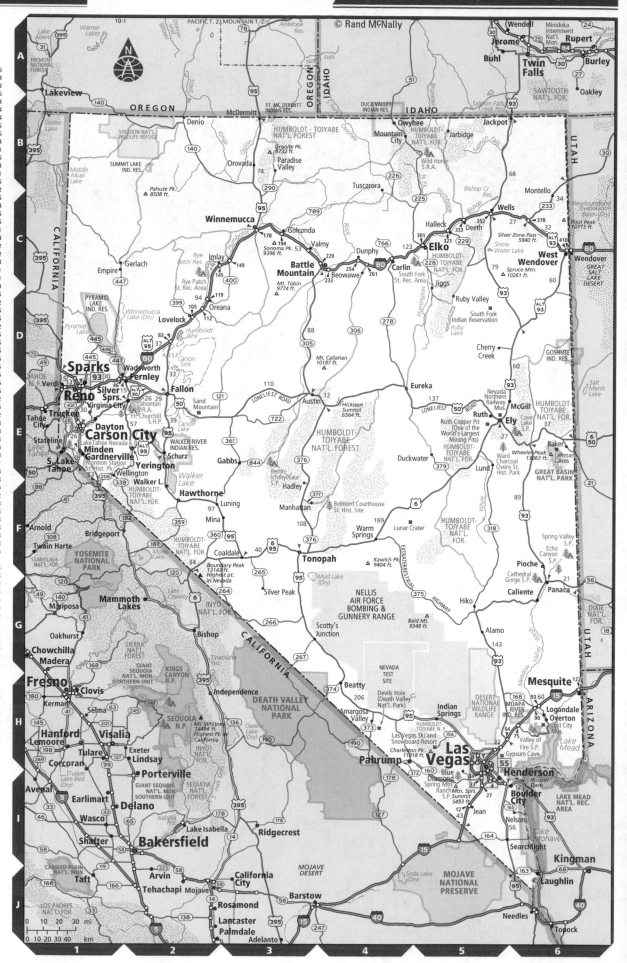

© Rand McNally

For border crossing information, please see p. 177.

New Hampshire

Population: 1,315,828
Land area: 8,968 sq. mi.
Capital: Concord

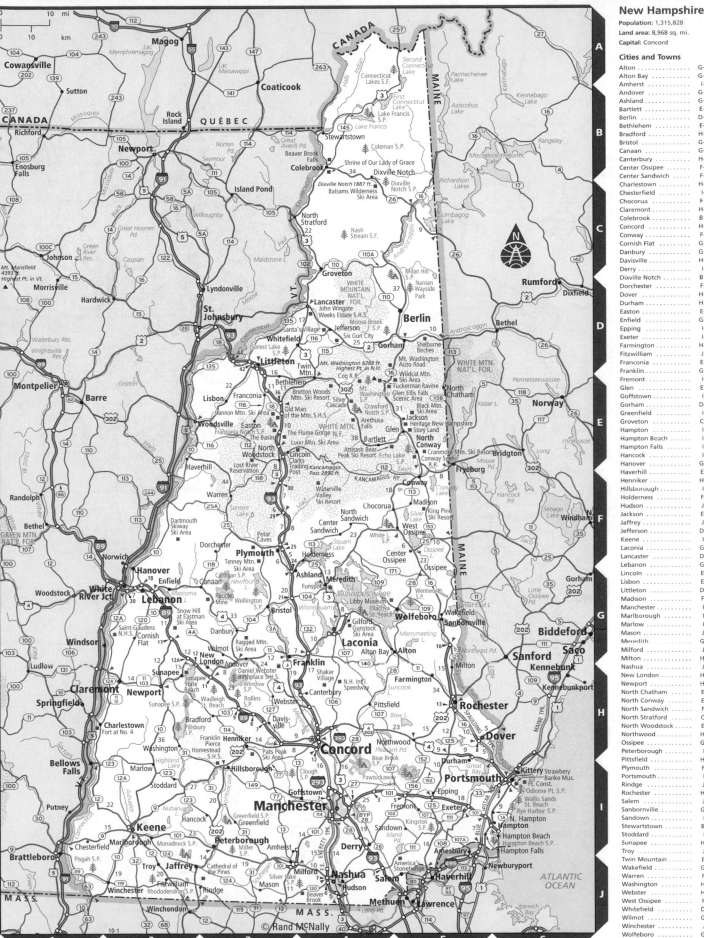

© Rand McNally

Get more New Jersey info at go.randmcnally.com/NJ

New Jersey
Population: 8,685,920
Land area: 7,417 sq. mi.
Capital: Trenton

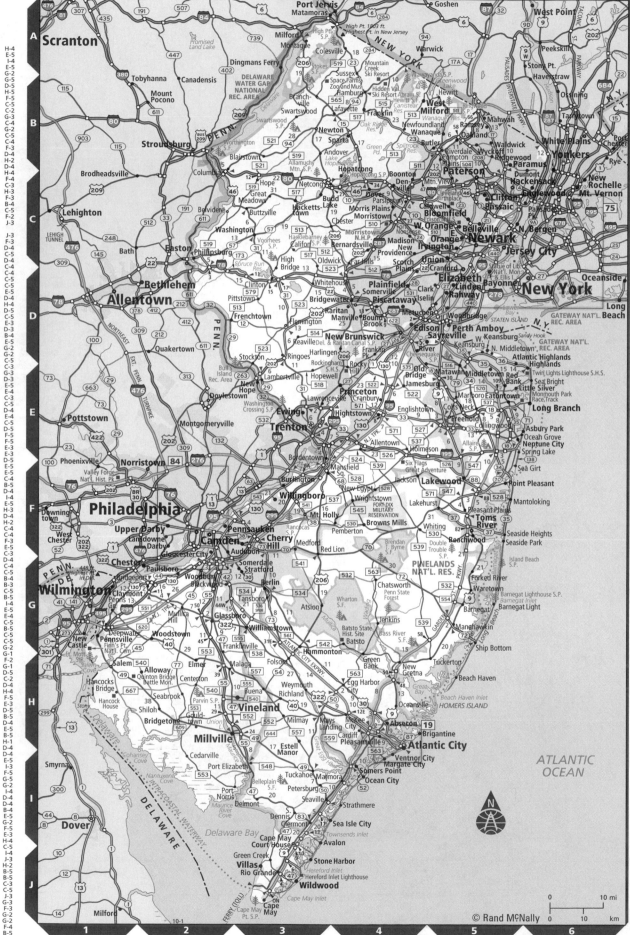

© Rand McNally

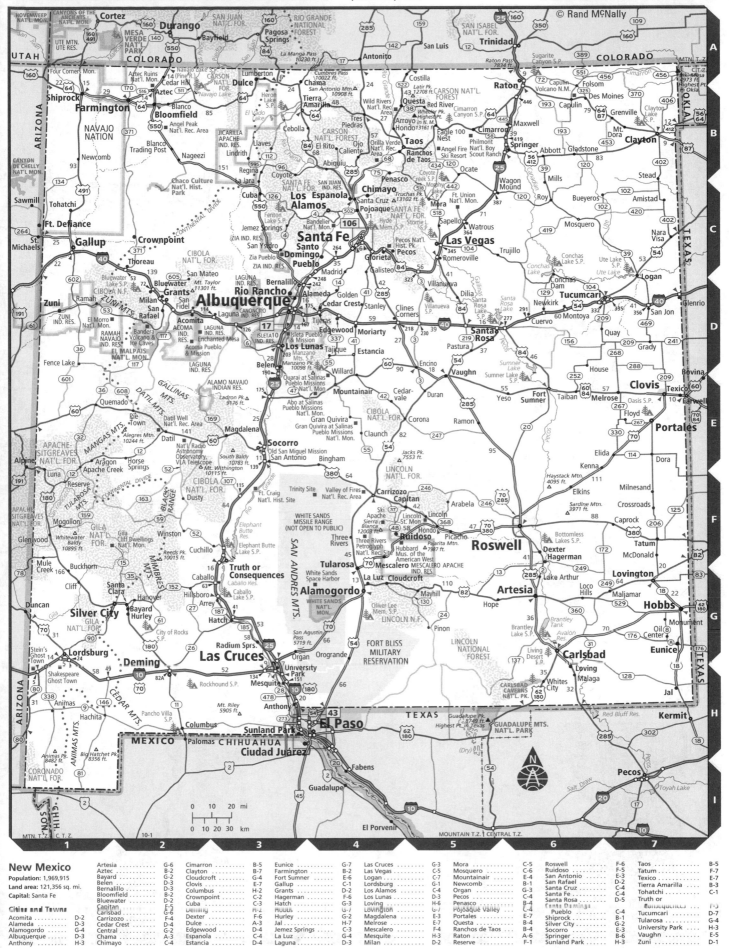

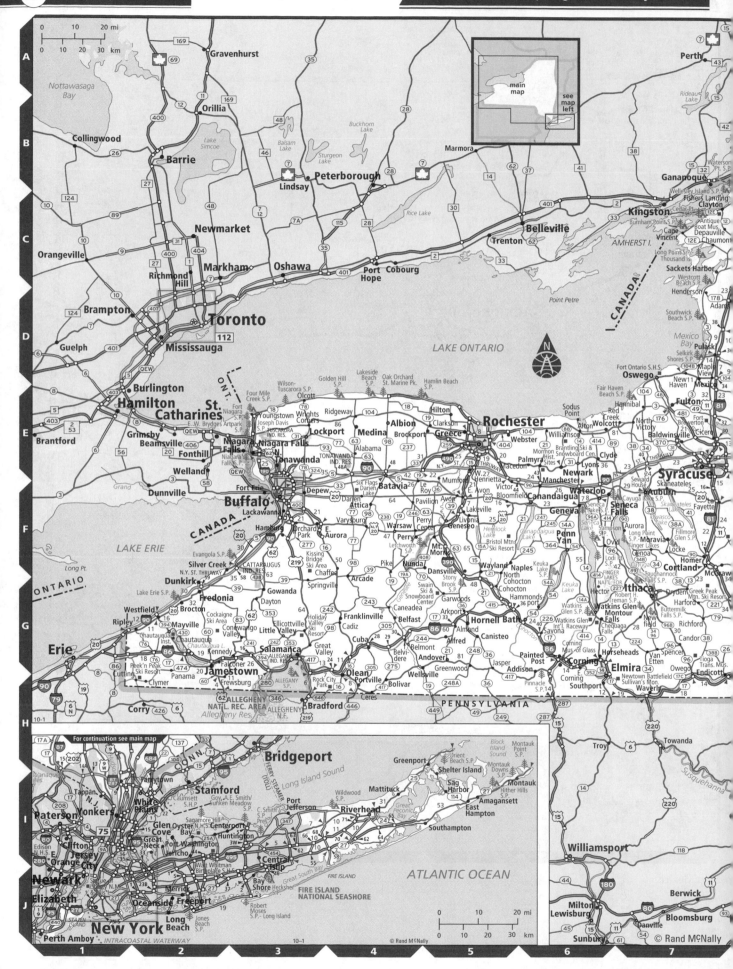

© Rand McNally

For border crossing information,
please see p. 177.

New York

Population: 19,297,729
Land area: 47,214 sq. mi.
Capital: Albany

Cities and Towns

Adams	D-7
Adams Center	D-8
Addison	G-6
Albany	F-11
Albion	E-4
Alexandria Bay	B-8
Alfred	G-5
Amagansett	I-5
Amenia	H-11
Amsterdam	F-10
Andover	G-5
Antwerp	C-8
Arcade	F-4
Attica	F-4
Au Sable Forks	B-11
Auburn	F-7
Avon	F-5
Bainbridge	G-8
Baldwinsville	E-7
Ballston Spa	E-11
Batavia	E-4
Bath	G-6
Bay Shore	J-3
Beacon	I-11
Belfast	G-4
Belmont	G-4
Binghamton	G-8
Blue Mountain Lake	C-10
Bolivar	H-4
Bolton Landing	D-11
Boonville	D-8
Brewster	I-11
Brockport	E-5
Brocton	G-2
Buffalo	F-3
Cadyville	B-11
Cairo	G-11
Cambridge	E-12
Camden	E-8
Canajoharie	F-10
Canandaigua	F-6
Canastota	E-8
Candor	G-7
Canisteo	G-5
Canton	B-9
Cape Vincent	C-7
Carthage	C-8
Catskill	G-11
Cazenovia	F-8
Centerport	J-12
Central Islip	I-3
Central Valley	I-10
Champlain	A-11
Chateaugay	A-10
Chaumont	C-7
Chautauqua	G-2
Cicero	E-7
Claverack	G-11
Clayton	C-7
Clinton	E-8
Clyde	E-6
Cobleskill	F-10
Cohocton	G-5
Cohoes	F-11
Congers	J-11
Cooperstown	F-9
Corinth	E-11
Corning	G-6
Cornwall on Hudson	I-11
Cortland	F-7
Croton Falls	I-11
Croton-on-Hudson	J-11
Crown Point	C-11
Cuba	G-4
Dannemora	B-11
Dansville	F-5
Delhi	G-9
Depew	F-3
Deposit	H-8
Dolgeville	E-9
Dover Plains	H-11
Downsville	H-9
Dryden	G-7
Dunkirk	G-2
East Aurora	F-3
East Greenbush	F-11
East Hampton	I-5
Elizabethtown	C-11
Ellenville	H-10
Elmira	H-6
Endicott	G-7
Falconer	G-2
Fayetteville	E-8
Fishkill	I-11
Fonda	F-10
Fort Plain	F-10
Franklinville	G-4
Fredonia	G-2
Freeport	J-11
Frewsburg	H-2
Fulton	E-7
Geneseo	F-5
Geneva	F-6
Glen Cove	J-11
Glens Falls	E-11
Gloversville	E-10
Goshen	I-10
Gouverneur	B-8
Gowanda	G-3
Grand Gorge	G-10
Granville	D-12
Great Neck	I-2
Greene	G-8
Greenport	H-5
Greenwich	E-11
Greenwood Lake	I-0
Hamburg	F-3
Hamilton	F-8
Hammondsport	G-6
Hancock	H-9
Herkimer	E-9
Highland	H-11
Hilton	E-5
Homer	F-7
Hoosick Falls	F-12
Hornell	G-5
Horseheads	G-6
Hudson	G-11
Hudson Falls	E-11
Huntington	J-12
Hyde Park	H-11
Ilion	E-9
Ithaca	G-7
Jamestown	G-2
Jericho	I-2
Johnstown	E-10
Keeseville	B-11
Kerhonkson	H-11
Kingston	H-11
Lackawanna	F-3
Lake George	D-11
Lake Luzerne	E-11

Lake Placid	C-11
Lake Pleasant	D-10
Lakeville	E-4
Le Roy	F-5
Liberty	H-9
Little Falls	E-9
Little Valley	G-3
Livingston Manor	H-9
Livonia	F-5
Loch Sheldrake	H-10
Lockport	E-3
Long Beach	J-2
Lowville	D-8
Lyon Mountain	A-11
Lyons	E-6
Macedon	E-6
Mahopac	I-11
Malone	A-10
Mamaroneck	J-11
Manchester	F-6
Massena	A-9
Mattituck	I-4
Mayfield	E-10
Mayville	G-2
Mechanicville	F-11
Medina	E-4
Merrick	J-2
Mexico	D-7
Middleburgh	F-10
Middletown	H-11
Millbrook	H-11
Millerton	H-11
Monroe	I-10
Montauk	I-5
Monticello	H-10
Montour Falls	G-6
Moravia	F-7
Mount Kisco	I-11
Mount Morris	F-5
Naples	F-5
New Berlin	F-8
New Hartford	E-8
New Paltz	H-11
New Rochelle	J-11
New York	J-1
Newark	E-6
Newburgh	I-11
Niagara Falls	E-3
North Tonawanda	E-3
Northville	E-10
Norwich	F-8
Norwood	B-9
Nunda	F-5
Oceanside	J-2
Ogdensburg	B-8
Olcott	E-3
Old Forge	D-9
Olean	H-4
Oneida	E-8
Oneonta	G-9
Orchard Park	F-3
Ossining	J-11
Oswego	D-7
Owego	G-7
Oxford	G-8
Oyster Bay	J-12
Painted Post	G-6
Palmyra	E-6
Paul Smiths	B-10
Pawling	I-11
Peekskill	I-11
Penn Yan	F-6
Perry	F-4
Plattsburgh	B-11
Port Henry	C-11
Port Jefferson	I-3
Port Jervis	I-10
Port Washington	I-2
Portville	H-4
Potsdam	B-9
Poughkeepsie	H-11
Pulaski	D-7
Red Hook	H-11
Rhinebeck	H-11
Richfield Springs	F-9
Ripley	G-2
Riverhead	I-4
Rochester	E-5
Rome	E-8
Roscoe	H-9
Rouses Point	A-12
Sackets Harbor	C-7
Sag Harbor	I-5
St. Regis Falls	B-10
Salamanca	G-3
Salem	E-12
Saranac Lake	B-10
Saratoga Springs	E-11
Saugerties	G-11
Schenectady	F-11
Schoharie	F-10
Schroon Lake	C-11
Schuylerville	E-11
Seneca Falls	F-6
Shelter Island	I-5
Sherburne	F-8
Sidney	G-8
Silver Creek	F-2
Skaneateles	F-7
Sodus Point	E-6
Southampton	I-5
Southport	H-6
Springville	G-3
Stamford	G-10
Star Lake	C-9
Stillwater	E-11
Stony Point	I-11
Syracuse	E-7
Tarrytown	J-11
Theresa	C-8
Ticonderoga	C-11
Troy	F-11
Tupper Lake	C-10
Utica	E-9
Victor	E-5
Walden	I-10
Walton	G-9
Warsaw	F-4
Warwick	I-10
Washingtonville	I-10
Waterloo	F-6
Watertown	C-8
Waterville	F-8
Watervliet	F-11
Watkins Glen	G-6
Waverly	H-7
Wayland	F-5
Webster	E-5
Wellsville	G-4
Westfield	F-2
White Plains	J-11
Whitehall	D-12
Whitney Point	G-8
Williamson	E-6
Wolcott	E-6
Woodstock	H-10
Wurtsboro	I-10
Yonkers	J-11
Youngstown	E-3

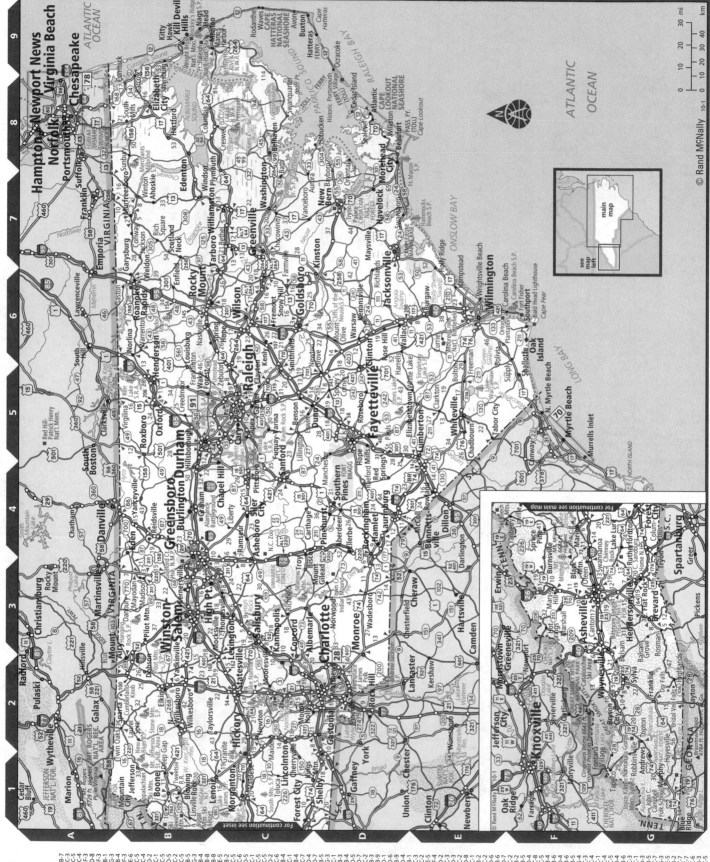

© Rand McNally

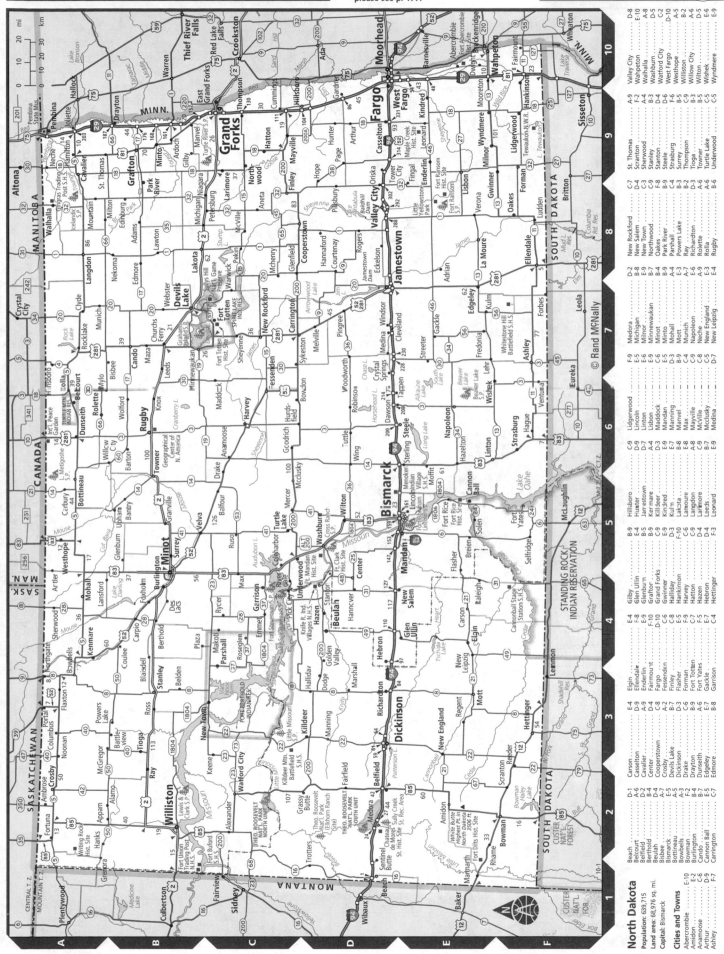

© Rand McNally

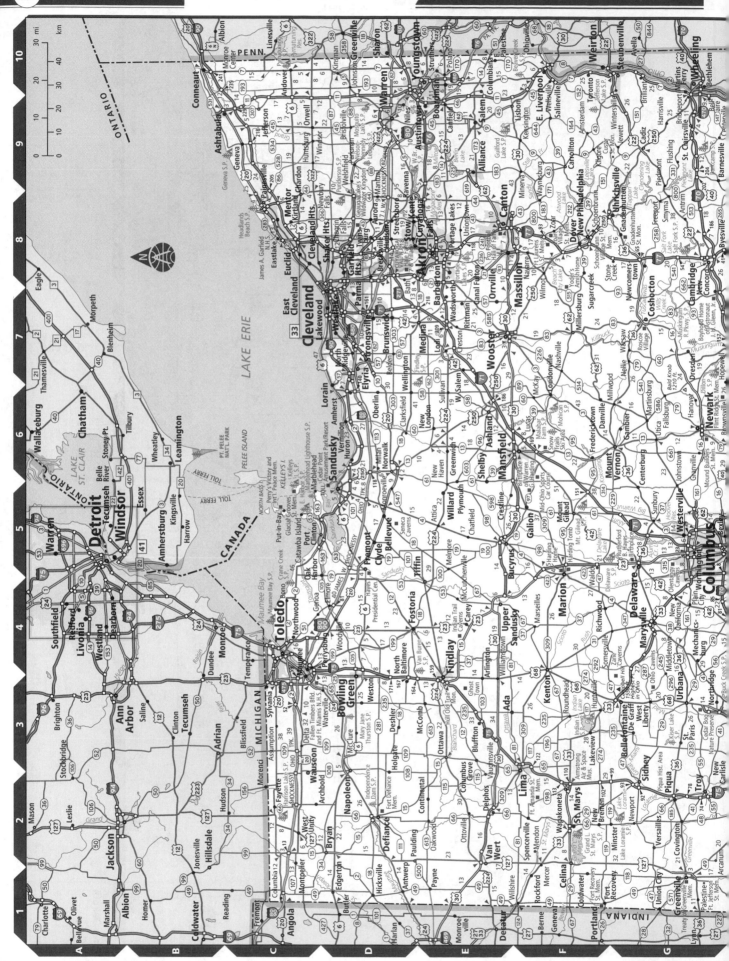

Ohio

Population: 11,466,917
Land area: 40,948 sq. mi.
Capital: Columbus

Cities and Towns

Aberdeen	K-3
Ada	G-3
Akron	E-8
Alliance	E-8
Amherst	D-6
Antwerp	G-2
Arcanum	G-2
Archbold	G-3
Ashland	E-6
Ashtabula	C-9
Athens	I-7
Aurora	D-8
Austintown	E-9
Baltimore	G-6
Barberton	E-8
Barnesville	G-9
Beavercreek	H-3
Bellaire	G-10
Bellefontaine	G-3
Bellevue	D-5
Belpre	I-8
Bethel	H-3
Bexley	G-5
Blanchester	H-3
Bluffton	G-3
Boardman	E-10
Bowling Green	D-3
Bremen	H-6
Bridgeport	G-9
Brilliant	G-10
Brookville	H-2
Brunswick	D-7
Bryan	C-2
Bucyrus	E-5
Cadiz	G-9
Caldwell	G-8
Cambridge	G-8
Camden	H-1
Canal Fulton	E-8
Canfield	E-9
Canton	E-8
Carey	E-4
Carrollton	F-9
Cedarville	H-3
Celina	G-10
Centerburg	G-5
Centerville	H-2
Chardon	C-8
Chillicothe	H-5
Chillicothe	I-5
Cincinnati	I-2
Circleville	H-5
Cleveland	D-7
Cleveland Heights	D-8
Clyde	D-5
Coldwater	G-2
Columbiana	E-9
Columbus	G-5
Columbus Grove	G-3
Conneaut	C-9
Corning	H-7
Coshocton	F-7
Covington	G-2
Crestline	E-5
Creston	E-7
Crooksville	G-7
Cuyahoga Falls	D-8
Dayton	H-2
De Graff	G-3
Defiance	G-2
Delaware	F-5
Delphos	G-2
Delta	F-2
Deshler	G-5
Dover	F-8
Dresden	G-7
East Cleveland	D-7
East Liverpool	F-10
East Palestine	E-10
Eastlake	D-7
Eaton	H-1
Edgerton	D-4
Elmore	D-5
Elyria	F-1
Englewood	E-10
Euclid	E-8
Fairfield	H-1
Fayette	D-3
Findlay	G-7
Forest Park	G-2
Fort Recovery	E-5
Fostoria	D-7
Franklin	G-3
Fredericktown	H-2
Fremont	G-3
Galion	F-2
Gallipolis	C-9
Gambier	C-4
Gates Mills		
Genoa	D-4
Georgetown	D-3
Germantown	H-2
Glouster	G-7
Granville	G-6
Greenville	F-10
Greenwich	E-10
Greenwich	E-6
Hamilton	H-1
Harrison	D-7
Hicksville	D-4
Hillsboro	C-8
Holgate	E-7
Hudson	H-4
Huron	I-3
Ironton	J-2
Jackson	I-2
Jamestown	D-4
Jefferson	F-6
Johnstown	D-5
Kent	F-6
Kenton	E-7
Kettering	G-4
Lakewood	E-5
Lancaster	C-9
Lebanon	C-8
Lewisburg	C-4
Lima	J-3
Lisbon	I-7
Logan	H-6
London	H-4
Lorain	G-6
Loudonville	E-6
Loveland	I-1
Lucasville	D-1
Manchester	K-4
Mansfield	E-6
Marietta	J-6
Marion	I-8
Martins Ferry	G-10
Marysville	E-3
Mason	I-6
Massillon	K-5
Maumee	G-5
McArthur	H-3
McComb	G-7
McConnelsville	G-7
Mechanicsburg	H-3
Medina	G-4
Mentor	E-5
Miamisburg	E-5
Middleport	D-8
Middletown	J-7
Milan	F-3
Milford	E-9
Millersburg	E-7
Minerva	H-6
Monroeville	D-6
Montgomery	E-6
Montpelier	I-5
Mount Gilead	K-4
Mount Healthy	D-1
Mount Orab	J-3
Mount Sterling	I-8
Mount Vernon	H-4
Napoleon	G-10
Navarre	F-8
Nelsonville	I-6
New Boston	E-8
New Bremen	K-5
New Carlisle	H-3
New Concord	H-2
New Lexington	G-7
New London	E-7
New Paris	H-1
New Philadelphia	G-8
New Richmond	J-2
Newark	H-2
Newcomerstown	G-8
Niles	I-2
North Baltimore	G-7
North Ridgeville	D-3
North Ridge	I-2
Northfield	D-5
Northwood	C-4
Norton	I-2
Norwalk	F-5
Norwood	D-6
Oak Harbor	J-6
Oak Hill	D-1
Oberlin	E-7
Ontario	F-9
Orrville	H-4
Ottawa	G-6
Oxford	D-3
Painesville	D-8
Parma	I-6
Paulding	K-5
Peebles	H-3
Perrysburg	H-3
Piketon	G-7
Piqua	I-5
Plain City	E-5
Plymouth	E-5
Poland	H-1
Pomeroy	C-8
Port Clinton	J-7
Portage Lakes	G-6
Portsmouth	G-8
Powhatan Point	D-9
Ravenna	D-3
Reading	D-7
Richwood	C-4
Ripley	K-3
Rittman	G-9
St. Clairsville	G-9
St. Marys	D-5
St. Paris	D-6
Salem	E-3
Salineville	E-7
Sandusky	H-1
Shaker Heights	E-4
Shelby	D-8
Sidney	D-7
Somerset	G-2
South Charleston	J-4
South Lebanon	J-5
South Russell	I-3
Springdale	P-8
Springfield	G-10
Steubenville	E-5
Stow	D-8
Streetsboro	D-7
Strongsville	D-5
Struthers	E-10
Sugarcreek	K-5
Sunbury	H-9
Sylvania	C-3
Toledo	C-4
Toronto	K-3
Trenton	G-3
Trotwood	G-9
Troy	H-2
Twinsburg	G-3
Uhrichsville	D-8
Union City	G-8
Uniontown	G-1
Upper Sandusky	D-8
Urbana	E-4
Utica	G-6
Van Wert	G-2
Vandalia	H-2
Vermilion	G-6
Versailles	E-7
Wadsworth	F-2
Wapakoneta	P-8
Warren	G-10
Washington Court House	D-8
Waterville	H-4
Wauseon	E-10
Waverly	F-5
Waynesville	H-3
Wellington	C-3
Wellston	J-6
Wellsville	F-10
West Liberty	G-3
West Salem	E-7
West Union	J-4
West Unity	C-2
Westerville	D-8
Westlake	D-7
Whitehall	H-5
Weston	E-4
Willard	G-6
Williamsburg	H-2
Wilmington	E-2
Withamsville	G-6
Woodsfield	E-7
Woodville	F-2
Wooster	D-9
Worthington	H-3
Xenia	H-3
Yellow Springs	H-3
Youngstown	E-10
Zanesville	C-2

Oklahoma

Population: 3,617,316
Land area: 68,667 sq. mi.
Capital: Oklahoma City

Cities and Towns

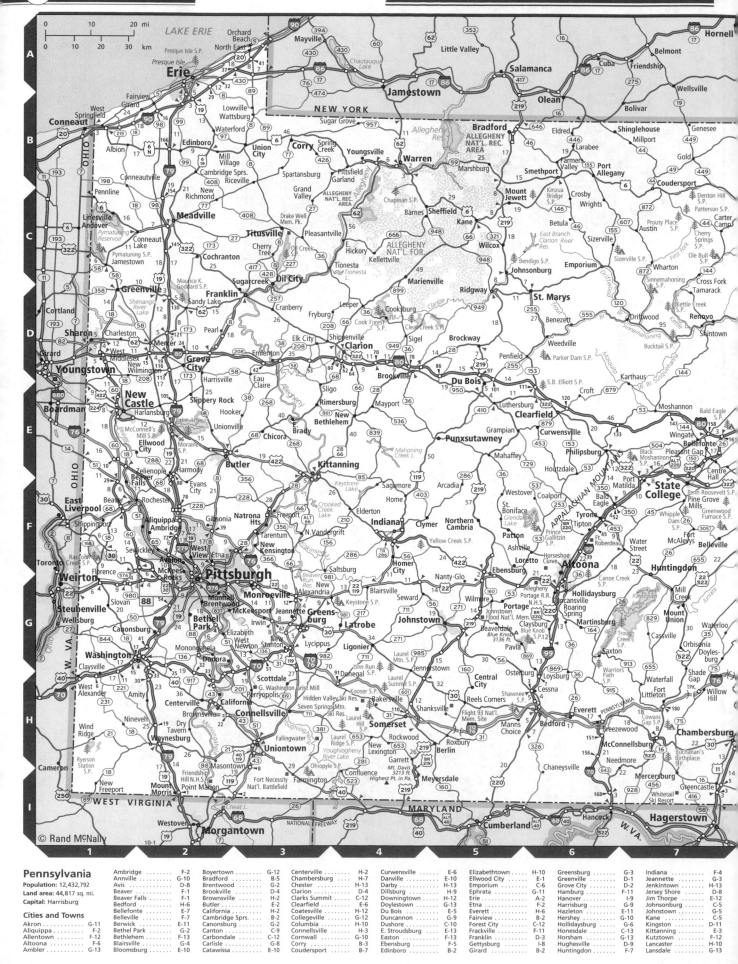

Pennsylvania

Population: 12,432,792
Land area: 44,817 sq. mi.
Capital: Harrisburg

Cities and Towns

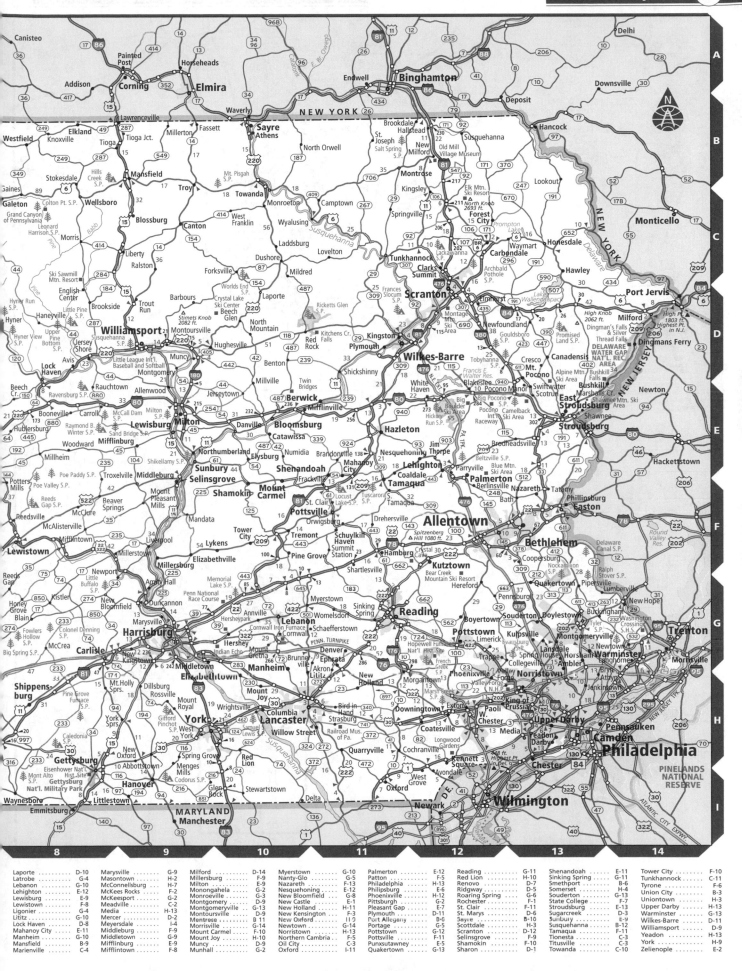

Laporte D-10
Latrobe G-4
Lebanon G-10
Lehighton E-12
Lewisburg E-9
Lewistown F-8
Ligonier G-4
Lititz G-10
Lock Haven D-8
Mahanoy City E-11
Manheim G-10
Mansfield B-9
Marienville C-4

Marysville G-9
Masontown H-2
McConnellsburg ... H-7
McKees Rocks F-2
McKeesport G-2
Meadville C-2
Media H-13
Mercer D-2
Meyersdale I-4
Middleburg F-9
Middletown G-9
Mifflinburg E-9
Mifflintown F-8

Milford D-14
Millersburg F-9
Milton E-9
Monongahela G-2
Monroeville G-3
Montgomery D-9
Montgomeryville .. G-13
Montoursville D-9
Montrose .... B 11
Morrisville G-14
Mount Carmel F-10
Mount Joy H-10
Muncy D-9
Munhall G-2

Myerstown G-10
Nanty-Glo G-5
Nazareth F-13
Nesquehoning E-12
New Bloomfield ... G-8
New Castle E-1
New Holland H-11
New Kensington ... F-3
New Oxford H9
Newtown G-14
Norristown H-13
Northern Cambria . F-5
Oil City C-3
Oxford I-11

Palmerton E-12
Patton F-5
Philadelphia H-13
Philipsburg E-6
Phoenixville H-12
Pittsburgh G-2
Pleasant Gap E-7
Plymouth D-11
Port Allegany B-6
Portage G-5
Pottstown G-12
Pottsville F-11
Punxsutawney E-5
Quakertown G-13

Reading G-11
Red Lion H-10
Renovo D-7
Ridgway D-5
Roaring Spring ... F-6
Rochester F-1
St. Clair F-11
St. Marys D-6
Sayre B-9
Scottdale G-3
Scranton D-12
Selinsgrove F-9
Shamokin F-10
Sharon D-1

Shenandoah E-11
Sinking Spring ... G-11
Smethport B-6
Somerset H-4
Souderton G-13
State College F-7
Stroudsburg E-13
Sugarcreek D-3
Sunbury E-9
Tamaqua F-11
Tionesta C-3
Titusville C-3
Towanda C-10

Tower City F-10
Tunkhannock C-11
Tyrone F-6
Union City B-3
Uniontown H-3
Upper Darby H-13
Warminster G-13
Wilkes-Barre D-11
Williamsport D-9
Yeadon H-13
York H-9
Zelienople D-1

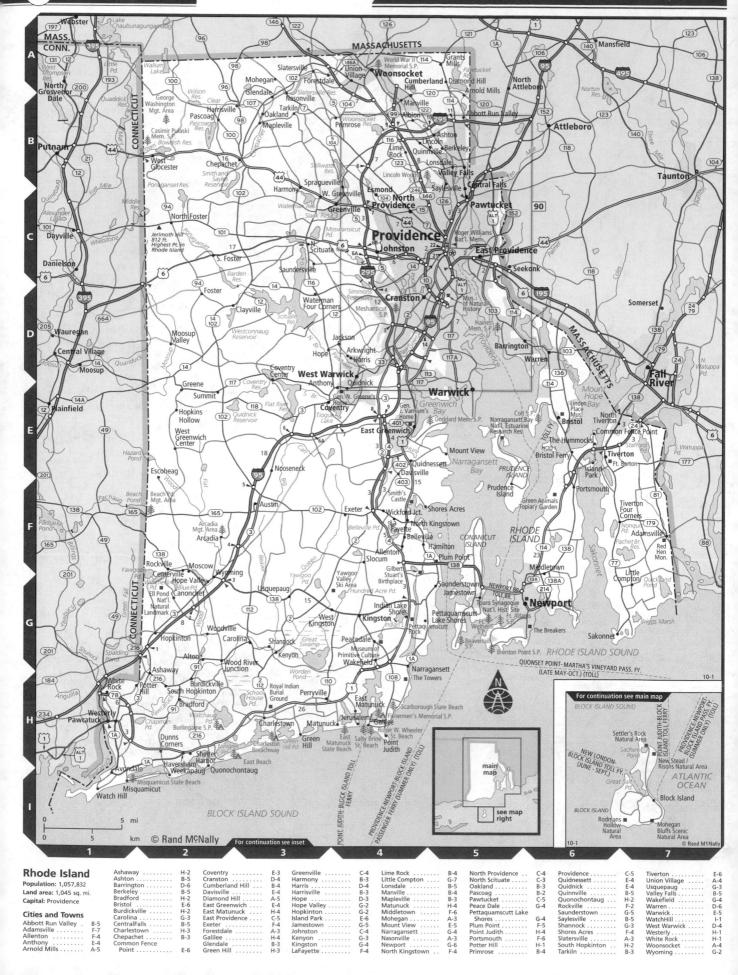

Rhode Island

Population: 1,057,832
Land area: 1,045 sq. mi.
Capital: Providence

Cities and Towns

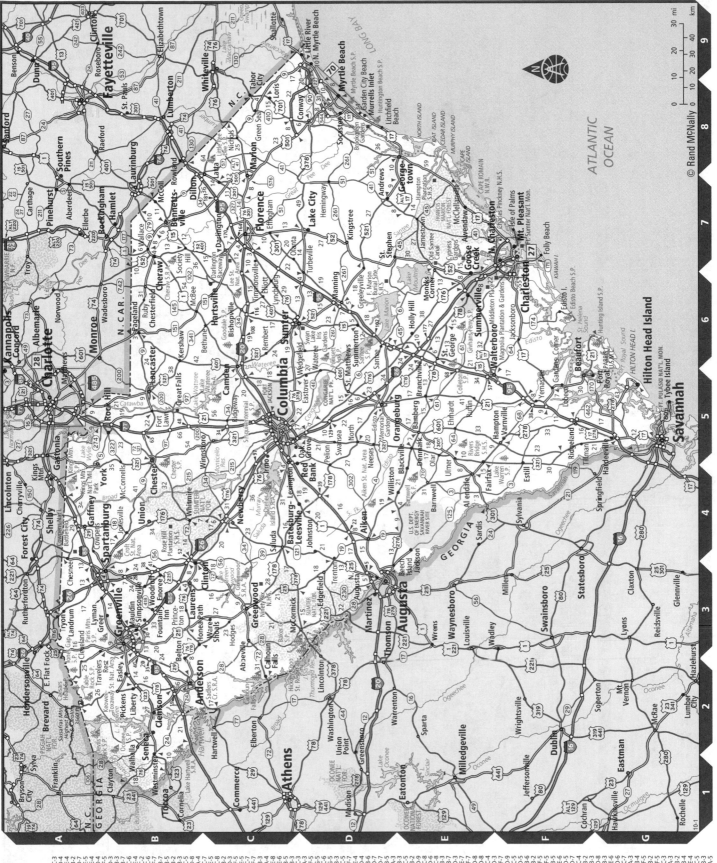

South Dakota

Population: 796,214
Land area: 75,885 sq. mi.
Capital: Pierre

Cities and Towns

Aberdeen	C-8
Alexandria	D-8
Armour	E-8
Avon	F-8
Belle Fourche	C-1
Beresford	E-10
Big Stone City	B-10
Bison	B-4
Blunt	C-6
Bonesteel	E-7
Bowdle	B-6
Bridgewater	D-9
Bristol	B-8
Britton	B-8
Brookings	C-10
Bryant	C-9
Buffalo	A-2
Burke	E-7
Canton	E-10
Castlewood	B-10
Cherry Creek	C-6
Chamberlain	D-7
Clark	C-8
Clear Lake	B-10
Colman	D-10
Colome	E-6
Custer	D-2
De Smet	C-8
Deadwood	C-2
Dell Rapids	D-10
Doland	C-8
Dupree	C-5
Eagle Butte	C-5
Edgemont	E-1
Elk Point	F-10
Estelline	C-9
Eureka	A-6
Faith	C-4
Faulkton	C-7
Flandreau	C-10
Fort Pierre	D-6
Fort Thompson	D-6
Gannvalley	D-7
Gettysburg	C-6
Gregory	E-7
Groton	B-8
Hecla	B-8
Herreid	A-6
Highmore	D-7
Hill City	D-2
Hoven	B-6
Howard	D-9
Ipswich	B-7
Iroquois	D-8
Isabel	B-5
Kadoka	D-4
Kennebec	D-6
Kimball	D-7
Kyle	E-4
Lake Andes	E-8
Lake Preston	C-9
Langford	B-8
Lead	C-2
Lemmon	A-4
Leola	B-7
Madison	D-9
Martin	E-4
McIntosh	A-5
McLaughlin	B-5
Menno	E-8
Milbank	B-10
Miller	D-7
Mission	E-5
Mitchell	D-8
Mobridge	B-5
Mount City	A-5
Mount Vernon	D-8
Murdo	D-5
New Underwood	D-2
Newell	C-2
Oglala	F-3
Olivet	E-8
Onida	D-6
Parker	E-9
Parkston	E-8
Philip	D-4
Piedmont	C-2
Pierre	D-6
Pine Ridge	F-3
Plankinton	D-7
Platte	E-7
Presho	D-5
Rapid City	D-2
Redfield	C-7
Roscoe	B-7
Rosebud	E-6
Rosholt	A-10
St. Francis	E-5
Salem	D-9
Scotland	E-8
Selby	B-6
Sisseton	B-9
Spearfish	C-1
Sturgis	C-2
Summit	B-10
Timber Lake	B-5
Tripp	E-8
Tyndall	E-8
Veblen	B-9
Vermillion	F-9
Viborg	E-9
Wagner	E-8
Wall	D-3
Watertown	C-9
Waubay	B-9
Webster	B-9
Wessington Sprs.	D-7
White Lake	E-5
White River	E-5
Willow Lake	C-9
Wilmot	B-10
Winner	E-6
Wolsey	D-8
Woonsocket	D-8
Yankton	F-9

© Rand McNally

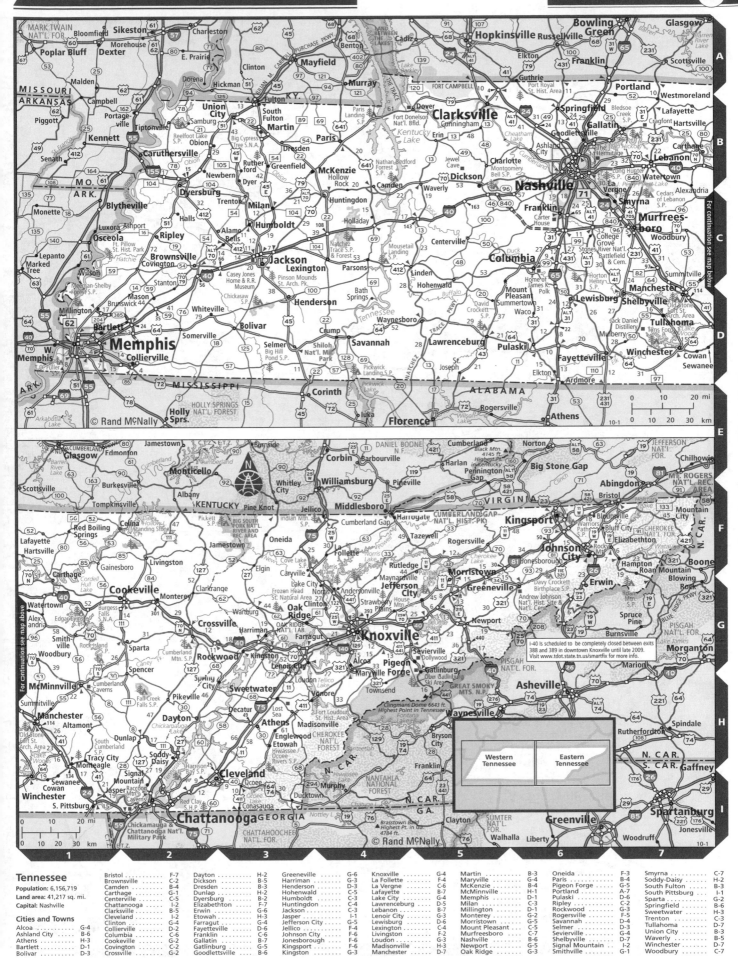

I-40 is scheduled to be completely closed between exits 388 and 389 in downtown Knoxville until late 2009. Visit www.tdot.state.tn.us/smartfix for more info.

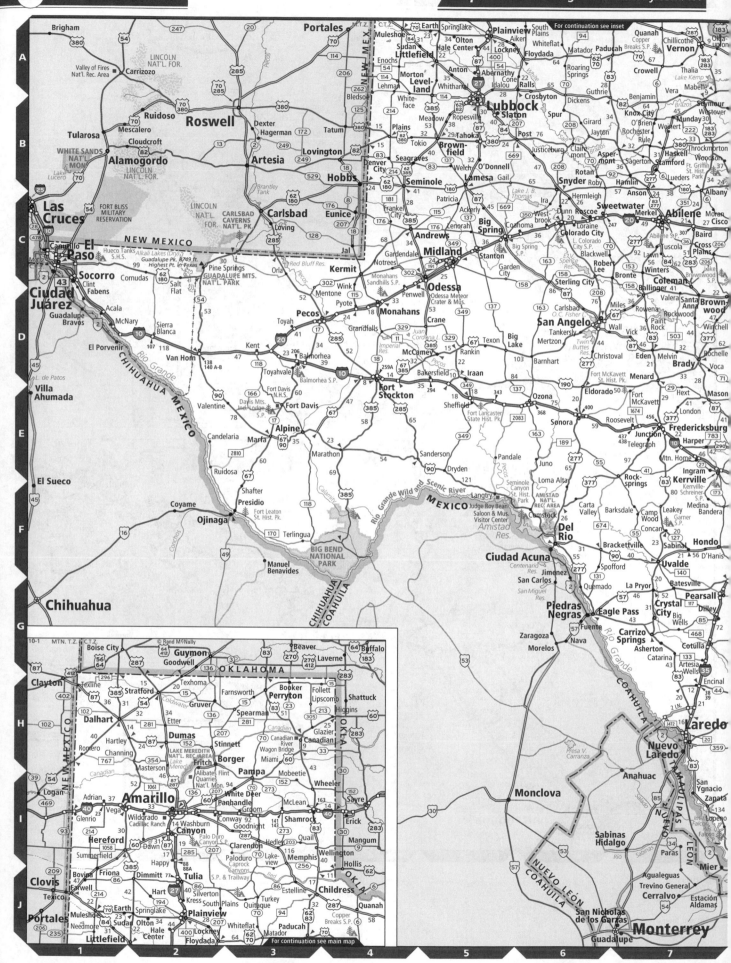

For border crossing information,
please see p. 177.

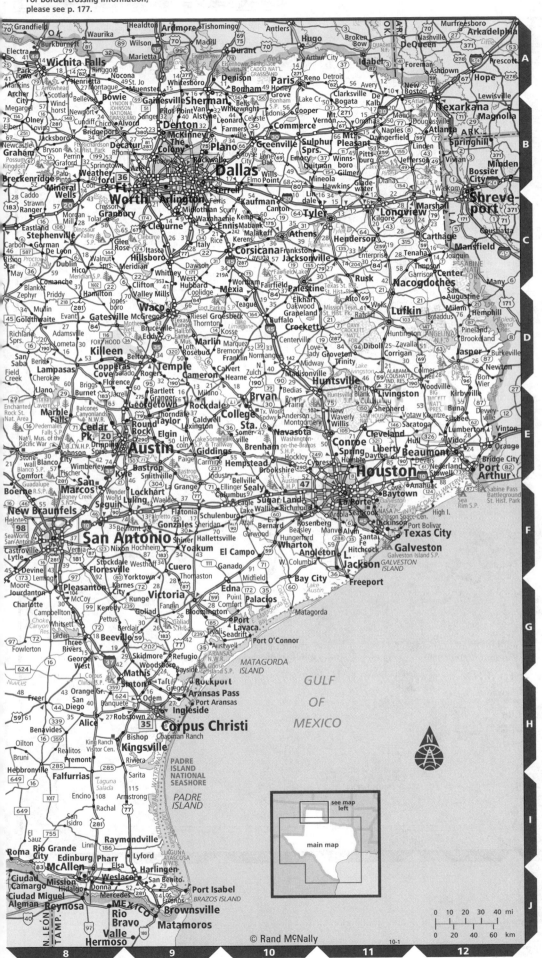

© Rand McNally

| 0 | 10 | 20 | 30 | 40 mi |
| 0 | 20 | 40 | 60 km |

see map left

main map

10-1

Texas

Population: 23,904,380
Land area: 261,797 sq. mi.
Capital: Austin

Cities and Towns

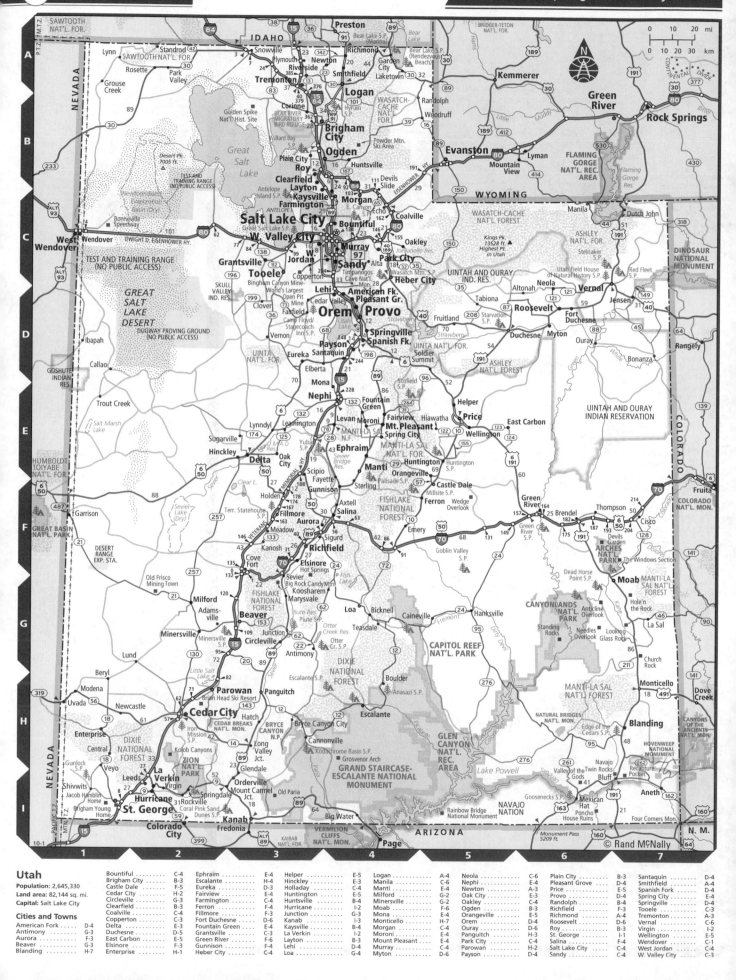

© Rand McNally

Vermont

Population: 621,254
Land area: 9,250 sq. mi.
Capital: Montpelier

Cities and Towns

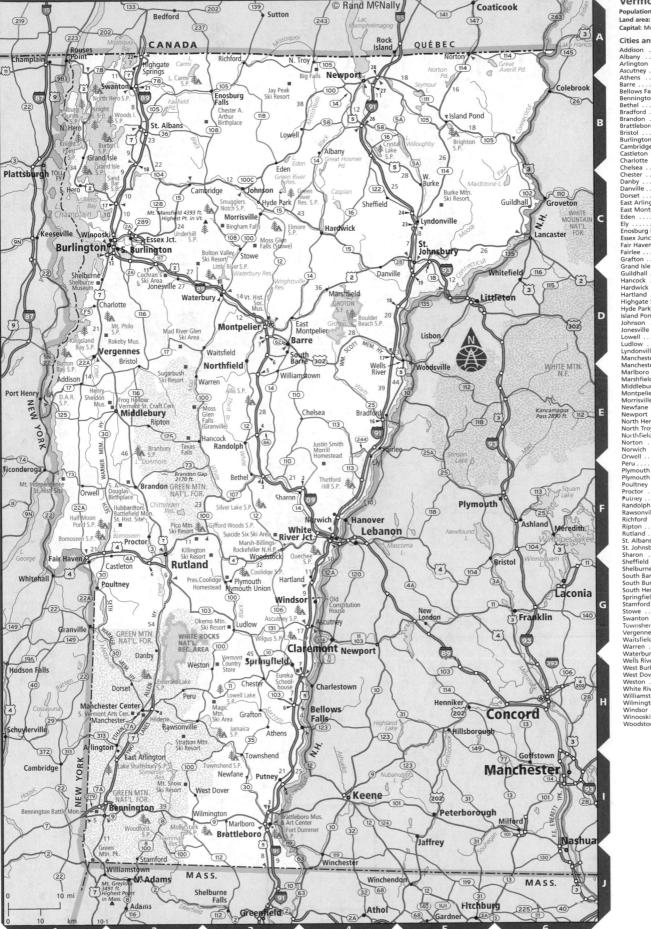

Virginia

Population: 7,712,091
Land area: 39,594 sq. mi.
Capital: Richmond

Cities and Towns

For continuation see main map

main map

see map above

For continuation see inset

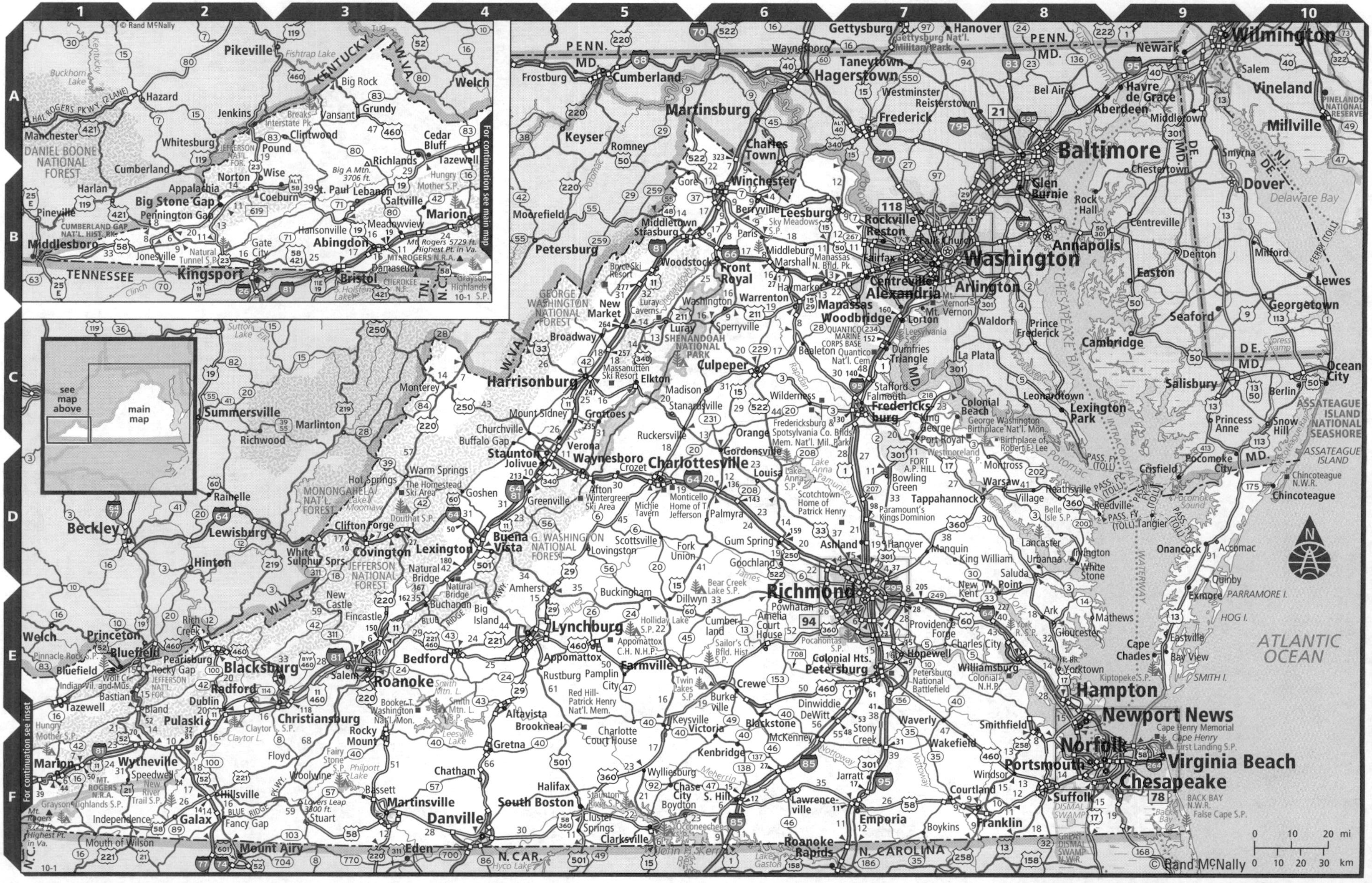

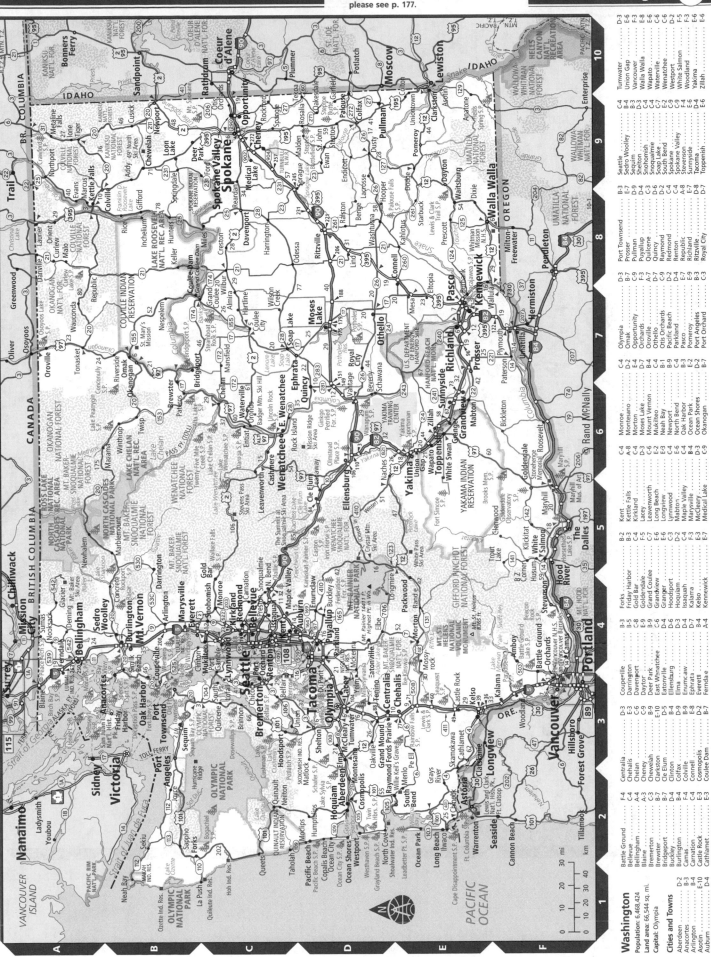

Rand McNally

West Virginia

Population: 1,812,035
Land area: 24,078 sq. mi.
Capital: Charleston

Cities and Towns

Town	Grid
Alderson	F-4
Ansted	E-3
Barboursville	E-2
Beckley	F-3
Belington	D-6
Belle	E-3
Berkeley Springs	C-8
Bethlehem	B-4
Buckhannon	D-5
Buffalo	D-2
Cameron	B-4
Cedar Grove	E-3
Chapmanville	E-2
Charles Town	C-9
Charleston	E-3
Clarksburg	D-5
Clay	E-4
Clendenin	E-3
Craigsville	E-5
Davis	D-6
Dunbar	E-3
Elkins	D-6
Elizabeth	D-3
Fairmont	D-4
Fayetteville	E-3
Follansbee	A-4
Fort Ashby	C-7
Fort Gay	E-1
Franklin	E-6
Gauley Bridge	E-3
Glenville	D-4
Grafton	D-5
Grantsville	D-4
Green Bank	E-6
Hamlin	E-2
Harpers Ferry	C-9
Harrisville	C-3
Hinton	F-4
Huntington	E-2
Keyser	C-7
Kingwood	C-6
Lewisburg	F-4
Logan	E-2
Madison	E-3
Malden	E-3
Man	E-2
Mannington	C-5
Marlinton	E-6
Marmet	E-3
Martinsburg	C-8
Middlebourne	C-3
Milton	E-2
Moorefield	D-7
Morgantown	C-6
Moundsville	B-4
Mount Hope	F-3
Mullens	F-3
New Martinsville	C-3
Nitro	E-2
Northfork	G-3
Nutter Fort	D-5
Oak Hill	E-3
Parkersburg	D-3
Parsons	D-6
Pennsboro	C-3
Petersburg	D-7
Piedmont	C-7
Pineville	F-3
Point Pleasant	D-2
Princeton	G-3
Rainelle	F-4
Rand	E-3
Ravenswood	D-3
Richwood	E-5
Ripley	D-2
Romney	C-7
St. Albans	E-3
St. Marys	C-3
Salem	D-4
Shady Spring	F-3
Shepherdstown	C-9
Shinnston	D-5
Sistersville	C-3
Sophia	F-3
South Charleston	E-3
Spencer	D-3
Summersville	E-5
Sutton	E-4
Union	F-4
Vienna	D-3
War	G-3
Wayne	E-2
Webster Springs	E-5
Weirton	A-4
Welch	G-2
Wellsburg	B-4
West Hamlin	E-2
West Union	C-3
Weston	D-5
Wheeling	B-4
White Sulphur Springs	F-4
Whitesville	E-3
Williamson	G-2
Williamstown	D-2
Winfield	E-3

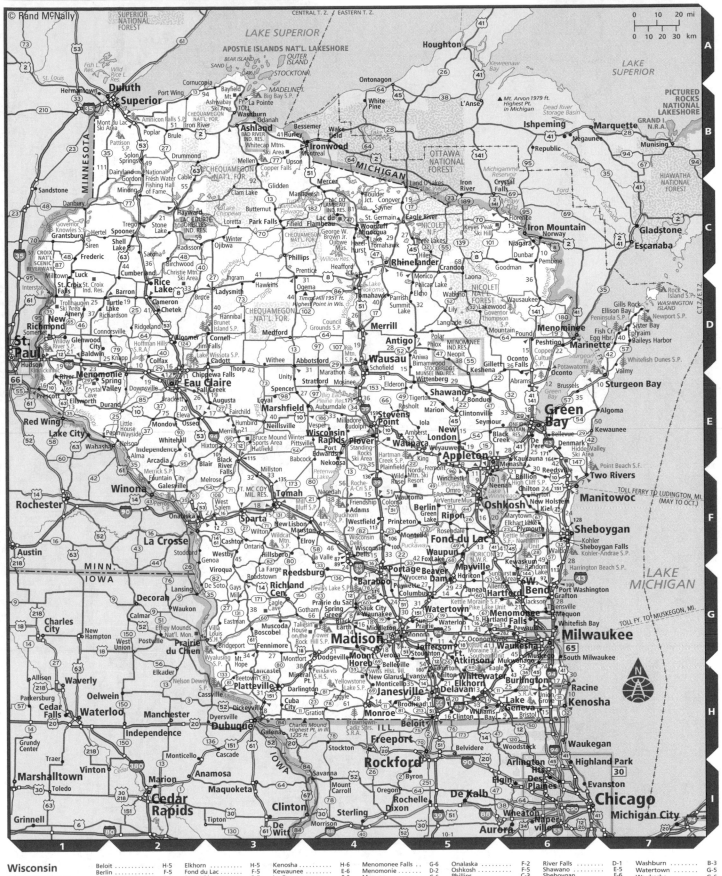

© Rand McNally

Wisconsin

Population: 5,601,640
Land area: 54,310 sq. mi.
Capital: Madison

Cities and Towns

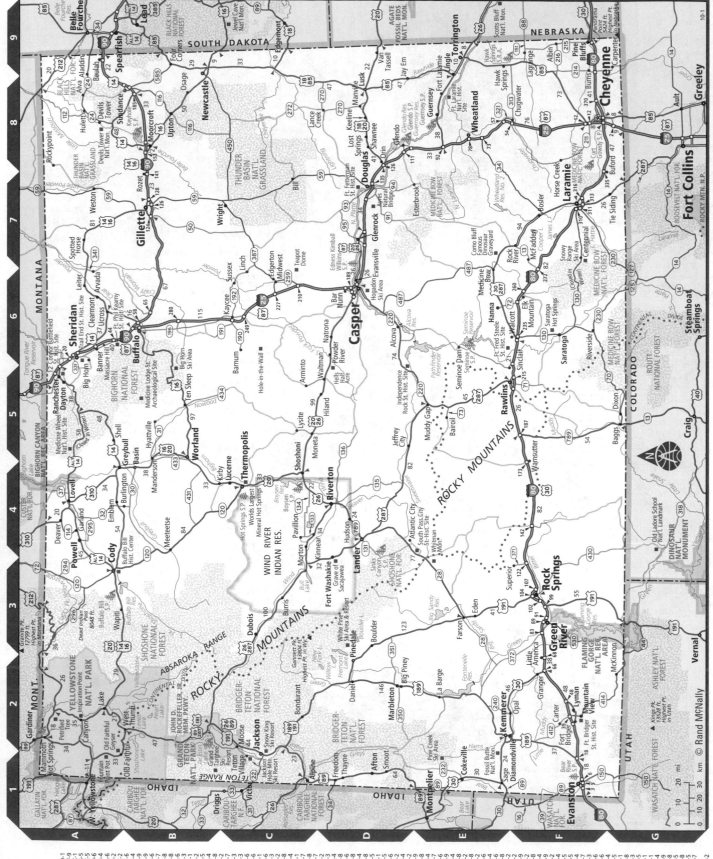

BORDER CROSSING INFORMATION

With advance planning, crossing the border to Mexico or Canada can be easier than you think.

Citizenship Documents

A U.S. passport or proof of citizenship, such as an original or certified birth certificate and photo identification is required for entry into Mexico or Canada. Naturalized U.S. citizens should carry citizenship papers; permanent residents of the United States must bring proof of residency and photo identification.

Traveling with Kids

For children under the age of 18, parents should be prepared to provide evidence, such as a birth certificate or adoption decree, to prove they are indeed the parents. Single or divorced parents and parents traveling without spouses should carry a letter of consent from the absent parent or guardian to bring a child across either border. Mexico requires the letter to be original and notarized. Divorced parents should also bring copies of their custody decree. Adults who are not the parents or guardians of the children they are traveling with must have written permission from the parents or guardians to supervise the children.

Minors traveling alone to Canada must have proof of citizenship and a letter from both parents detailing the length of stay, providing the parents' telephone number, and authorizing the person waiting for them to take care of them.

Re-entry to the U.S.

Proof of both citizenship and identity is required for entry into the United States.

The Western Hemisphere Travel Initiative (WHTI) is changing the requirements for re-entry into the U.S.

Since January 31, 2008, citizens of the United States, Canada, Mexico, and Bermuda traveling between the U.S. and Canada, Mexico, the Caribbean, and Bermuda by land or sea are required to present either a WHTI-compliant document (www.dhs.gov/xtrvlsec/crossingborders/#0), or a government-issued photo ID, such as a driver's license, plus proof of citizenship, such as a birth certificate, in order to re-enter the U.S. Children age 18 and under will be able to enter with proof of citizenship.

Beginning June 1, 2009, the U.S. government will implement the full requirements of the land and sea phase of WHTI. U.S. and Canadian citizens who are 16 years old and older traveling between the U.S. and Canada, Mexico, Central and South America, the Caribbean, and Bermuda by land or sea (including ferries), will be required to present a valid passport or other alternative documents as determined by the Department of Homeland Security (www.dhs.gov/xtrvlsec/crossingborders). U.S. and Canadian citizens who are 15 years old or younger will still be allowed to travel with only a copy of their birth certificate, as will teens ages 16-18 if they are part of an adult-supervised school, religious, cultural, or athletic group.

U.S. Passport Card

Since July 14, 2008, the U.S. passport card has been in production. The passport card facilitates entry and expedites document processing at U.S. land and sea ports-of-entry when arriving from Canada, Mexico, the Caribbean and Bermuda. The card may not be used to travel by air. Otherwise, it carries the rights and privileges of the U.S. passport book and is adjudicated to the exact same standards (www.travel.state.gov/passport/ppt_card/ppt_card_3926.html).

Mexico Only

Driving in Mexico

According to the U.S. Department of State, tourists traveling beyond the border zone must obtain a temporary import permit or risk having their car confiscated by Mexican customs officials. To acquire a permit, you must submit evidence of citizenship, title for the car, a car registration certificate, driver's license, and a processing fee to either a Banjercito (Mexican Army Bank) branch located at a Mexican Customs office at the port of entry, or at one of the Mexican consulates in the U.S. Mexican law also requires posting a bond at a Banjercito office to guarantee departure of the car from Mexico within a period determined at the time of application. In order to recover this bond or avoid credit card charges, travelers must go to any Mexican Customs office immediately prior to departing Mexico. Carry proof of car ownership (the current registration card or a letter of authorization from the finance or leasing company). Mexican law also requires that owners either drive their vehicles or be inside the vehicle when it is being driven. Auto insurance policies, other than Mexican, are not valid in Mexico. A short-term liability policy is obtainable at the border.

Tourist Cards

Tourist cards are valid up to six months, require a fee, and are required for all persons, regardless of age, who are traveling in Mexico outside the "border zone." Cards may be obtained from Mexican border authorities, Consuls of Mexico, or Federal Delegates in major cities. Cards are also distributed to passengers en route to Mexico by air.

Fast Pass for Frequent Travelers

For frequent travelers, it is possible to apply for a SENTRI card, which allows pre-screened, low-risk travelers to be processed with little or no delay at land border crossings. Approved applicants are issued an identification card and they can quickly cross the border in a dedicated traffic lane without routine customs and immigration questioning (unless they are randomly selected).

For additional information on traveling in Mexico, contact the Mexican Embassy in Washington, D.C.: (202) 736-1000; or visit http://portal.sre.gob.mx/usa/. You also can visit the U.S. Department of State Website, http://travel.state.gov/travel/cis_pa_tw/cis/cis_970.html.

Canada Only

Driving in Canada

Drivers need proof of ownership of the vehicle or documentation of its rental, a valid U.S. driver's license, and automobile insurance.

Fast Pass for Frequent Travelers

For frequent travelers, the United States and Canada have instituted the NEXUS program, which allows pre-screened, low-risk travelers to be processed with little or no delay by U.S. and Canadian border officials.

For additional information on traveling in Canada, contact the Canadian Embassy in Washington, D.C.: (202) 682-1740; www.canadianembassy.org or go to the U.S. Department of State Website, http://travel.state.gov/travel/cis_pa_tw/cis/cis_1082.html.

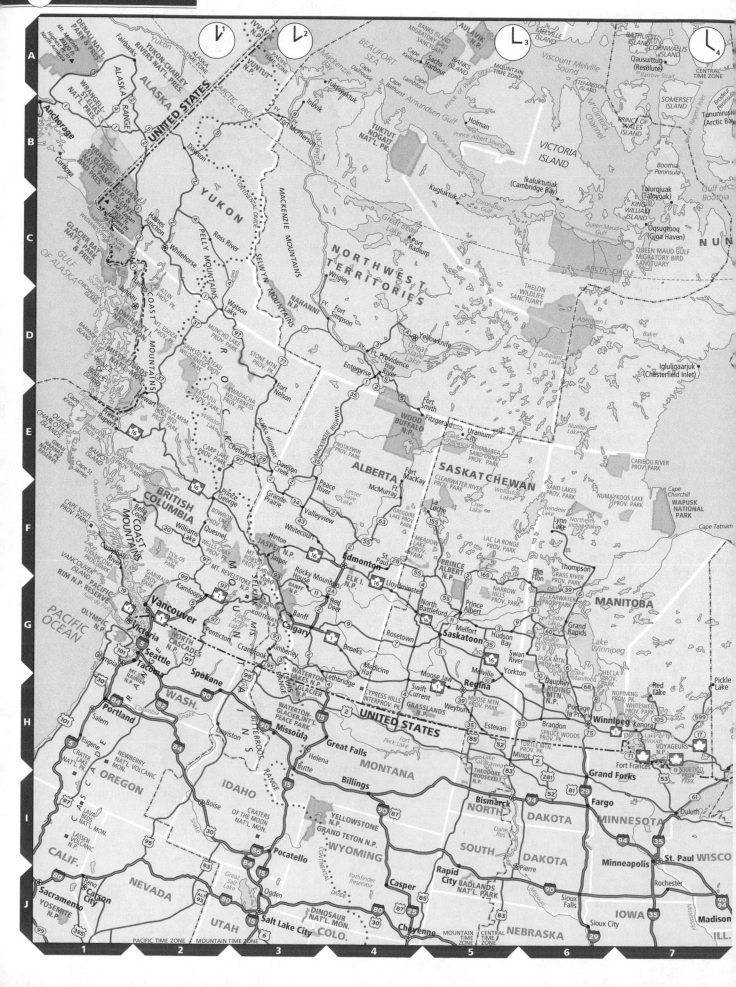

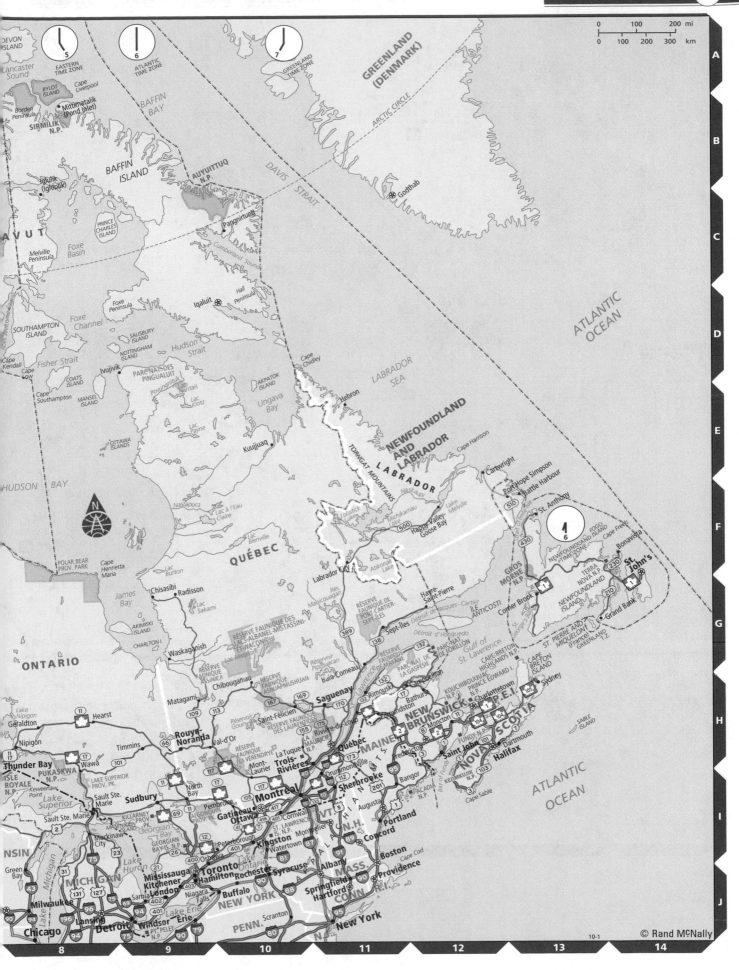

GREENLAND
(DENMARK)

0   100   200 mi
0   100   200   300 km

5 EASTERN TIME ZONE
6 ATLANTIC TIME ZONE
7 GREENLAND TIME ZONE

DEVON ISLAND
Lancaster Sound
Cape Liverpool
Borden Peninsula
BYLOT ISLAND
Mittimatalik (Pond Inlet)
SIRMILIK N.P.

BAFFIN BAY

BAFFIN ISLAND

AUYUITTUQ N.P.

DAVIS STRAIT

ARCTIC CIRCLE

Godthåb

Melville Peninsula
PRINCE CHARLES ISLAND
Pangnirtung

Cumberland Sound

SOUTHAMPTON ISLAND
Foxe Channel
Foxe Basin

NUNAVUT

SALISBURY ISLAND
NOTTINGHAM ISLAND

Foxe Peninsula

Hall Peninsula
Iqaluit

ATLANTIC OCEAN

Cape Kendall
Cape Low
Fisher Strait
COATS ISLAND
MANSEL ISLAND
Cape Southampton

Hudson Strait

Cape Chidley

LABRADOR SEA

Ivujivik
PARC NAT. DES PINGUALUIT
Povungnituk
Nantais
Lac Klotz

Hebron

OTTAWA ISLANDS
Lac Payne
Ungava Bay

NEWFOUNDLAND AND LABRADOR

HUDSON BAY

Kuujjuaq

Cape Harrison

Cartwright

AKIMISKI ISLAND

Nastapoca
Lac à l'Eau Claire

TORNGAT MOUNTAINS

Nasskaupi

Port Hope Simpson
Battle Harbour
510
St. Anthony
430

FOGO ISLAND
Cape Freels

James Bay

Lac Bienville

Lobstick Lake
Michikamau
Lake Melville
500
Happy Valley-Goose Bay

6
NEWFOUNDLAND TIME ZONE
Bonavista

POLAR BEAR PROV. PARK
Cape Henrietta Maria

QUÉBEC

230
St. John's
1
210

Chisasibi
Radisson
Lac Burton

Labrador City
Atikonak Lake
Rés. Manicouagan

Havre-Saint-Pierre

GROS MORNE N.P.
1
Corner Brook

TERRA NOVA N.P.
NEWFOUNDLAND ISLAND

Lac Sakami

ÎLE ANTICOSTI
Détroit d'Honguedo

Grand Bank

CHARLTON I.
Waskaganish

RÉSERVE FAUNIQUE DES LACS-ALBANEL-MISTASSINI-ET-WACONICHI
Lac Mistassini

389
138
Sept-Îles
Détroit de Jacques-Cartier

ST. PIERRE AND MIQUELON (France)

ONTARIO

RÉSERVE FAUNIQUE ASSINICA
RÉSERVE FAUNIQUE ASHUAPMUSHUAN

Réservoir Pipmuacan

PARC NAT. DE LA GASPÉSIE
132
Gaspé

CAPE BRETON HIGHLANDS N.P.
CAPE BRETON ISLAND

Matagami
Chibougamau

167   169
Saguenay

132
Baie-Comeau

RÉSERVE FAUNIQUE DE PORT-CARTIER-SEPT-ÎLES

105
Sydney

Lake Nipigon
11
Hearst

109   113

170
Rimouski
17
Matane

SABLE ISLAND

Geraldton
Nipigon

66
Rouyn-Noranda
Val-d'Or

Réservoir Gouin
Saint-Félicien
RÉSERVE FAUNIQUE DES LAURENTIDES

155   175
LA MAURICIE N.P.
173
Québec

Rivière-du-Loup

Bathurst
Edmundston
8
Moncton
104
1
Charlottetown
P.E.I.
104

Timmins

RÉSERVE FAUNIQUE LA VÉRENDRYE

2
NEW BRUNSWICK

KOUCHIBOUGUAC N.P.
PRINCE EDWARD I.
NOVA SCOTIA

11   17
Thunder Bay
Wawa
101

La Tuque
Mont-Laurier

Drummondville

MAINE

FUNDY N.P.
Fredericton

101
Dartmouth
Halifax

11   17

Trois-Rivières
40
117

112
Sherbrooke
201

1
Saint John
BAY OF FUNDY

103
KEJIMKUJIK N.P.

ISLE ROYALE N.P.
PUKASKWA N.P.
LAKE SUPERIOR PROV. PK.

North Bay

105
Montréal
417

Bangor

Cape Sable

ATLANTIC OCEAN

Keweenaw Point
Lake Superior

11
KILLARNEY PROV. PARK
69

Pembroke
ALGONQUIN PROV. PARK
416
401
Ottawa
Gatineau
7

133
Cornwall
ST. LAWRENCE IS. N.P.

APPALACHIAN MTS.
Augusta

1
ACADIA N.P.

Sault Ste. Marie
2
Mackinaw City
23

GEORGIAN BAY IS. N.P.
Georgian Bay
12

Peterborough
401
Kingston
Watertown

VT.
N.H.

Montpelier
Portland

MICHIGAN
31
Green Bay
21
Lake Huron
400

Oshawa
Lake Ontario
81
Syracuse
Rochester

Concord
89

Boston
Cape Cod

Milwaukee
43
196
Lansing
96
131   127
London
Sarnia
402
401

Toronto
403
Hamilton
Mississauga
Kitchener

Albany
90
MASS.
R.I.
CONN.
Providence
Springfield
Hartford

Lansing

Niagara Falls
Buffalo

90
Scranton

Chicago
94
75
Detroit
Windsor
Erie
PELEE N.P.
90   79

NEW YORK
PENN.
80
N.J.
New York

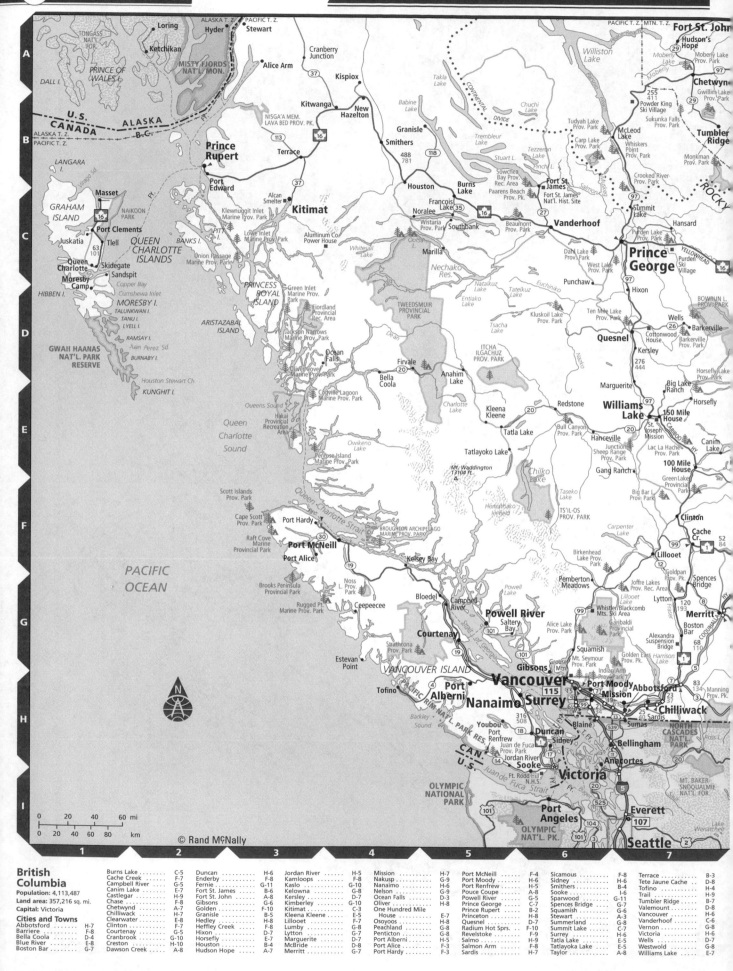

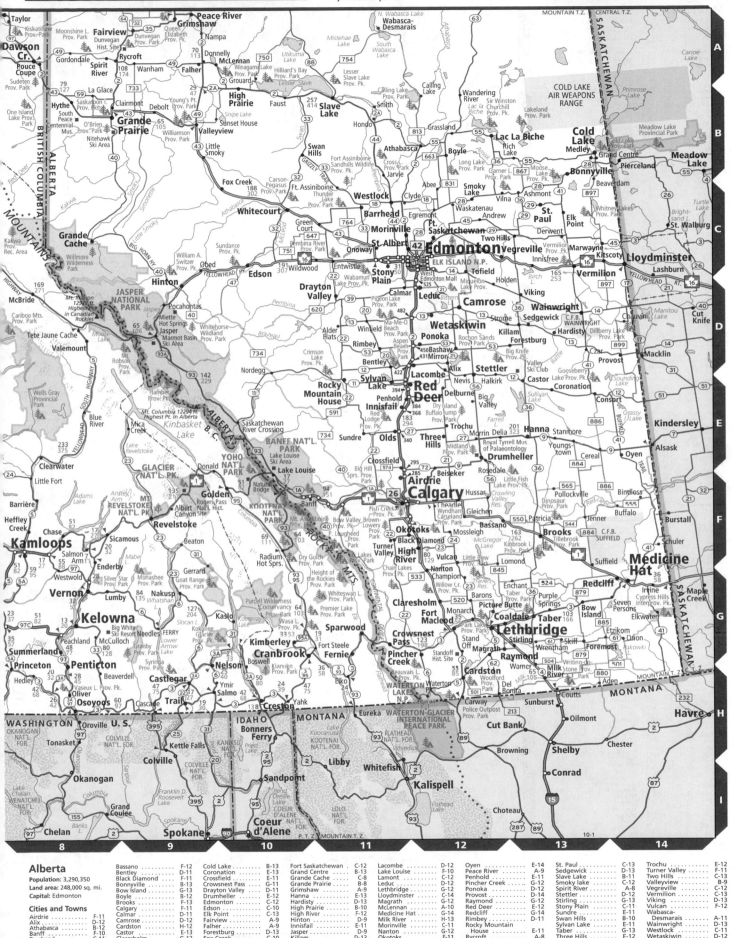

Alberta

Population: 3,290,350
Land area: 248,000 sq. mi.
Capital: Edmonton

Cities and Towns

Manitoba

Population: 1,148,401
Land area: 213,729 sq. mi.
Capital: Winnipeg

Cities and Towns

Saskatchewan

Population: 968,157
Land area: 228,445 sq. mi.
Capital: Regina

Cities and Towns

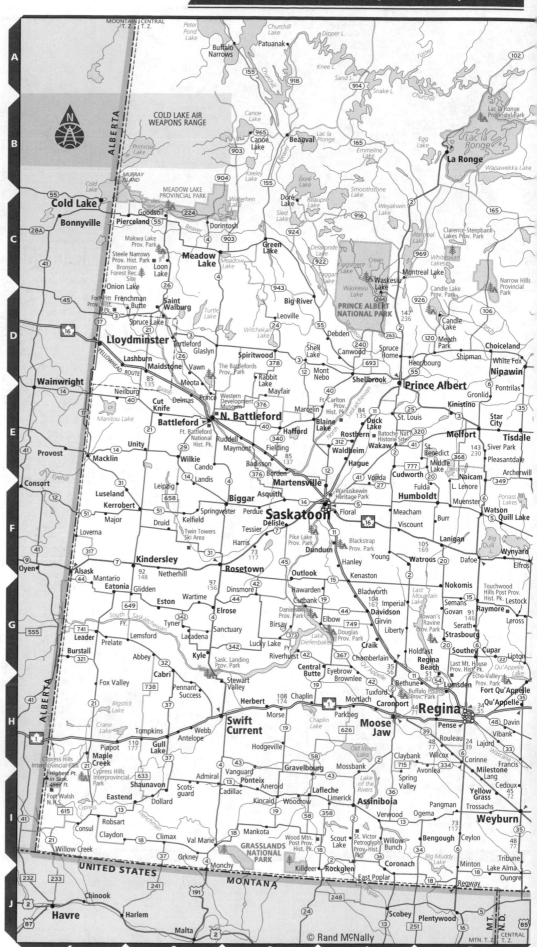

0   20   40 mi
0   20   40   60 km

SASKATCHEWAN

MANITOBA

ONTARIO

LAKE WINNIPEG

Lake Winnipegosis

Lake Manitoba

RIDING MOUNTAIN NATIONAL PARK

UNITED STATES

N. DAK.

MINN.

Thompson
Flin Flon
Creighton
Channing
Cranberry Portage
The Pas
Snow Lake
Wabowden
Pipun
Cross Lake
Norway House
Warren Landing
Grand Rapids
Easterville
Moose Lake
Cormorant
Wanless
Pelican Narrows
Sandy Bay
Cumberland House
Carrot River
Arborfield
Crooked River
Prairie River
Hudson Bay
Westgate
Powell
Mafeking
Birch River
Novra
Swan River
Minitonas
Bowsman
Duck Bay
Camperville
Winnipegosis
Skownan
Meadow Portage
Gypsumville
Grahamdale
Steep Rock
Hilbre
Hodgson
Moosehorn
Ashern
Dallas
Fisher River
Pine Dock
Berens River
Matheson Island
Jackhead
Dauphin River
Manigotagan
Bissett
Preeceville
Sturgis
Canora
Kamsack
Yorkton
Roblin
Grandview
Dauphin
Ste. Rose du Lac
Ochre River
McCreary
Alonsa
Reykjavik
Ashern
Camper
Fisher Branch
Riverton
Arborg
Gimli
Hecla
Melville
Russell
Angusville
Rossburn
Erickson
Neepawa
Gladstone
Woodlands
Selkirk
Beausejour
Winnipeg
Portage la Prairie
Brandon
Souris
Carberry
MacGregor
Austin
Steinbach
Carman
Morden
Winkler
Morris
Emerson
Pembina
Moosomin
Virden
Elkhorn
Hartney
Deloraine
Boissevain
Killarney
Estevan
Carlyle
Arcola
Redvers
Oxbow
Crosby
Mohall
Bottineau
Dunseith
Rolla
Langdon
Roseau
Warroad

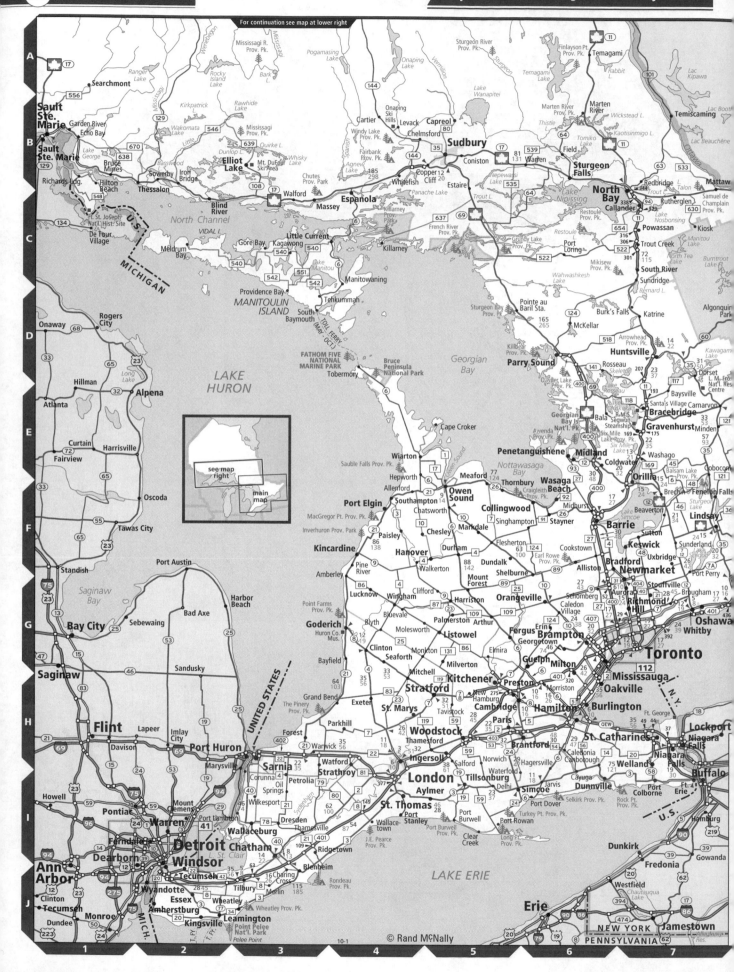

For continuation see map at lower right

LAKE HURON

Georgian Bay

LAKE ERIE

MANITOULIN ISLAND

MICHIGAN

UNITED STATES

U.S.

Saginaw Bay

see map right

main map

© Rand McNally

PENNSYLVANIA

NEW YORK

N.Y.

10-1

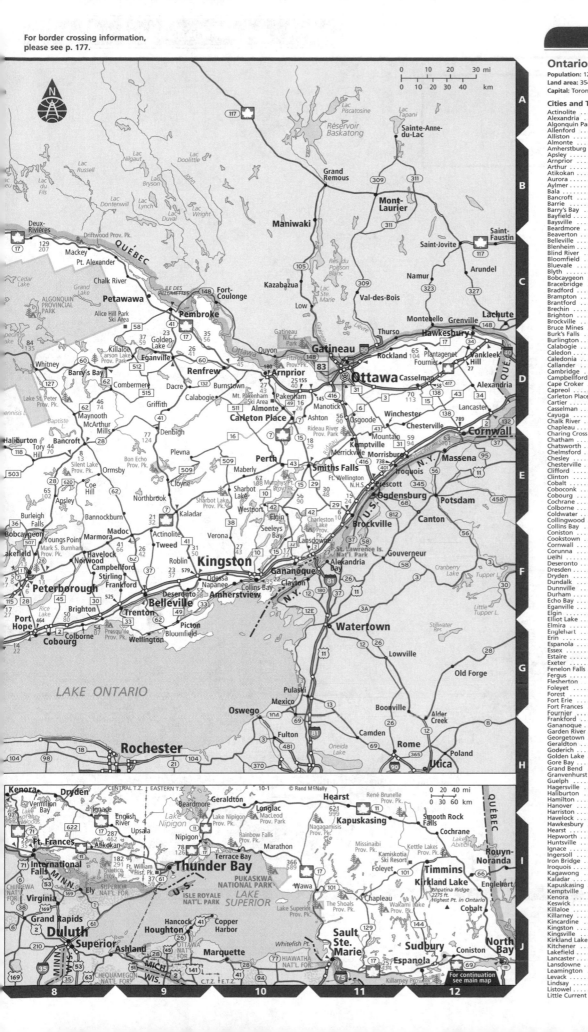

For border crossing information,
please see p. 177.

For border crossing information, please see p. 177.

Ontario

Population: 12,160,282
Land area: 354,342 sq. mi.
Capital: Toronto

Cities and Towns

Québec

Population: 7,546,131
Land area: 527,079 sq. mi.
Capital: Québec

For border crossing information, please see p. 177.

© Rand McNally

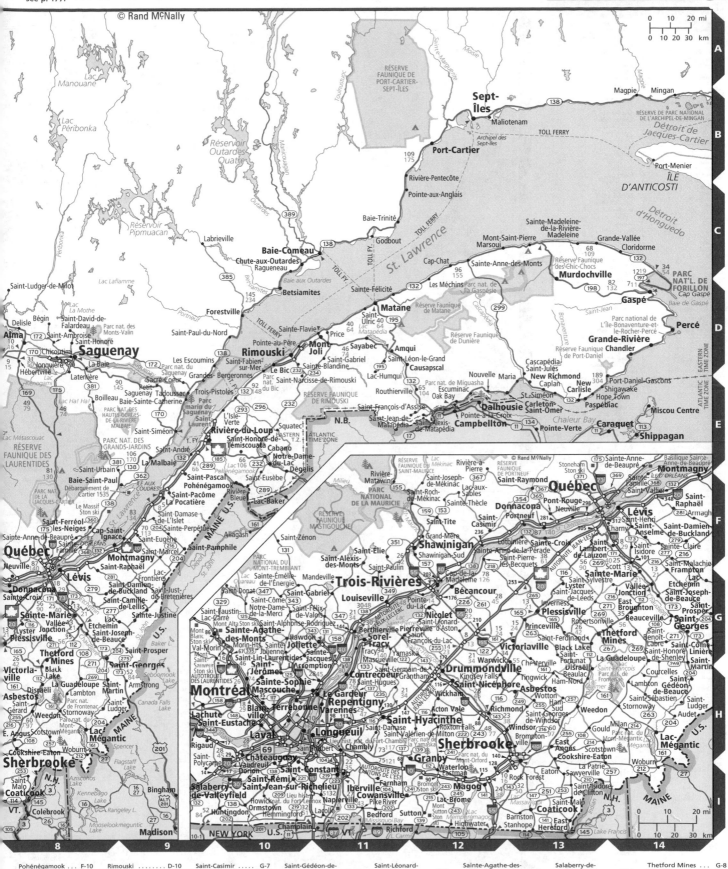

Pohénégamook	F-10	Rimouski	D-10	Saint-Casimir	G-7	Saint-Gédéon-de-	
Pointe-du-Lac	G-12	Rivière-Bleue	F-10	Saint-Côme-		Beauce	H-14
Pont-Rouge	F-13	Rivière-du-		Linière	G-14	Saint-Georges	G-8
Port-Cartier	B-12	Loup	E-9	Saint-Constant	H-10	Saint-Germain-de-	
Portneuf	G-7	Rivière-Rouge	G-5	Saint-Eustache	H-10	Grantham	H-12
Price	D-11	Robertsonville	G-14	Saint-Félicien	D-7	Saint-Hubert	H-11
Princeville	G-13	Roberval	D-7	Saint-Félix-de-		Saint-Hyacinthe	H-7
Québec	G-8	Rock Forest	I-13	Valois	G-11	Saint-Jean-sur-	
Rawdon	G-10	Roxton Falls	H-12	Saint-Ferréol-les-		Richelieu	H-6
Repentigny	H-6	Rouyn-Noranda	D-1	Neiges	F-8	Saint-Jérôme	H-6
Richmond	H-7	Saguenay	D-8	Saint-François-du-		Saint-Joseph-de-	
Rigaud	H-9	Saint-Ambroise	D-8	Lac	G-11	Beauce	G-8
		Saint-Anselme	F-14	Saint-Gabriel	G-6		

Saint-Léonard-		Sainte-Agathe-des-		Salaberry-de-		Thetford Mines	G-8
d'Aston	G-12	Monts	G-5	Valleyfield	H-6	Thurso	H-4
Saint-Lin-		Sainte-Anne-de-		Sayabec	D-11	Trois-Pistoles	E-10
Laurentides	H-10	Beaupré	F-8	Senneterre	D-3	Trois-Rivières	G-7
Saint-Pacôme	F-9	Sainte-Anne-des-		Sept-Îles	B-12	Val-d'Or	D-2
Saint-Pamphile	F-9	Monts	C-12	Shawinigan	G-7	Varennes	H-6
Saint-Pascal	F-9	Sainte-Blandine	D-10	Shawinigan-		Victoriaville	G-7
Saint-Prime	D-7	Sainte-Marie	G-8	Sud	F-12	Ville-Marie	E-1
Saint-Raphaël	F-8	Sainte-Perpétue	F-9	Sherbrooke	H-7	Warwick	G-13
Saint-Raymond	F-7	Sainte-Sophie	H-10	Sorel-Tracy	G-7	Weedon	H-8
Saint-Rémi	I-10	Sainte-Thècle	F-12	Sutton	I-12	Windsor	H-7
Saint-Tite	G-7	Terrebonne	H-10				

New Brunswick

Population: 729,997
Land area: 27,587 sq. mi.
Capital: Fredericton

Cities and Towns

Newfoundland and Labrador

Population: 505,469
Land area: 144,353 sq. mi.
Capital: St. John's

Cities and Towns

Prince Edward Island

Population: 135,851
Land area: 2,185 sq. mi.
Capital: Charlottetown

Cities and Towns

Nova Scotia

Population: 913,462
Land area: 20,594 sq. mi.
Capital: Halifax

Cities and Towns

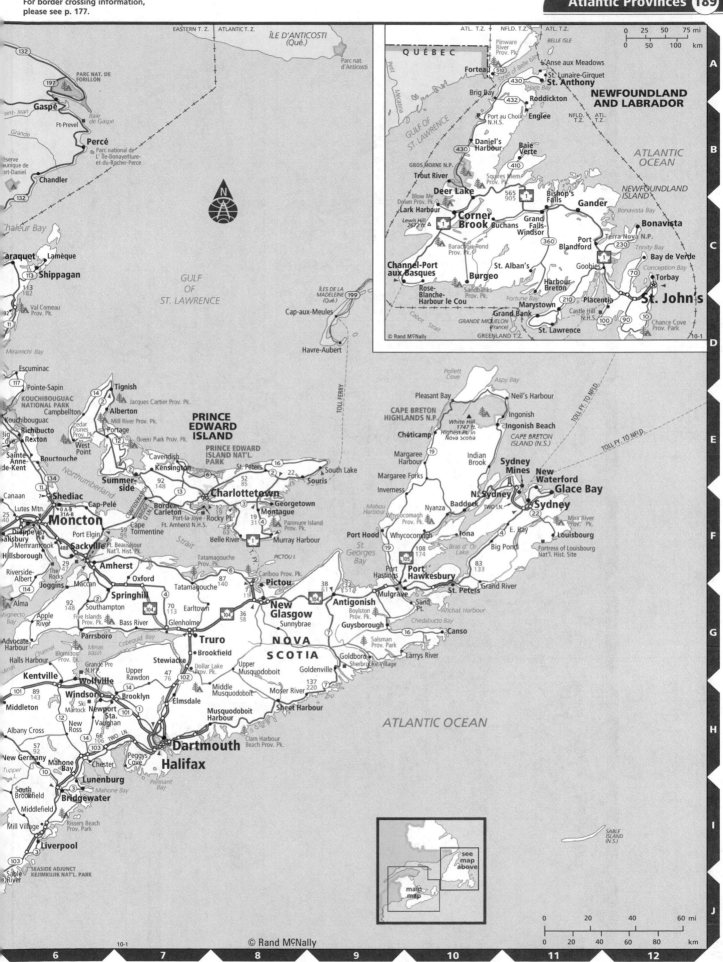

EASTERN T. Z. | ATLANTIC T. Z.

ÎLE D'ANTICOSTI
(Qué.)

Parc nat.
d'Anticosti

QUÉBEC

ATL. T.Z. | NFLD. T.Z. | ATL. T.Z.

0   25   50   75 mi
0   50   100 km

Pinware
River
Prov. Pk.
Forteau
510
L'Anse aux Meadows
St. Lunaire-Girquet
St. Anthony
Brig Bay
430
Roddickton
432
Englée
**NEWFOUNDLAND
AND LABRADOR**

Port au Choix
N.H.S.

Daniel's
Harbour
Baie
Verte
430
410

GROS MORNE N.P.
Trout River
Squires Mem.
Prov. Pk.

ATLANTIC
OCEAN

NEWFOUNDLAND
ISLAND

Blow Me
Down Prov. Pk.
Deer Lake
565
905
**Bishop's
Falls**
Gander
Bonavista Bay
Lark Harbour
Lewis Hill
2672 ft.
Buchans
Grand
Falls-
Windsor
Bonavista
**Corner
Brook**
360
Port
Blandford
Terra Nova N.P.
230
Trinity Bay
Bay de Verde
Conception Bay
Baraciois Pond
Prov. Pk.
St. Alban's
70
Torbay
**Channel-Port
aux Basques**
Burgeo
Goobies
Harbour
Breton
210
Placentia
St. John's
Rose-
Blanche-
Harbour le Cou
Sandbanks
Prov. Pk.
Fortune Bay
Marystown
Castle Hill
N.H.S.
100
90
10
Chance Cove
Prov. Park
**Grand
Bank**
GRANDE MIQUELON
(France)
St. Lawrence
GREENLAND T.Z.
Cabot Strait
© Rand McNally
10-1

Gaspé
132
PARC NAT. DE
FORILLON
197
Ft-Prevel
Baie
de Gaspé
Saint-Jean
Grande
Percé
Parc national de
L' Île-Bonaventure-
et-du-Rocher-Percé
Réserve
faunique de
Port-Daniel
Chandler
132
Chaleur Bay

GULF OF
ST. LAWRENCE

ÎLES DE LA
MADELEINE
(Qué.)
199
Cap-aux-Meules

Havre-Aubert

Miramichi Bay

Escuminac
117
Pointe-Sapin
**KOUCHIBOUGUAC
NATIONAL PARK**
14
Campbellton
2
Kouchibouguac
Cedar
Dunes
Prov. Pk.
Big
Cove
Richibucto
Rexton
12
Sainte-
Anne-
de-Kent
Bouctouche
134
Canaan
11
Shediac
Cap-Pelé
Lutes Mtn.
9 A B
25
40
Dieppe
Moncton
Salisbury
Memramcook
488
Port Elgin
Sackville
Hillsborough
29
47
Riverside-
Albert
The
Rocks
Amherst
114
Joggins
Maccan
2
Oxford
Springhill
Alma
92
148
Southampton
104
chignecto
Apple
River
Five Islands
Prov. Pk.
70
113
Earltown
Advocate
Harbour
Parrsboro
Bass River
Glenholme
104
Halls Harbour
channel
Minas
Basin
Blomidon
Prov. Pk.
Grande Pre
N.H.P.
Cobequid Bay
Truro
Minas
Brookfield
Kentville
89
143
Upper
Rawdon
Stewiacke
Dollar Lake
Prov. Pk.
101
Wolfville
47
76
102
Middleton
Windsor
Ski
Martock
Newport
Sta.
Brooklyn
101
1
Elmsdale
12
New Ross
Vaughan
Albany Cross
14
106
TWO LN.
66
103
Middlefield
Baraquet
Lamèque
113
Shippagan
113
182
Val Comeau
Prov. Pk.
11
92

Tignish
14
Alberton
2
Mill River Prov. Pk.
Portage
Green Park Prov. Pk.
12
West
Point
Cavendish
**PRINCE
EDWARD
ISLAND**
PRINCE EDWARD
ISLAND NAT'L.
PARK
Kensington
St. Peters
16
6
**Summer-
side**
92
148
13
Charlottetown
South Lake
Souris
52
85
2
22
Borden
Carleton
3
Georgetown
19
31
Montague
Port-la-Joye - Rocky Pt.
Ft. Amherst N.H.S.
Panmure Island
Prov. Pk.
59
63
Cape
Tormentine
1
Belle River
Murray Harbour
Ft. Beauséjour
Nat'l. Hist. Site
Tatamagouche
Prov. Pk.
PICTOU I.
St.
Georges
Bay
59
95
Strait
Caribou Prov. Pk.
38
32
61
Pictou
87
140
51
Tatamagouche
11
Mulgrave
Sand
Pt.
**New
Glasgow**
36
58
Antigonish
104
Boylston
Prov. Pk.
Sunnybrae
Chedabucto Bay
**NOVA
SCOTIA**
Guysborough
7
Achat Harbour
Southampton
Salsman
Prov. Park
Canso
Goldboro
Larrys River
16
Sherbrooke Village
Goldenville
137
220
7
Upper
Musquodoboit
Middle
Musquodoboit
Moser River
Musquodoboit
Harbour
Clam Harbour
Beach Prov. Pk.
Sheet Harbour

ATLANTIC OCEAN

TOLL FERRY

Pollett
Cove
Aspy Bay
TOLL FY. TO NFLD.
Pleasant Bay
Neil's Harbour
**CAPE BRETON
HIGHLANDS N.P.**
Ingonish
White Hill
1747 ft.
Highest Pt. in
Nova Scotia
Ingonish Beach
Chéticamp
19
CAPE BRETON
ISLAND (N.S.)
TOLL FY. TO NFLD.
Margaree
Harbour
Indian
Brook
Margaree Forks
**Sydney
Mines**
**New
Waterford**
Inverness
Nyanza
Baddeck
TWO LN.
Glace Bay
Mabou
Harbour
Whycocomagh
Prov. Pk.
Sydney
22
Iona
Mira River
Prov. Pk.
Port Hood
Whycocomagh
19
E. Bay
4
Big Pond
Louisbourg
St.
Georges
Bay
108
174
Bras d'Or
Lake
Fortress of Louisbourg
Nat'l. Hist. Site
**Port
Hawkesbury**
105
Port
Hastings
83
133
St. Peters
Grand River

SABLE
ISLAND
(N.S.)

Halifax
Dartmouth
103
Peggys
Cove
Chester
Lunenburg
Mahone
Bay
Mahone Bay
Pennant
Bay
New Germany
Tupper
10
Bridgewater
3
South
Brookfield
Mill Village
Rissers Beach
Prov. Park
Sable
River
103
Liverpool
3
SEASIDE ADJUNCT
KEJIMKUJIK NAT'L. PARK

see
map
above
main
map

0   20   40   60 mi
0   20   40   60   80   km

© Rand McNally
10-1

6   7   8   9   10   11   12

A B C D E F G H I J

Mexico

Population: 103,263,388
Land area: 758,450 sq. mi.
Capital: Mexico City

Cities and Towns

Acaponeta	D-5
Acapulco	F-6
Acayucan	F-8
Aguascalientes	D-5
Arriaga	F-8
Atlixco	E-7
Autlán de Navarro	E-5
Bahía Kino	B-3
Bermejillo	C-5
Buenaventura	B-4
Campeche	E-9
Cancún	D-10
Champotón	E-9
Chetumal	E-10
Chihuahua	B-4
Chilpancingo	F-6
Choix	C-4
Cholula	E-7
Cintalapa	F-8
Ciudad Camargo	C-6
Ciudad del Carmen	E-9
Ciudad de México	E-6
Ciudad Juárez	A-4
Ciudad Madero	D-7
Ciudad Mante	C-6
Ciudad Obregón	B-3
Ciudad Valles	D-6
Ciudad Victoria	D-6
Coatzacoalcos	E-8
Colima	E-5
Cozumel	D-10
Cuajinicuilapa	F-7
Cuauhtémoc	B-4
Cuernavaca	E-6
Culiacán	C-4
Durango	D-5
El Fuerte	C-4
El Sueco	B-4
Ensenada	A-2
Escárcega	E-9
Fresnillo	D-5
Gómez Palacio	C-5
Guadalajara	E-5
Guamúchil	C-4
Guanajuato	D-6
Guaymas	B-3
Guerrero	B-4
Guzmán	E-5
Hermosillo	B-3
Hidalgo del Parral	C-4
Huajuapan de León	E-7
Iguala	E-6
Irapuato	E-6
Jalpa	D-5
Jiménez	C-5
Juan Aldama	C-5
La Paz	C-3
La Pesca	D-7
León	D-6
Linares	C-6
Loreto	C-3
Los Mochis	C-3
Manzanillo	E-5
Matamoros	C-7
Matehuala	D-6
Mazatlán	D-4
Mérida	D-9
Mexicali	A-2
Mexico City	E-6
Monclova	C-6
Monterrey	C-6
Morelia	E-6
Navojoa	B-3
Nogales	A-3
Nueva Rosita	B-6
Nuevo Casas Grandes	A-4
Nuevo Laredo	B-6
Oaxaca	F-7
Ojinaga	B-5
Orizaba	E-7
Pachuca	E-6
Parras	C-5
Piedras Negras	B-6
Pitiquito	A-3
Poza Rica	E-7
Puebla	E-7
Puerto Ángel	F-7
Puerto Escondido	F-7
Puerto Morelos	D-10
Puerto Peñasco	A-2
Puerto Vallarta	E-5
Punta Prieta	B-2
Querétaro	E-6
Reynosa	C-7
Río Lagartos	D-10
Rosario	A-2
Sabinas	B-6
Sabinas Hidalgo	C-6
Sahuaripa	B-4
Salamanca	E-6
Saltillo	C-6
San Blas	D-5
San Carlos	C-3
San Felipe	A-2
San Fernando	C-7
San Francisco del Orco	C-4
San José del Cabo	D-3
San Luis Potosí	D-6
Santa Ana	A-3
Santa Bárbara	C-4
Santa Rosalia	B-3
Santo Domingo Tehuàntepec	F-8
Tamazunchale	D-6
Tampico	D-7
Tapachula	F-8
Taxco	E-6
Tepehuanes	C-4
Tepic	D-5
Tijuana	A-1
Tlaxcala	E-7
Toluca	E-6
Tónichi	B-3
Topolobampo	C-3
Torreón	C-5
Tuxpan	D-7
Tuxtla Gutiérrez	F-8
Uruapan del Progreso	E-5
Veracruz	E-7
Villahermosa	E-8
Villagrán	C-6
Xalapa	E-7
Zacatecas	D-5
Zihuatanejo	F-6

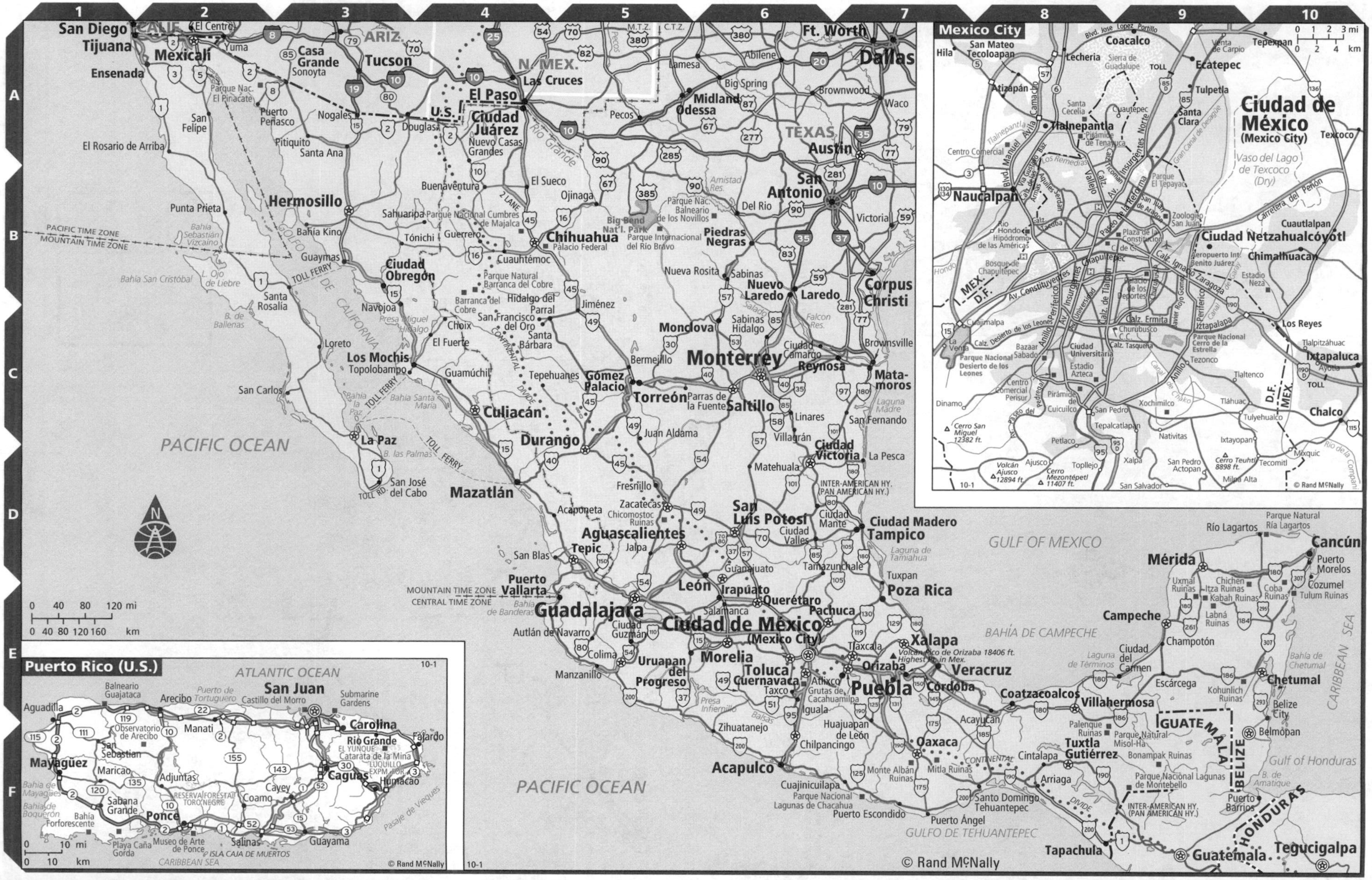

Mexico City
Ciudad de México (Mexico City)
Ciudad Netzahualcóyotl
Naucalpan
Tlalnepantla
Ecatepec
Coacalco
Chimalhuacán
Los Reyes
Ixtapaluca
Chalco
Vaso del Lago de Texcoco (Dry)
Puerto Rico (U.S.)
San Juan
Carolina
Caguas
Ponce
Mayagüez
Arecibo
ATLANTIC OCEAN
CARIBBEAN SEA
PACIFIC OCEAN
GULF OF MEXICO
BAHÍA DE CAMPECHE
GOLFO DE CALIFORNIA
GULFO DE TEHUANTEPEC
CARIBBEAN SEA
Gulf of Honduras
PACIFIC TIME ZONE
MOUNTAIN TIME ZONE
CENTRAL TIME ZONE
TEXAS
ARIZ.
N. MEX.
CALIF.
GUATEMALA
BELIZE
HONDURAS
© Rand McNally

For border crossing information, please see p. 177..

TOURISM CONTACTS

On the road or before you go, log on to the official tourism website of your destination. These websites offer terrific ideas about organizing a visit and often include calendars of special events and activities. Prefer calling? Most states offer toll-free numbers.

Alabama Bureau of Tourism & Travel
(800) 252-2262
(334) 242-4169
www.800alabama.com

Alaska Travel Industry Association
(907) 929-2200
www.travelalaska.com

Arizona Office of Tourism
(866) 275-5816
www.arizonaguide.com

Arkansas Department of Parks & Tourism
(800) 628-8725
www.arkansas.com

California Travel & Tourism Commission
(800) 862-2543*
(916) 444-4429
www.visitcalifornia.com

Colorado Tourism Office
(800) 265-6723
www.colorado.com

Connecticut Tourism
(888) 288-4748
www.ctvisit.com

Delaware Tourism Office
(866) 284-7483
www.visitdelaware.com

Visit Florida
(888) 735-2872
(050) 400-5007
www.visitflorida.com

Georgia On My Mind (Georgia Department of Economic Development)
(800) 847-4842
www.georgiaonmymind.org

Hawaii Visitors & Convention Bureau
(800) 464-2924
www.gohawaii.com

Idaho Division of Tourism Development
(800) 847-4843
(208) 334-2470
www.visitidaho.org

Illinois Bureau of Tourism
(800) 226-6632
www.enjoyillinois.com

Indiana Office of Tourism Development
(800) 677-9800
www.visitindiana.com

Iowa Tourism Office
(800) 345-4692*
(888) 472-6035
(515) 242-4705
www.traveliowa.com

Kansas Department of Commerce, Travel & Tourism
(800) 252-6727
www.travelks.com

Kentucky Department of Travel
(800) 225-8747
www.kentuckytourism.com

Louisiana Office of Tourism
(800) 334-8626
www.louisianatravel.com

Maine Office of Tourism
(888) 624-6345
www.visitmaine.com

Maryland Office of Tourism
(866) 639-3526
www.visitmaryland.org

Massachusetts Office of Travel & Tourism
(800) 227-6277
(617) 973-8500
www.massvacation.com

Travel Michigan
(800) 644-2489
www.michigan.org

Explore Minnesota Tourism
(888) 868-7476
(651) 296-5029
www.exploreminnesota.com

Mississippi Division of Tourism
(800) 927-6378
(866) 733-6477
www.visitmississippi.org

Missouri Division of Tourism
(800) 519-2100
(573) 751-4133
www.visitmo.com

Travel Montana
(800) 847-4868
www.visitmt.com

Nebraska Division of Travel & Tourism
(877) 632-7275
(800) 228-4307
www.visitnebraska.org

Nevada Commission on Tourism
(800) 638-2328
(775) 687-4322
www.travelnevada.com

New Hampshire Division of Travel and Tourism Development
(800) 386-4664
www.visitnh.gov

New Jersey Division of Travel & Tourism
(800) 847-4865
www.visitnj.org

New Mexico Tourism Department
(800) 733-6396
www.newmexico.org

New York State Division of Tourism
(800) 225-5697
www.iloveny.com

North Carolina Division of Tourism
(800) 847-4862
(919) 733-8372
www.visitnc.com

North Dakota Tourism Division
(800) 435-5663
www.ndtourism.com

Ohio Division of Travel & Tourism
(800) 282-5393
www.discoverohio.com

Oklahoma Tourism & Recreation Department
(800) 652-6552
www.travelok.com

Travel Oregon
(800) 547-7842
www.traveloregon.com

Pennsylvania Tourism Office
(800) 847-4872
www.visitpa.com

Rhode Island Tourism Division
(888) 886-9463*
(800) 556-2484*
(800) 250-7384
www.visitrhodeisland.com

South Carolina Department of Parks, Recreation & Tourism
(888) 727-6453*
(803) 734-1700
www.discoversouthcarolina.com

South Dakota Office of Tourism
(800) 732-5682
www.travelsd.com

Tennessee Department of Tourist Development
(800) 462-8366*
(615) 741-2159
www.tnvacation.com

Texas Tourism
(800) 888-8839*
www.traveltex.com

Utah Office of Tourism
(800) 200-1160
(801) 538-1030
www.utah.com

Vermont Department of Tourism and Marketing
(800) 837-6668
www.vermontvacation.com

Virginia Tourism Corporation
(800) 847-4882
www.virginia.org

Washington State Tourism
(800) 544-1800
www.experiencewashington.com

Destination DC
(800) 422-8644
(202) 789-7000
www.washington.org

West Virginia Division of Tourism
(800) 225-5982
(304) 558-2200
www.wvtourism.com

Wisconsin Department of Tourism
(800) 432-8747
(608) 266-2161
www.travelwisconsin.com

Wyoming Travel & Tourism
(800) 225-5996
(307) 777-7777
www.wyomingtourism.org

Canada

Travel Alberta
(800) 252-3782
www.travelalberta.com

Tourism British Columbia
(800) 435-5622
www.hellobc.com

Travel Manitoba
(800) 665-0040
(204) 927-7800
www.travelmanitoba.com

Tourism New Brunswick
(800) 561-0123
www.tourismnewbrunswick.ca

Newfoundland & Labrador Tourism
(800) 563-6353
(709) 729-2830
www.newfoundlandlabrador.com

Nova Scotia Department of Tourism, Culture & Heritage
(800) 565-0000
(902) 425-5781
novascotia.com

Ontario Travel
(800) 668-2746
www.ontariotravel.net

Tourism Prince Edward Island
(800) 463-4734
www.gentleisland.com

Tourisme Québec
(877) 266-5687
(514) 873-2015
www.bonjourquebec.com

Tourism Saskatchewan
(877) 237-2273
www.sasktourism.com

Mexico

Mexico Tourism Board
(800) 446-3942
www.visitmexico.com

*To request travel materials only

MILE MARKERS — MILEAGE CHART

This handy chart offers more than 2,400 mileages covering 77 North American cities. Want more mileages? Visit go.randmcnally.com/MC and type in any two cities or addresses.

	Albuquerque, NM	Atlanta, GA	Billings, MT	Boston, MA	Charlotte, NC	Chicago, IL	Cincinnati, OH	Dallas, TX	Denver, CO	Detroit, MI	Houston, TX	Indianapolis, IN	Kansas City, MO	Los Angeles, CA	Memphis, TN	Miami, FL	Milwaukee, WI	Minneapolis, MN	New Orleans, LA	New York, NY	Omaha, NE	Orlando, FL	Philadelphia, PA	Phoenix, AZ	Pittsburgh, PA	Portland, OR	Saint Louis, MO	Salt Lake City, UT	San Francisco, CA	Seattle, WA	Washington, DC	Wichita, KS
Albuquerque, NM		1386	998	2219	1626	1333	1387	647	446	1570	884	1279	784	786	1008	1952	1354	1225	1165	2001	863	1730	1924	462	1641	1363	1037	599	1086	1438	1885	591
Amarillo, TX	284	1102	965	1935	1342	1049	1103	363	424	1286	589	995	570	1072	720	1668	1132	1009	881	1716	647	1446	1640	746	1357	1669	752	883	1370	1743	1600	382
Atlanta, GA	1386		1831	1095	244	715	461	780	1404	722	794	533	800	2174	379	661	809	1127	468	882	992	440	780	1844	684	2603	555	1878	2472	2649	637	955
Atlantic City, NJ	1985	831	2072	338	590	818	632	1518	1792	644	1598	703	1187	2774	1063	1248	910	1232	1273	126	1272	1038	60	2447	365	2922	948	2201	2934	2889	188	1379
Austin, TX	705	920	1495	1959	1164	1121	1128	193	950	1358	157	1007	702	1381	643	1341	1204	1136	503	1737	839	1204	1658	1010	1411	2068	825	1304	1763	2143	1524	542
Baltimore, MD	1887	683	1953	400	442	699	513	1368	1673	524	1448	584	1082	2670	914	1082	792	1112	1124	192	1153	889	98	2349	246	2804	829	2081	2816	2771	39	1260
Billings, MT	998	1831		2236	1990	1246	1546	1425	551	1535	1652	1435	1026	1240	1477	2497	1173	838	1868	2041	845	2275	2011	1210	1713	891	1278	552	1173	818	1951	1064
Birmingham, AL	1241	146	1780	1177	390	660	466	636	1329	724	668	478	749	2030	235	746	754	1072	343	960	939	534	880	1700	748	2551	502	1826	2327	2598	745	810
Boise, ID	938	2177	621	2660	2336	1693	1943	1702	830	1960	1930	1835	1372	842	1825	2844	1732	1461	2216	2465	1225	2622	2435	914	2137	428	1622	339	639	503	2375	1338
Boston, MA	2219	1095	2236		841	983	870	1764	1970	724	1844	937	1391	2983	1312	1482	1074	1396	1526	207	1436	1288	306	2681	550	3086	1182	2365	3098	3054	439	1613
Branson, MO	864	652	1241	1433	868	545	601	435	806	784	602	493	209	1651	274	1284	630	643	597	1201	402	1062	1138	1326	851	2013	249	1288	1950	2060	1081	292
Calgary, AB	1542	2357	541	2615	2400	1627	1925	1967	1096	1916	2209	1814	1567	1557	2028	3018	1555	1221	2419	2439	1387	2797	2391	1524	2093	787	1820	869	1500	678	2334	1606
Charleston, SC	1703	317	2133	970	207	908	620	1099	1706	826	1105	726	1103	2491	696	583	1002	1324	742	768	1294	380	668	2165	654	2904	857	2180	2789	2951	532	1272
Charlotte, NC	1626	244	1990	841		769	477	1023	1566	616	1038	583	961	2414	619	728	867	1180	712	641	1151	526	539	2088	446	2712	714	2037	2712	2808	398	1092
Chicago, IL	1333	715	1246	983	769		289	926	1002	280	1085	181	526	2015	531	1381	90	408	923	787	470	1153	757	1795	459	2118	296	1398	2130	2063	697	724
Cincinnati, OH	1387	461	1546	870	477	289		934	1187	259	1055	108	584	2172	482	1127	381	703	804	637	722	905	571	1849	288	2369	348	1647	2380	2363	512	779
Cleveland, OH	1598	714	1597	638	514	342	248	1194	1330	168	1315	315	799	2342	729	1240	434	756	1057	460	797	1043	428	2060	131	2446	560	1725	2458	2414	370	992
Columbus, OH	1457	567	1606	763	426	354	106	1039	1261	191	1174	176	657	2244	587	1164	455	766	910	533	792	954	468	1920	184	2439	421	1718	2451	2425	411	851
Corpus Christi, TX	855	1001	1622	2051	1244	1338	1262	410	1077	1542	207	1228	919	1494	782	1394	1421	1353	554	1844	1056	1172	1754	1222	1561	2218	1042	1454	1873	2292	1619	758
Dallas, TX	647	780	1425	1764	1023	926	934		880	1163	228	873	489	1437	453	1307	1010	928	519	1548	656	1086	1467	1066	1221	2218	630	1403	1734	2193	1332	361
Denver, CO	446	1404	551	1970	1566	1002	1187	880		1270	1035	1083	603	1015	1097	2069	1042	913	1398	1775	534	1851	1732	908	1447	1256	854	533	1268	1320	1671	519
Des Moines, IA	983	902	946	1299	1057	332	580	683	670	599	938	474	193	1682	617	1567	371	242	1008	1105	137	1339	1074	1445	777	1786	354	1065	1798	1764	1015	391
Detroit, MI	1570	722	1535	724	616	280	259	1163	1270		1319	286	764	2281	742	1354	374	696	1066	613	736	1144	583	2032	285	2385	533	1664	2397	2353	522	961
Duluth, MN	1375	1187	860	1370	1239	446	760	1092	1063	754	1331	651	586	2076	963	1852	394	152	1354	1246	530	1632	1230	1838	932	1749	679	1458	2033	1677	1171	785
Edmonton, AB	1724	2391	722	2549	2443	1670	1968	2149	1278	1968	2391	1857	1626	1755	2147	3058	1598	1264	2538	2482	1445	2836	2434	1721	2136	966	1878	1069	1695	793	2377	1787
El Paso, TX	260	1418	1257	2373	1662	1455	1569	635	707	1702	744	1398	929	796	1089	1934	1497	1377	1095	2202	1004	1712	2102	424	1774	1630	1157	866	1175	1705	1967	730
Fargo, ND	1318	1361	607	1629	1414	641	937	1079	873	930	1321	825	600	1848	1054	2025	569	235	1445	1438	420	1807	1405	1780	1107	1497	841	1160	1781	1424	1348	685
Gatlinburg, TN	1439	196	1803	922	202	578	290	884	1376	552	964	396	773	2226	431	865	672	994	640	707	964	640	625	1901	493	2574	527	1850	2525	2621	490	905
Guadalajara, JA	1194	1739	2194	2789	1982	1954	1962	1028	1639	2191	948	1901	1535	1501	1482	2131	2037	1969	1292	2592	1672	1910	2492	1212	2261	2545	1658	1792	1963	2631	2356	1377
Gulfport, MS	1221	399	1912	1482	643	896	767	562	1386	1025	403	780	883	1949	365	792	988	1196	78	1266	1073	572	1180	1577	1052	2633	647	1909	2307	2730	1036	867
Houston, TX	884	794	1652	1844	1038	1085	1055	228	1035	1319		1021	732	1550	575	1186	1163	1171	347	1632	898	965	1547	1178	1354	2356	784	1634	1929	2431	1411	595
Indianapolis, IN	1279	533	1435	937	583	181	108	873	1083	288	1021		482	2068	464	1198	272	591	818	707	613	968	643	1742	359	2260	243	1541	2273	2253	582	674
Jacksonville, FL	1636	346	2183	1146	379	1068	796	962	1756	1002	871	874	1152	2421	677	349	1163	1474	547	939	1344	141	844	2050	825	2954	907	2230	2723	3001	706	1312
Kansas City, MO	784	800	1026	1421	961	526	584	489	603	764	732	482		1616	451	1466	565	436	844	1196	187	1246	1127	1246	840	1797	250	1073	1808	1844	1066	193
Key West, FL	2099	809	2646	1659	886	1534	1275	1455	2222	1515	1334	1348	1617	2884	1159	162	1632	1944	1010	1446	1807	387	1357	2514	1332	3417	1370	2693	3186	3464	1213	1735
Las Vegas, NV	572	1959	973	2714	2199	1746	1932	1220	747	2013	1457	1828	1349	270	1581	2525	1786	1656	1739	2518	1278	2303	2480	286	2190	1023	1600	419	569	1128	2428	1164
Lexington, KY	1371	369	1610	917	400	370	83	876	1186	344	996	184	581	2158	423	1030	464	782	745	701	771	817	638	1833	370	2381	334	1657	2392	2428	533	773
Little Rock, AR	877	515	1407	1447	754	650	617	319	965	885	439	533	381	1666	137	1147	724	815	425	1230	574	925	1150	1340	905	2211	345	1488	1963	2275	1015	446
Los Angeles, CA	786	2174	1240	2983	2414	2015	2172	1437	1015	2281	1550	2068	1616		1794	2735	2055	1925	1894	2787	1546	2515	2713	370	2428	963	1821	688	380	1134	2670	1377
Memphis, TN	1008	379	1477	1312	619	531	482	453	1097	742	575	464	451	1794		1012	622	831	394	1094	641	778	1014	1471	768	2245	283	1524	2095	2299	879	577
Mexico City, DF	1404	1718	2301	2768	1962	2017	1979	1090	1756	2254	924	1963	1598	1839	1500	2111	2100	2032	1272	2571	1735	1889	2471	1469	2279	2768	1721	2003	2218	2842	2336	1440
Miami, FL	1952	661	2497	1482	728	1381	1127	1307	2069	1354	1186	1198	1466	2735	1012		1475	1791	861	1288	1658	229	1180	2362	1173	3260	1221	2544	3038	3315	1044	1587
Milwaukee, WI	1354	809	1173	1074	867	90	381	1010	1042	374	1163	272	565	2055	622	1475		336	1015	879	509	1258	849	1817	551	2062	379	1437	2170	1990	788	763
Minneapolis, MN	1225	1127	838	1396	1180	408	703	928	913	696	1171	591	436	1925	831	1791	336		1223	1204	372	1573	1111	1687	874	1727	563	1308	2040	1655	1110	634
Mobile, AL	1234	328	1874	1427	571	917	721	589	1414	978	468	733	850	2014	382	719	1011	1224	144	1202	1038	497	1101	1643	1000	2661	645	1936	2320	2727	965	894
Montréal, QC	2129	1218	2099	310	980	847	824	1722	1832	560	1884	847	1330	2845	1314	1647	938	1262	1640	382	1302	1437	454	2591	603	2948	1092	2228	2960	2916	587	1529
Nashville, TN	1219	248	1586	1099	407	469	273	664	1158	534	786	287	555	2006	212	913	564	881	532	884	747	692	802	1682	560	2357	310	1633	2304	2404	667	688
New Orleans, LA	1165	468	1868	1520	712	923	804	519	1398	1066	347	818	844	1894	394	861	1015	1223		1304	1032	641	1222	1523	1090	2642	675	1920	2252	2716	1087	880
New York, NY	2001	882	2041	207	641	787	637	1548	1775	613	1632	707	1196	2787	1094	1288	879	1204	1304		1245	1089	97	2463	369	2891	954	2170	2902	2858	228	1391
Norfolk, VA	1910	558	2132	569	328	878	605	1350	1758	704	1362	720	1155	2707	898	950	969	1295	1026	370	1335	755	271	2373	425	2962	911	2238	2973	2949	189	1349
Oklahoma City, OK	542	844	1203	1678	1084	792	846	204	631	1029	437	739	348	1326	466	1476	876	788	722	1460	452	1254	1384	1005	1101	1922	496	1200	1627	1948	1344	158
Omaha, NE	863	992	845	1436	1151	470	722	656	534	736	898	613	187	1658	509	1658	509	372	1032	1245		1436	1212	1325	919	1650	439	930	1662	1663	1151	292
Orlando, FL	1730	440	2275	1288	526	1153	905	1086	1851	1144	965	968	1246	2515	778	229	1258	1573	641	1089	1436		986	2145	975	3048	999	2323	2816	3093	849	1365
Ottawa, ON	2039	1158	1768	428	920	760	732	1632	1748	471	1804	757	1240	2763	1230	1618	859	1032	1582	440	1213	1408	447	2501	546	2660	1002	2142	2877	2586	566	1439
Philadelphia, PA	1924	780	2011	306	539	757	571	1467	1732	583	1547	643	1127	2713	1014	1180	849	1171	1222	97	1212	986		2387	304	2861	888	2140	2873	2828	137	1319
Phoenix, AZ	462	1844	1210	2681	2088	1795	1849	1066	908	2032	1178	1742	1246	370	1471	2362	1817	1687	1523	2463	1325	2145	2387		2104	1332	1499	653	749	1414	2348	1053
Pittsburgh, PA	1641	684	1713	570	446	459	288	1221	1447	285	1354	359	840	2428	768	1173	551	874	1090	369	919	1475	304	2104		2563	604	1842	2574	2530	244	1035
Portland, ME	2315	1192	2304	110	938	1079	967	1861	2067	825	1940	1034	1518	3082	1408	1585	1176	1492	1616	304	1533	1385	402	2778	666	3186	1279	2461	3196	3151	535	1710
Portland, OR	1363	2603	891	3086	2761	2118	2369	2128	1256	2385	2356	2260	1797	963	2245	3260	2062	1727	2642	2891	1650	3048	2861	1332	2563		2050	765	635	172	2800	1764
Rapid City, SD	843	1508	323	1900	1670	912	1208	1061	397	1200	1291	1100	704	1312	1160	2173	840	575	1551	1708	525	1956	1675	1305	1378	1215	959	649	1384	1142	1618	699
Reno, NV	1019	2396	958	2881	2555	1913	2163	1668	1051	2180	1904	2056	1591	470	2029	3063	1953	1818	2186	2685	1445	2841	2656	733	2357	578	1844	518	217	720	2595	1558
Richmond, VA	1832	532	2051	547	293	797	512	1278	1671	622	1329	627	1069	2620	824	944	888	1210	1002	334	1259	742	245	2294	340	2868	822	2145	2880	2868	108	1267
Saint Louis, MO	1037	555	1278	1182	714	296	348	630	854	533	784	243	250	1821	283	1221	379	563	675	954	439	999	888	1499	604	2050		1326	2061	2096	827	442
Salt Lake City, UT	599	1878	552	2365	2037	1398	1647	1403	533	1664	1634	1541	1073	688	1524	2544	1437	1308	1920	2170	930	2323	2140	653	1842	765	1326		735	839	2079	1042
San Antonio, TX	712	986	1480	2039	1230	1202	1210	276	935	1439	197	1149	766	1357	727	1379	1285	1205	541	1822	920	1160	1742	985	1495	2076	906	1311	1736	2150	1607	625
San Diego, CA	810	2138	1302	3046	2381	2080	2196	1359	1077	2346	1402	2080	1599	127	1819	2656	2118	1986	1816	2809	1613	2436	2738	352	2542	1083	1845	750	501	1256	2693	1401
San Francisco, CA	1086	2472	1173	3098	2721	2130	2380	1734	1268	2397	1929	2273	1808	380	2095	3038	2170	2040	2252	2902	1662	2816	2873	749	2574	635	2061	735		807	2812	1775
Santa Fe, NM	58	1379	943	2212	1618	1313	1379	640	391	1562	877	1272	766	846	998	1944	1336	1207	1158	1994	891	1723	1917	520	1634	1388	1029	625	1144	1463	1879	572
Sault Ste. Marie, ON	1777	1040	1273	923	947	471	577	1370	1428	347	1527	540	951	2465	972	1685	398	538	1355	921	850	1475	921	2240	614	2166	740	1848	2581	2090	854	1150
Seattle, WA	1438	2649	818	3054	2808	2063	2363	2193	1320	2353	2431	2253	1844	1134	2299	3315	1990	1655	2716	2858	1663	3093	2828	1414	2530	172	2096	839	807		2768	1828
Spokane, WA	1320	2369	541	2774	2528	1785	2084	1964	1091	2075	2192	1973	1564	1216	2018	3035	1712	1377	2409	2580	1383	2814	2550	1381	2814	351	1817	730	1441	351	2517	1548
Tampa, FL	1746	451	2293	1342	578	1166	916	1102	1860	1178	980	984	1252	2525	779	255	1260	1578	651	1138	1445	84	1040	2153	1023	3064	1008	2340	2832	3111	904	1381
Toronto, ON	1800	963	1771	548	756	519	493	1393	1504	232	1551	518	1001	2517	983	1483	609	933	1306	489	974	1284	497	2262	316	2620	763	1899	2632	2588	486	1188
Tulsa, OK	645	782	1234	1576	1022	687	738	258	692	927	487	635	243	1433	402	1414	773	704	671	1350	380	1192	1282	1107	994	1938	392	1215	1731	2012	1234	173
Vancouver, BC	1575	2785	953	3188	2944	2198	2499	2338	1465	2487	2565	2389	1980	1275	2437	3451	2125	1790	2851	2993	1799	3229	2963	1550	2665	313	2232	973	947	141	2903	1973
Washington, DC	1885	637	1951	439	398	697	512	1322	1671	522	1411	582	1066	2670	879	1044	788	1110	1087	228	1151	849	137	2348	244	2800	827	2079	2812	2768		1258
Wichita, KS	591	955	1064	1613	1092	724	779	361	519	964	595	674	193	1377	577	1587	763	634	880	1391	298	1365	1319	1053	1035	1764	442	1042	1775	1828	1258	

Mileages in this chart are based upon the routes usually followed by motorists. Highway systems include interstate, U.S., and state highways.

Mileages ©Rand McNally